D0131808

Mac OS X 10.5 Leopard

Peachpit Learning Series

Mac OS X 10.5 Leopard

Robin Williams

 Peachpit Press

Mac OS X 10.5 Leopard: Peachpit Learning Series

ROBIN WILLIAMS

Copyright ©2008 Robin Williams

Peachpit Press
1249 Eighth Street
Berkeley, CA 94710
510.524.2178   voice
510.524.2221   fax

Find us on the web at www.peachpit.com
To report errors, please send a note to errata@peachpit.com
Peachpit Press is a division of Pearson Education

Interior layout design: Kim Scott
Production: Robin Williams
Compositor: Robin Williams

NOTICE OF RIGHTS

All rights reserved. No part of this book may be reproduced or transmitted in any form by any means, electronic, mechanical, photocopying, recording, or otherwise, without the prior written permission of the publisher. For information on getting permission for reprints and excerpts, contact permissions@peachpit.com.

NOTICE OF LIABILITY

The information in this book is distributed on an "As Is" basis without warranty. While every precaution has been taken in the preparation of the book, neither the author nor Peachpit Press shall have any liability to any person or entity with respect to any loss or damage caused or alleged to be caused directly or indirectly by the instructions contained in this book or by the computer software and hardware products described in it.

TRADEMARKS

Many of the designations used by manufacturers and sellers to distinguish their products are claimed as trademarks. Where those designations appear in this book, and Peachpit Press was aware of a trademark claim, the designations appear as requested by the owner of the trademark. All other product names and services identified throughout this book are used in editorial fashion only and for the benefit of such companies with no intention of infringement of the trademark. No such use, or the use of any trade name, is intended to convey endorsement or other affiliation with this book.

ISBN 13: 978-0-321-50263-6
ISBN 10: 0-321-50263-9
9 8 7 6 5 4 3
Printed and bound in the United States of America

It's great to be a Mac user.

Robin

Contents at a Glance

Contents

MAC OS X APPLICATIONS IN LEOPARD

Contents

MAKE IT **YOUR OWN MAC**

TECH STUFF

Contents

THE END **MATTERS**

Mac OS X Basics for New Mac Users

1

GOALS

Become familiar and
comfortable with the
Desktop and Finder

Get to know the Finder
windows and how
to use them

Create your own folders

Understand the Dock

Use the Trash basket

Know how and when to
use keyboard shortcuts

Learn to watch for tool tips
and other visual clues

Know where to go for
more information

Introduction to the Mac OS X Desktop

If you have a Mac running Leopard (Mac OS X version 10.5), you're ready to jump right in! In this lesson you'll become familiar with using the basic features of your Mac and its Desktop/Finder.

This book assumes you are familiar with how to operate a computer—how to use a mouse, select items from menus, distinguish one icon from another, move files and folders and windows around, how and why to save the documents you create, etc. If you're brand new to computers in general, I strongly suggest you use *The Little Mac Book, Leopard Edition* instead of this book—*The Little Mac Book* introduces you to using a computer in much more detail and at a much slower pace than this book.

Get to Know your Desktop and Finder

When you turn on your Mac, you'll always see your **Desktop,** shown below. This is also called the **Finder,** although technically the Finder is the application that runs the Desktop. Whenever you see a direction that tells you to go to the Desktop or to the Finder, this is where you need to go.

Apple menu.

Application menu.
This menu changes depending on which application is "active" at the moment.

Finder window.
See pages 5–7.

Spotlight.
See Lesson 19.

Menu bar.

Hard disk icon.

Desktop.
This whole background area is the Desktop.

Finder icon.
See the next two pages.

Dock.
See pages 20–21.

Trash.
See pages 22–23.

TIP —— Because of the way the computer works, you might see the Desktop but not actually be in the Finder. Get in the habit of checking the application menu (shown top-left and on the opposite page). When you are really in the Finder or at the Desktop, the application menu will show "Finder."

Make sure you can get to the Desktop or Finder whenever necessary

As you work on your Mac, you will be using a number of applications in which you'll create your documents, but you'll often want to go back to the Finder, which is like home base. The name of the *active* application, the one that's currently open and available to use (including the Finder), will always be displayed in the application menu. Keep an eye on that menu.

To go to the Finder at any time, do one of these things:

- Single-click on any blank area of the Desktop.

- Single-click on any Finder window (shown below) that you see.

- Single-click the Finder icon in the Dock (shown on the opposite page).

Check to make sure the **application menu** says "Finder," as shown circled below.

Get to Know your Home and its Folders

When you open a Finder window, it usually opens to the Home window, as shown below. You can tell it's Home because your user name and the little house icon are in the title bar. It can be confusing that the Home icon isn't labeled "Home"—it's labeled with the "short name" that was chosen when the computer was first turned on and set up. In the example below, the Home icon is named "robin."

■ **To open a Finder window,** single-click on the Finder icon (shown to the left) in the Dock (the Dock is that row of icons that is usually found across the bottom of your screen).

If the window that opens doesn't display your Home folders, as shown below, single-click the Home icon you see in the Sidebar.

Your Home window displays a number of special folders. Do not change the names of these folders or throw them away unless you are very clear on what you're doing and why you're making that choice! For now, just let them be.

TIP —— If several people use your Mac or if you occasionally have a guest who wants to use it, you can create individual Homes for each user; everyone's files will be perfectly safe from any other user. See Lesson 18 for information about multiple users.

What each folder in your Home window is for

Desktop This folder holds any files that might be sitting directly on the Desktop (see page 4). Putting files on the Desktop is like keeping them on your office desk instead of putting them in a filing cabinet. Having this folder to hold the same files means you can get to them when you're not actually at the Desktop, as when you want to open a file from within an application.

Documents At first your Mac makes sure every document you create is safely tucked into this Documents folder. Later you can create your own folders (see pages 10–11) and store your documents in them.

Downloads This folder holds most of the files that you download through Bonjour, iChat, or the Internet. Files that come to you through email will also end up here if you click the "Save" button in an email message. The Downloads folder in the Dock holds the exact same files.

Library This folder is used by the operating system. *Do not rename this folder, do not throw it away, do not take anything out of it, and do not put anything in it* unless you know exactly what you are doing. Just ignore it for now. For details, see page 37.

Movies The iMovie application uses this folder to automatically store the files necessary for creating the movies you make.

Music The iTunes application uses this folder to automatically keep track of all the music files you buy and all of your playlists.

Pictures The iPhoto application uses this folder to automatically keep track of all your photos and albums.

Public You'll use this folder to share files with other people who also use your Mac, as explained in Lesson 18.

Sites You can create a web site, store it in this folder, and share it with anyone on the Internet. (Directions for that process are not in this book!)

TIP —— You can have as many Finder windows open as you like. This makes it easier to move files from one window to another. **To open another window,** make sure you are at the Finder (see pages 4–5), then go to the File menu and choose "New Finder Window."

Get to Know your Finder Window

Below, you see a typical **Finder window.** This is called a *Finder* window to
distinguish it from similar (but different) windows you will use in your applications.
The following pages go into further detail about this very important window.

Title bar.
*This is the name of the
folder whose contents
are shown in the window.*

Toolbar.

Quick Look button.
See page 19.

*See the opposite page
for these buttons.*

View buttons.
See pages 14–18.

Action button.
See page 43 and 55.

Hide/Show.
See page 9.

Your hard disk.
See page 36.

**Sharing files on
your network.**
See Lesson 21.

Home icon.
See page 6.

**Smart
Folders
for quick
searches.**
See page 336.

Spotlight.
See Lesson 19.

**To change
the view of
a window,**
*see pages
14–18.*

9 items, 44.45 GB available

Sidebar.
See pages 12–13.

Press-and-drag
this bar to **resize**
the Sidebar.

Press-and-drag any
edge to **move** the
window.

Press-and-drag
this corner to
resize the
entire window.

8

Use the buttons in the Finder Window

There are several buttons in the Toolbar of every Finder window.

Red, yellow, and green buttons

- ● Single-click the **red button to *close*** the window.

- ○ Single-click the **yellow button to *minimize*** the window, which sends a tiny icon down into the Dock, on the right side. Try it.

  To open that window again, single-click its icon in the Dock.

- ● Single-click the **green button to *resize*** the window bigger or smaller.

Back and Forward buttons

These buttons go back and forward through the contents of windows you have viewed (just like the back and forward buttons on web pages). Every time you open a new window, these buttons start over.

Hide/Show the Toolbar and Sidebar

In the upper-right corner of every Finder window is a small gray button. Single-click this button to hide the Toolbar and the Sidebar, as shown below. When you double-click on a folder while the Toolbar and Sidebar are hidden, a new and separate window will open. Try it. **To show the Toolbar and Sidebar again,** click the small gray button again.

TIP —— If you *always* want a new and separate window to open, change your Finder preferences; see pages 262–263.

Create your Own Folders

At any time you can create your own **folders** where you can **store** your documents and **organize** your files. For instance, you might want a folder in which to store all your financial documents. And another folder for all your newsletter files. And yet another for the screenplays you're writing. All of these documents *could* go inside the Documents folder, but that's like putting every document in your office in one big manila folder.

Use digital folders on your Mac as you would use manila folders in a metal filing cabinet. See pages 44–45 for tips on how to save files directly into your custom folders.

- **To make a new folder,** go to the File menu and choose "New Folder." The new folder appears *inside the window whose name is in the title bar* (shown circled, below). That is, if you want to put the new folder into the Documents folder, first open the Documents folder before you make a new one.

In my Documents folder, I made a new folder called "The Shakespeare Papers." Inside that folder, I made these six new folders.

■ **To rename a folder:**

1 Single-click on the folder to select it.

This is a new,
untitled folder.

untitled folder

This folder is highlighted,
or selected.

untitled folder

2 Then single-click directly on the name to highlight the name
(you'll see a blue outline around the name).

This folder is ready
for a new name.

untitled folder

3 Type to replace the existing name. (You don't need to delete the original
name first.)

As in any other text, you can double-click a word
to select the entire word, or use the Delete key
to backspace and delete characters.

Mermaid Tavern

4 Hit Return or Enter to set the name.

Mermaid Tavern

Mermaid Tavern

Click on any blank spot
in the Finder window to
unhighlight the folder.

■ **To open a folder,** double-click on it.

■ **To go back** to the contents of the previous folder, single-click the left-pointing
triangle, called the Back button (circled on the opposite page).

■ **To move a folder,** just drag it to another window or another folder.

11

Take Advantage of the Sidebar

The **Sidebar** of every Finder window is customizable—you can add or remove any folder or document as often as you like. Items in the Sidebar are always *aliases,* or icons that merely *represent* the real file. This means you can delete an icon from the Sidebar and it does not delete the actual file that it represents.

As shown below, each of the current icons in the Sidebar actually represents a file or folder somewhere else on your hard disk.

Because a folder or document in the Sidebar is a *picture* (alias) of the real thing, you can put files into the icon in the Sidebar (just drag them in and drop them) *or* into the original folder and they go to the same place. **Try it:** Drop a file into the Documents folder in the Sidebar, then open the Documents folder in the Home window and you'll see the new document.

Add a folder or document to the Sidebar. This makes it easier to put other files into that folder, and it makes that document easier to open (just single-click on it). It's easier, not only on the Desktop, but also when you are working in an application and want to open or save a file (as shown on pages 44–45).

Remove folder or document icons from the Sidebar that you don't use. Don't worry—removing the picture of a folder from the Sidebar does not throw away the original folder nor anything in it!

- **To add a folder or document to the Sidebar,** simply drag the icon from any window or from the Desktop and drop it into the Sidebar.

    Use the Finder preferences to add hard disk icons and more; see page 265.

- **To remove an item from the Sidebar,** simply press on it with the mouse and drag it out of the Sidebar. Let go when the mouse pointer is on the Desktop. As you can see below, the icon disappears in a puff of smoke. Notice that although I removed the Pictures folder from the Sidebar, the original Pictures folder is still safe and sound in the Home window.

Change the View of the Finder Window

You can change how the items inside any window are displayed. That is, you can show them as icons, as a list of items, or in columns of information. You might prefer one view for certain things and a different view for others—with the click of a button, you can switch from one to the other. Experiment with the **three different views** and decide for yourself how you like to work.

- **To change views,** single-click one of the four little View buttons.

 From left to right, the View buttons display Icon View, List View, Column View, Cover Flow view.

The Icon View

Obviously, this displays every file as an **icon,** or small picture.

Icon View button

Sidebar

Home folders

In the Icon View, double-click to open files:

 Folder icon: Double-click a folder to display its contents in the window. (But *not* in the Sidebar; single-click those icons.)

Downloads

 Document icon: Double-click a document to open not only that document, but also the application it was created in.

Mabel.rtf

 Application icon: Double-click an application icon to open that application, ready for you to create wonderful projects.

TextEdit.app

The List View

In the **List View,** you can organize the list of files alphabetically by names, by the dates the files were last modified, by what kind of items they are, and other options. You can also see the contents of more than one folder at once.

List View button

The **blue column heading** is a *visual clue* that the contents are organized, or "sorted," by that heading. You can see, above, that the files in this window are sorted by "Name." To organize the contents by the dates they were modified, their size or kind, single-click that column heading (you might have to open the window wider or drag the blue scroll bar to the right to see the other columns and headings).

The **tiny triangle** in the column heading (circled above) is a *visual clue* that tells you whether the information is sorted from first to last or last to first. Single-click the triangle to reverse the order. Try it.

In the List View, single-click vs. double-click:

Folder icon: Single-click the **disclosure triangle** to the left of a folder to display its contents as a sublist, as shown circled above. You can view the contents of more than one folder at once.

Double-click a tiny **folder icon** to display its contents in the window, which will *replace* the contents you currently see in the window.

Document icon: Double-click a document to open not only that document, but also the application it was created in.

Application icon: Double-click an application icon to open it.

The Column View

Viewing a Finder window in **columns** allows you to see not only the contents of a selected folder or hard disk, but you can easily keep track of where each file is located. You can also view the contents of another folder without losing sight of the first one. This view helps you understand where everything is kept in your computer.

If you have photographs, graphic images, or movies in your folders, the last column displays **previews** of the items. You can even play a small movie in this preview column. Some documents can display previews as well.

Column View button

To resize an individual column, drag one of these "thumbs."

To resize all columns, Option-drag a thumb (hold down the Option key while you drag with the mouse).

You won't see a column to the right until you **single-click** a folder or a file—then a new column to the right appears to display the contents of that folder or a preview of the file. A triangle indicates that file is a folder that can contain other files.

In the example above, you can see that the "top level" folder is my Home folder, "robin." In "robin," I selected the folder "Pictures" (I clicked once on it) and in that folder I selected "Rosetta," and in that folder I selected "Rosetta playing pool.JPG," and the last column displays a preview of the selected file and information about it. (That's my dog.)

In the Column View, single-click files to display columns:

Documents ▸   **Folder icon:** Single-click a folder to display its contents in the column to the right. If there is no column to the right, one will appear.

Mabel.rtf   **Document icon:** Single-click a document to see a preview in the column to the right. Not all documents can provide picture previews, but the preview will at least give you information about that file.

Double-click a document to open not only that document, but also the application it was created in.

TextEdit.app   **Application icon:** Single-click an application icon to preview information about it, such as its version and date of modification.

Double-click an application icon to open that application.

TIP ——— You can customize many features about the Finder windows, such as the font size, the icon size, even the color inside the window. You can organize the List View by different columns of information, choose to turn off the preview in Column View, and more. See Lesson 15.

TIP ——— No matter which view you are in, you can always open a folder into a **new, separate window:** Hold down the Command key and double-click on any folder in any view.

The Cover Flow View

The Cover Flow View displays your files graphically in a slideshow-like format at the top of the window. You can "toss" the files on either side of the center image to flip through them, or use the slider bar.

For the columns below the cover images, organize and use them just as you would in Column View, as described on the previous pages.

Cover Flow View button.

Double-click an icon here to open that document or application.

While in Cover Flow view, single-click on any item in the Sidebar to display it or its contents in the window.

Single-click an icon here to display it in the Cover Flow view window above.

Double-click an icon here to open that document or application.

Quick Look/Slideshow button

The button in the toolbar with an eyeball on it is the **Quick Look/Slideshow** button. This is a terrific feature that lets you preview any file, photograph, graphic, PDF, or whatever. An image appears immediately in front of you and no application opens. With the click of the mouse, the preview disappears.

If you preview a text file, you can actually scroll through the document. If you preview a Keynote presentation, you'll see your slides and your notes. If you preview a PDF with lots of pages, you can scroll through the pages.

Once you have a Quick Look preview open, you can click on other files in the Finder and they will appear in that preview.

Select more than one file and your Quick Look automatically becomes a Slideshow with back and forward buttons.

Click these arrows to enlarge the preview to full screen or reduce it to the smaller size.

There are three other ways to open a Quick Look:

- Select one or more items and go to the File menu and choose "Quick Look."
- Select files and press Command Y *or* hit the Spacebar
- Control-click (or right-click) and choose "Quick Look *filename*."

To put away a Quick Look:

- Press Command Y *or* hit the Spacebar.
- Click the **X** in the upper-left corner of the Quick Look window.

Use the Dock

The **Dock** is that strip of icons across the bottom of the screen*. The specific icons that appear in the Dock will change as you open and close applications, view photos, or customize what's in the Dock. "Hover" your mouse over an icon (just position the pointer and hold it there, but don't click) to see a label appear that tells you the name of the application or file.

- **To open an application or document** from the Dock, single-click its icon.

The **tiny blue light** underneath an icon indicates that particular application is open and available. Even if you don't see that application on your screen, you can single-click the Dock icon and that application comes forward, ready for you to work in. Keep an eye on the application menu (as explained on pages 4–5) to verify which application is "active" at any moment.

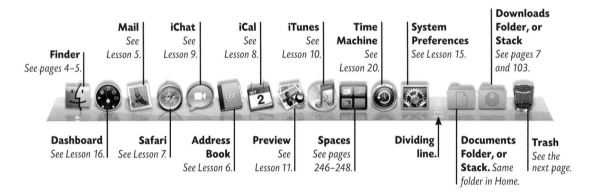

You can **rearrange** any of the icons. You can **add** or **remove** applications from the *left* side of the dividing line (see callout, above), and you can **add** or **remove** folders, documents, and web page locations from the *right* side of the dividing line. Do all this by dragging:

- **To rearrange an icon,** press the mouse on it and drag it left or right. The other icons will move over to make room.

- **To add an application,** first open the Applications folder: single-click on the Applications icon in the Sidebar of any Finder window. Then drag an application icon down to the Dock, to the *left* side of the dividing line.

- **To add a folder or a document,** drag it to the *right* side of the dividing line.

- **To remove any icon from the Dock,** press on it with the mouse and drag it upwards, off the Dock. Let go of the mouse and the icon will disappear in a poof of smoke. This doesn't hurt anything! *Never* will you delete any original item by removing its icon from the Dock.

- **To add a web page,** open your browser application, Safari (see Lesson 7 about Safari). Go to the web page that you want to have easy access to in your Dock. Drag the tiny icon that you see on the left of the web page address in the location field (circled, below) and drop it in the Dock—on the *right* side of the dividing line.

The advantage of putting a web page icon in your Dock is that you can be using any application on your Mac, and if you click that icon, your web browser opens to that page—you don't have to go find your browser first and then find the bookmark.

*Is the Dock missing?

The Dock can be customized in many ways. It might be along either side of the screen instead of at the bottom, or it might even be hidden. If you don't see the Dock anywhere, push your mouse to the far left, the far right, or the deep bottom of the screen and the hidden Dock will appear from one of those edges. See Lesson 15 for details about how to customize the Dock to fit your needs.

Use the Trash

The **Trash basket** in the Dock is where you throw away any files you don't want.

- **To put a file in the Trash,** press on any file and drag it to the Trash basket. When the *tip of the pointer* touches the basket, the basket changes color— this means you're in the right place. Let go of the mouse button and that file is in the Trash. Remember, it's the *tip of the pointer,* not the icon image, that selects the Trash basket.

- **To empty the Trash,** press *(don't click)* on the Trash icon and a little menu pops up with an option that says, "Empty Trash." Choose that option, or go to the Finder menu and choose "Empty Trash."

When you empty the Trash, you'll get a warning asking if that's what you really want to do. Some people like to have this reminder; others hate it. You can tell your Mac to stop reminding you about emptying the Trash (next page).

Are you sure you want to remove the items in the Trash permanently?
You cannot undo this action.

Cancel   OK

■ **To turn off (or on) the Trash warning:**

   1 From the Finder menu, choose "Preferences...."

   2 Click the "Advanced" icon in the toolbar at the top.

   3 Uncheck (or check) the box to "Show warning before emptying the Trash."

   4 Click the red button in the upper-left of the preferences pane to put it away.

■ **To take an item out of the Trash,** click once on the Trash icon in the Dock to open its window. Assuming you have not yet emptied the Trash, you can drag the item you want to retrieve out of the window and put it back where you want it.

Take Advantage of Keyboard Shortcuts

Most actions that you can do with the mouse and menus can also be done with **keyboard shortcuts.** Often this is not only faster, but more convenient because you don't have to take your hands off the keyboard to pick up and maneuver the mouse. You will see lots of keyboard shortcuts in the menus across the top of the screen, such as the ones shown below in the Edit menu. Use a keyboard shortcut *instead* of going to the menu.

Take careful notice of which modifier keys are used and which character keys are used.

Recognize the common modifier keys

Keyboard shortcuts work with **modifier keys,** which are those keys that don't do anything by themselves. For instance, the Shift key doesn't do anything when you press it down by itself, *but it modifies the behavior of other keys.*

Each key has a **symbol** by which it is known. These are the key symbols you will see in menus and charts:

⇧	**Shift**	↻	**Escape (esc)**
⌘	**Command**	⇞ ⇟	**PageUp or PageDown**
⌥	**Option**	⌫	**Delete**
^	**Control**	↑↓←→	**Arrow keys**
↵	**Return**	⌅	**Enter**

Fkeys are those keys across the top of the keyboard that are labeled with the letter F and a number, such as F2 or F13.

The **fn** key (function key) is on a laptop in the bottom-left corner. It helps individual keys do more than one function.

Keyboard shortcuts typically use one or more modifier key(s), plus one number, character, or Fkey, as you can see in the example of the Edit menu above: the keyboard shortcut to copy *selected* text is Command C, or ⌘ C.

Use a keyboard shortcut

The trick to using a keyboard shortcut is this: *Hold down* the modifier keys all together and keep them held down, then *tap* the associated letter, number, or Fkey *just once* for each time you want to perform an action.

For instance, the keyboard shortcut to close a window is Command W, so hold the Command key down and tap the letter W just once. If there are three windows open on your Desktop, you can hold the Command key down and tap the letter W three times and it will close three windows.

Notice gray vs. black commands

When commands in a menu are gray instead of black, the Mac is giving you an important visual clue. Here's a short exercise to demonstrate.

1 Click on an empty spot on the Desktop.

2 Now take a look through the Finder menus and notice the shortcuts for different actions, or commands. Notice how many commands are gray.

   If a command is **gray,** that means you cannot use that command at the moment. Often this is because you have not *selected* an item first, an item to which the command should apply. For instance, you can't use the command to close a window unless an open window is *selected.*

3 Now open a Finder window (if there isn't one already) and *select* a folder icon (click *once* on it).

4 Look at the File menu again, and notice how many more commands are available (they're in **black,** not gray).

5 In the File menu, find the keyboard shortcut to "Open," but don't choose the command—just remember the shortcut (Command O). Click somewhere off the menu to make the menu go away.

6 Make sure a folder is selected. Now use the keyboard shortcut, Command O, to open it.

Learn More About Mac OS X

There are a number of ways to learn more about your Mac and how to use it, all available right from your Desktop. Keep these tips in mind as you spend time on your Mac—you will learn a lot from them.

Tool tips

Most applications and dialog boxes provide little **tool tips** that pop up when you "hover" your mouse over an item. They tell you what the items do. Just hold the mouse still over a button or icon for about three seconds and if there is a tool tip, it will appear, as shown in the examples below.

TextEdit toolbar.

Font Panel toolbar.

Preview toolbar.

Hover tips

As mentioned in the previous paragraph, tool tips appear when you hover your mouse. For instance, you've probably already noticed that when you hover over an item in the Dock, the name of that item appears. Actually, all kinds of things appear when you hover—try it on everything! Below are some examples. Remember, "hover" means to hold your mouse still while pointing to an item—don't click or press the button.

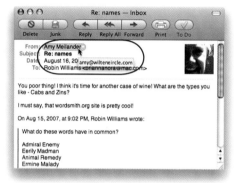

In Mail, hover over a name in an email to see what address it came from.

In iChat, hover over a name in your Buddy List or Bonjour List to see that person's information.

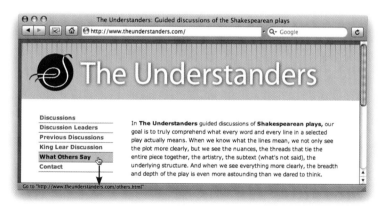

In Safari (your web browser), hover over a link name to see exactly where it goes—the destination will appear in the Status Bar at the bottom of the window. (If you don't see this Status Bar, go to the View menu in Safari and choose "Show Status Bar.")

Visual clues

Keep a constant eye out for the **visual clues** that the Mac is always providing. Every little visual extra means something! When the pointer turns into a double-headed arrow, that's a clue. When you see a little dot in a divider bar, that's a clue. When you see a triangle anywhere, that's a clue.

You are probably already aware of visual clues such as the underline beneath text on a web page to indicate a link, or the line of little colored dots in your word processor that indicates a word is misspelled. Here are a few others that will help you start noticing what your Mac is telling you.

This flashing insertion point is a clue that if you type, the text will appear at that point.

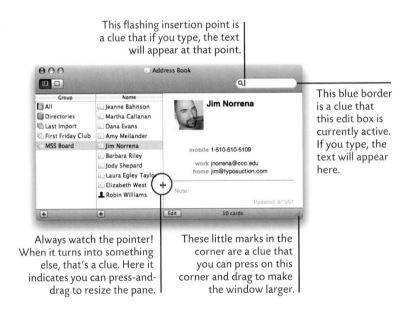

This blue border is a clue that this edit box is currently active. If you type, the text will appear here.

Always watch the pointer! When it turns into something else, that's a clue. Here it indicates you can press-and-drag to resize the pane.

These little marks in the corner are a clue that you can press on this corner and drag to make the window larger.

A tiny triangle on a blue background is a clue that you will see a menu appear when you click on it. Do you see the three menus in this toolbar?

Sometimes our eyes glaze over because there is so much visual stimulation on the Mac screen. Just keep in mind that everything means something, and slowly get to know the visual clues.

Below you see a typical title bar of a document. There are two visual clues in this title bar: the **red button** has a dark dot in it, and the **tiny icon** next to the title is gray. Both of these visual clues mean the same thing: this file has unsaved changes. Once you save the document, the dark dot goes away and the tiny icon is no longer gray.

You might see a **dot** next to a document name in an application's Window menu—that's another visual clue that the document has not been saved recently. The **checkmark** indicates the active document, or the one that is in front of all the others and that you're currently working on.

Everywhere on your Mac you will see buttons to save a document, to not save, to cancel a process, etc. One of these buttons is always **blue.** The blue is a visual clue that you can hit the Return or Enter key to activate that button instead of picking up the mouse to click on it.

Help files

No matter where you are on the Mac or what application you are working in, you'll always find **Help** just a click away. At the Finder, go to the Help menu to look up tips and techniques on just about anything.

Every application has a Help menu, and it's always at the far end of the menu choices, as shown below. Choose the Help option for that particular application, then type in a word or two that you want to look up. You see two different kinds of options available, "Menu Items" and "Help Topics."

Menu Items   This tells you where the item you're looking for can be found in the menus. It doesn't explain anything about that item. When you select an option in the "Menu Items" list, a menu drops down and a big moving arrow points to the item you're looking for.

Help Topics   If Apple has written information in the Help file, you will see a list of the possible topics. Choose one and the Help file opens to that piece of information.

Support pages

The Apple web site has a huge number of **support pages.** Here you can find manuals that you can view on screen or download (copy) to your computer. There are discussion pages where users talk about different products and software packages on the Mac, ask questions, and answer questions. You can sign up for training at a local Apple store, read the product question-and-answer pages for hardware and software, and more. Go to www.Apple.com/support.

.Mac Learning Center

If you are a .Mac (pronounced *dot mac*) member, take advantage of the **.Mac Learning Center** where you'll find dozens of tutorials and movies to help you learn more about all sorts of features of your computer. Log in to your .Mac account and then find the link called "Learning Center."

A .Mac membership costs $99.95 a year and includes lots of perks. Check Apple's .Mac web site for details, www.Apple.com/dotmac.

Although many of the tutorials are for .Mac members only, you'll find lots of great information for everyone.

2

GOALS

Become familiar with the
various disk icons in your
Finder windows

Understand the Library
folders

Learn how to select
multiple items in the
different window views

Use Exposé to access
a window easily

Take advantage of
contextual menus

Use keyboard shortcuts
to navigate Save As and
Open dialog boxes

Access menus at the
Finder without using
the mouse

A Bit Beyond the Basics

If you're feeling comfortable with the techniques and features described in the previous lesson, then carry on into this lesson and learn a few more advanced (but still everyday and useful) features. If anything overwhelms you in this lesson, feel free to skip it and come back later.

Understand the Various Disk Icons

In the **top portion of the Sidebar,** you probably see something similar to the example shown below—you might see more icons and you might see fewer. These icons represent hard disks, networks, a CD, a DVD, an iPod, or any other type of removable media.

Display the contents of each media item the same way you do any of the items in the lower portion of the Sidebar: single-click the icon.

You can choose what gets displayed in this upper portion of the Sidebar; see page 265.

The **Hard Disk** is your computer, the disk that holds the operating system and all your files. You can rename your hard disk at any time, just as you rename a folder (as explained on page 11).

The **iDisk** is your personal storage space on Apple's computers, which is something you get when you sign up for a .Mac account. A single click on the iDisk icon connects you to that storage space. If you don't have a .Mac account, you don't have any reason to display this icon.

"Chaucer" is a CD I inserted, as you can tell by the icon. To its right is the Eject symbol.

⏏ When you see the **eject symbol** to the right of an icon (the triangle with a bar under it), that means it is a removable disk of some sort. It might be a CD, a DVD, an iPod, or even another computer that you are connected to over the network. Click on the symbol to eject or disconnect the item.

TIP ———— By default, your Desktop displays the same icons that appear in the upper portion of the Sidebar. If you want to clear some or all of these icons off your Desktop, see page 262.

Shared

The **Shared** section (if you have it in your Sidebar) displays any other computers or disks that you can connect to through your *local* network. A local network is one in which computers in a small area, such as a home or office, are all connected via wires or a wireless connection.

Places

The **Places** section displays folders and files on your own computer.

Search For

The **Search For** folders are "smart folders" that automatically keep track of files for you to make it easier for you to find things. Please see page 336 for more details. Feel free to single-click on any icon in the "Search For" section to see the files it has organized for you.

View your Home folder from the hard disk

Below you see another way of looking at your Home folder, using the Column view (as explained on pages 16–17).

You can tell by the highlight that in the top portion of the Sidebar I clicked on the hard drive icon labeled "Hard Disk"; the hard disk is where all your files are stored (although you might have renamed your hard disk). This click displays the folders stored on that hard disk; you can see them in the column to the right.

Then I clicked on "Users," which displays my Home folder in the *next* column. If you make any other users, as explained in Lesson 18, you will see all of those users here.

Then I clicked on "robin," which displays my Home folders in the *next* column.

Do you see the Applications folder in the screen shot below? Notice that it's in the top level (first column) of the Hard Disk. Your Applications icon in the Sidebar makes it easy to access this folder.

Experiment with different ways of getting to your Home folders until you feel comfortable about where things are stored on your Mac.

Understand the Various Library Folders

As you work with your Mac, you'll run across a number of folders with the same name: **Library.** Do you see the two Library folders in the illustration below? And if you open the "System" folder, you'd see another Library folder.

Library folders contain information that the operating system and certain applications need to function. Unless you have a really good reason and know exactly what you're doing, **leave the Library folders alone—don't put anything in them and don't take anything out.**

The Library folder you see above, the one directly to the right of the "Hard Disk," is at the "top level" of your hard disk. It contains files that are critical to running your entire computer, and those files pertain to all users who use this Mac. For instance, this Library folder has a folder inside called "Fonts," and all fonts that are installed into this top level folder are available to all users. (For details about multiple users and how to create them, please see Lesson 18.)

The Library folder in the far-right column, above, is in my Home collection, my user folder. This is where all my application preferences, web page bookmarks, Address Book contact information, email, and other personal information is stored. Each user you set up will have her own Library folder with all her own data. There is even a Fonts folder in here; any fonts a user puts in her own Fonts folder will be available only to that user.

That's all you really need to know about your Library folders—and leave them alone for now!

Select Multiple Items in the Finder

To select an individual item in a Finder window, you simply single-click it, as you probably know. But often you'll want to select more than one item at a time. **To select multiple items,** there are two ways to do it, as explained below. Once items are a group, you can move, trash, or open all the selected files at once, change their labels (see page 264 about labels), and more.

In the Icon View

To select multiple items in the Icon View, hold down the **Command key** *or* the **Shift key** and single-click on as many items as you want to group together. You can only select items from one window while in the Icon View.

Or *press* on a blank spot in the window and *drag* the mouse around the items you want to select. Any icon that is completely or partially enclosed by the rectangle you draw with the mouse will be selected.

You can see that the rectangle I dragged is partially overlapping six files. When I let go of the mouse, all six of these files are selected.

In the List View or Column View

In these views, using the Shift key is different from using the Command key.

Hold down the **Command key** and single-click on multiple items.

In the *List View,* you can select items from several different folders in the same window, as long as their contents are showing in the list. See the example on the opposite page.

In the *Column View,* you can select multiple items from one column at a time.

Command-click to select non-contiguous items.

The **Shift key** lets you select a group of items that are *contiguous,* or next to each other in the list. Single-click on the *first* item you want to select in a list. Then hold down the Shift key and click on the *last* item you want in the list. *Everything between the two clicks will be selected.* See the example below.

Shift-click to select contiguous items.

To deselect an item from any group in any view: Command-click it.

To deselect all items from any group in any view: Single-click on any blank area in the window.

Exposé

Some of us like to keep only one window or two open at a time; others have a clutter of windows all over the place all the time. If you like to keep lots of windows open (application windows, preference panes, Finder windows, etc.), Exposé is a feature you'll enjoy because it helps you find everything even if it appears to be a mess.

Your Mac is already set up to use Exposé. Open several windows on your Mac, then try it—press the F11 key at the top of your keyboard (on a laptop, you might need to hold down the fn key while you tap F11). Don't be scared if every window on your Mac disappears! Just hit the F11 key to bring them all back.

The keyboard shortcuts for Exposé are explained below, but if you need to change them, use the Exposé & Spaces system preferences, as shown below (go to the Apple menu, choose "System Preferences...," and click on its icon).

In the System Preferences pane, click this icon to get the preferences where you can change the shortcuts.

Use these right-hand menus to assign an Exposé action to a two-button mouse and/or a mouse with a middle button.

- **To show every window on the screen at once,** as shown on the bottom of the opposite page, press F9.

- **To show just application windows** (no Finder windows), press F10.

- **To hide every window so you can see your entire Desktop,** press F11.

- **To use your mouse** to activate Exposé, assign the actions in the preferences, as shown above.

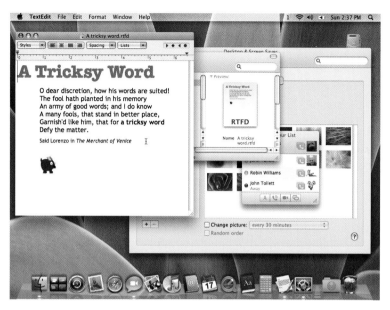

Above is my messy Desktop. Rather than move windows around to find what I want, I can hit F9 and they all line themselves up, as shown below. As my mouse slides over the top of each one, it turns blue (see below),

the title of the document or window appears, and the pointer turns into a browser hand. The browser hand is a visual clue that if I click on that particular item, it will come forward and everything else will hide behind it.

Look for Contextual Menus

These are great. You can Control-click just about anywhere (hold down the Control key—not the *Command key*—and click) and a menu pops up right where you click. This is a **contextual menu** that is specific to the item you Control-click on, meaning what you see in the pop-up menu depends on what you click on (as opposed to menus in the menu bar or in dialog boxes that always contain the same items).

To display a contextual menu, hold down the Control key and click on an icon, a blank spot on the Desktop, inside a Finder window, or just about anywhere. A little menu pops up, as you can see by the examples below.

If you have a **two-button mouse,** you don't need the Control key—just use the right-hand button to display a contextual menu.

There is *no visual clue* for a contextual menu—just keep checking. You'll find them in applications, on web pages, in toolbars, in the Sidebar, and elsewhere.

A contextual menu on a blank spot on the Desktop.

A contextual menu on a folder.

A contextual menu on a Toolbar.

This is an example of a contextual menu in an application.

Control-click on a misspelled word to get a contextual menu with possible spellings. Select the correct word, let go of the mouse button, and the misspelled word is instantly replaced with the correct one.

Try the "Speech" option—your text will be read out loud to you.

TIP —— In Finder windows, the **Action button** does many of the same things as the contextual menu. Try it: Single-click to select an icon, then click the Action button to see what the contextual options are.

Use Keyboard Shortcuts in Dialog Boxes

When creating and working with documents, you can use keyboard shortcuts in the **Save As** and **Open** dialog boxes. Use the Tab key to select different areas of the dialog box and the Arrow keys to select items in the columns. When you Save As, you can title your document, select the folder in which you want it stored, and save it—without using the mouse.

Visual Clues: Notice the **blue border** around this Save As edit box, and the blue highlight on the text; this means the edit box and text are **selected.** Simply type to replace the highlighted text.

If you don't see the full dialog box, as shown here, single-click this disclosure triangle.

You can search for the folder in which you want to save your file.

Your file will be saved in whatever folder or disk is named in this menu. So if you want to save the file in another folder, you must first select the other folder before you click the Save button.

I suggest that you uncheck this box so the extensions are visible to you. See the tip below.

You can create a new folder right now and your document will be saved inside of that new folder. But remember where you put that new folder!

TIP —— **Extensions** are the three- or four-letter abbreviations at the ends of file names. Your Mac needs these extensions so it knows what to do with the files. You can "hide" the extensions so you don't have to see them, but it's a good idea to get used to them. They will help *you* keep track of what kind of files you're creating.

Use the Tab key to select various parts of the Save As or Open dialog boxes:

❶ If the insertion point is in the field where you name the file, then the first Tab selects the Search field.

❷ The next Tab selects the Sidebar. Use the up and down Arrow keys to highlight the folder or disk you need.

❸ The next Tab selects the first column. Use the up and down arrows to select a file in the first column, then hit the right Arrow to select the next column.

❹ When you select the folder into which you want to save the file, hit the Return key to activate the Save button.

Navigate the Desktop and Finder Windows

If you so choose, you can get around your entire Desktop and inside Finder windows using the keyboard. For instance, you can get to every menu across the top of the screen and choose commands, without ever touching the mouse.

Access the menus on the Desktop or in any application:

1   Press Control F2 to select the menu bar across the top of the screen (on a laptop, you might need to press **fn Control F2**).

2   Use the left and right Arrow keys to select menu items across the menu bar, or type the first letter of the menu you want to select. When a menu is selected, you'll see it highlight.

3   When the menu name you want is highlighted, press the Return key to drop down its menu.

4   Press the down and up arrows to choose a command in the list, or type the first letter or two or three. (If there is more than one command that starts with the same letter, type the first two or three letters quickly to select a specific one.)

5   Hit Return to activate the selected command.

   To put the menu away without activating a command, press Command Period (Command .).

Try these shortcuts in a Finder window:

- Type the first letter or two or three to select files.
- When you're in the List View or Column View, use the Arrow keys to select the columns to the right or left, then use the letter keys to select files in that column.
- Select a document, hit Command O to open it, and get to work!

If you are interested in using more keyboard shortcuts, go to the "Keyboard & Mouse" preferences, as explained on pages 276. In that preference pane you see shown on the page, you'll find an extensive list of keyboard shortcuts. The shortcuts are not printed here in this book—they're in that preference pane on your Mac!

Mac OS X Applications in Leopard

3

GOALS

Understand the
common features
of Apple applications

Realize what can NOT be
covered in this book

Introduction to Mac OS X Applications

One of the greatest things about Mac applications is that they are consistent, which makes them easy to learn and easy to use— what you learn in one application applies easily to just about any other application.

In this short introductory lesson, I'm just going to present a brief overview of the major apps (applications) that you'll find in your Applications folder and the Dock. All of the Apple applications are integrated with other apps, and they all share certain features and tools. In the following chapters I'll go into more detail about individual programs, and in Lesson 13 of this section you'll learn how to use the tools that all Apple applications share.

Know your Applications Folder

In the Sidebar of any Finder window is an icon labeled **Applications.** Single-click this icon to display the contents of the Applications window. These are the programs you will use to create your work on your Mac.

At any time, you can put the application you use most often **in the Dock** so you'll have easy access to it: Just drag the application icon from this window and drop it on the Dock. If you accidentally lose something from the Dock, you can always come back to this Applications window to drag the item back in.

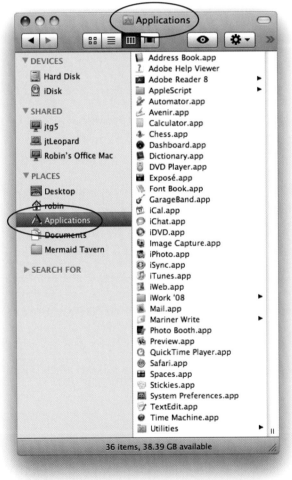

Some applications that you buy will display their *folders* here in the Applications window instead of the *applications' icons* (here, you can see the Mariner Write folder, the word processor I use).

If you see an application in a folder, open that folder and find the actual *application* icon to drag to the Dock.

Application Integration

All of the Apple applications share certain tools such as the Spell Checker and Grammar Checker, the Fonts palette, the Colors palette, the Special Character palette, and more. All of those common tool elements are explained in detail in Lesson 13.

Also keep in mind that all of these applications also work together in amazing ways. You can drag text and graphics from one app to another, save files into different formats, save to-do messages from Mail directly into iCal, create a PDF in TextEdit that you can read and annotate in Preview, and more. See the individual application chapters and Lesson 14 for details.

And be sure to read the last page of each of the application lessons to learn how many ways each app is integrated with others!

What I'm not Covering!

I introduce iTunes in Lesson 10, but I don't cover iPhoto, iWeb, iMovie, or iDVD because they are not part of the Mac operating system. John Tollett covers those, however, in a big fat book called *Cool Mac Apps,* which is essentially eighteen manuals in one book. There you'll find much more information than I can provide in this introductory book about such programs as Mail, iCal, and iChat—48 pages on iChat alone, and 76 pages on Mail. You can see why I don't cover all of that in this book!

Nor do I cover Pages, Numbers, or Keynote in this book because you have to buy those in the iWork package. If you have those programs, Peachpit publishes a book on iWork, plus the applications have pretty good Help files built right in.

Know the Common Features of Mac Apps

Most Mac applications have these features in common.

Windows and window controls

When you open an application, you'll actually be working in a **window.** If you worked through Lesson 1, you already know all about windows, even ones you haven't seen before. You see the same red, yellow, and green buttons to close, minimize, and resize the window. The document name and a tiny icon appear in the title bar. You can drag the title bar or any edge to move the window.

Application menu

The application menu (directly to the right of the blue Apple menu) always tells you the name of the currently **active application,** the one you're working in (even if there is no document window open on the screen). You'll always find the Quit command at the bottom of this menu.

File and Edit menus

You'll always find File and Edit as the first two menus to the right of the application menu.

Although each application includes specific features in its menus, in the *File menu* you'll always find the commands to *open* an existing document or create a *new* one, *save* the document or *save as* with another name, *close* the active window, and *print* the active document.

From the *Edit menu,* as shown below, you can always *undo or redo, cut, copy, paste, delete, select all,* check the *spelling and grammar,* and access the *Special Characters.*

Preferences Every application has its own preferences where you can **customize**
the application to suit yourself. You'll always open the preferences
from the application menu (see the previous page). Typically you'll
see a toolbar across the top of the preferences pane; single-click an
icon in that toolbar to set the preferences for that particular feature.

Safari preferences.
The Tabs pane
is selected.

Toolbars Many applications have a Toolbar across the top of the window.
Usually you can **customize** this Toolbar: check the **View menu**
for a command called "Customize Toolbar…," or use the contextual
menu (Control-click or right-click on the toolbar).

This is a typical
sheet that drops
down from a
toolbar so you can
customize it.

Sidebars or drawers

Many applications have a sidebar, a drawer, or some other sort of pane on the side of the window. Single-click the icons you see in a sidebar-like feature to display its particular contents in the window.

Here the iTunes Store is selected in the sidebar.

Special collections

Several applications use collection metaphors such as *Albums* in iPhoto, *Playlists* in iTunes, *Bookmark Collections* in Safari, *Mailboxes* in Mail, *Groups* in Address Book. Use these to store and organize your stuff.

Open and Save As dialog boxes

Whenever you open an existing document or save a new one, the dialog boxes you see to open a new document or save a document always look familiar. See pages 44–45 for tips on how to get around these dialog boxes and save into particular folders.

Help files   Every application has a Help menu with Help files specific to that application. You can either use the menu you see on your screen or press **Command ?** to bring up the files. You'll find a search box where you can type in key words, then hit Return to display the answers. See page 30 for more details.

Action button and menu

 In many applications, you'll see the Action button (shown to the left) that displays the Action menu. Every application has different options—always click on it to see what is available.

Preview before you print

At the bottom of the Print dialog box is a button called "Preview." Click this to open your document in the Preview application where you can see what it will look like when printed.

Search   Just about every application has a search feature. It's usually in the upper-right corner of the window, as you can see in the iTunes window on the opposite page and in the Address Book below. Just exactly what the search feature searches depends on the application. See the individual overviews in the lessons for each application.

Smart Folders

Many applications have some version of *Smart Folders* that automatically update themselves according to your specified criteria. See Lesson 19 on Spotlight to learn how to take advantage of this great feature.

Other applications have similar types of smart folders: The Address Book has *Smart Groups* that will add appropriate contacts to themselves; iTunes has *Smart Playlists* that will add music to themselves; Mail has *Smart Mailboxes.* See the individual lessons for each application.

This Smart Group finds people in my Address Book who have birthdays coming up. iCal will add these birthdays to a calendar; see page 152.

4

GOALS

TextEdit for Word Processing

TextEdit is a small yet surprisingly powerful word processor. Use it for writing memos, letters, diaries, novels, grocery lists, memoirs, or any other text documents. In TextEdit you can create simple tables and automatically numbered or bulleted lists. You can put shadows on type, insert images, search and replace text, and more. But it's not a full-blown word processor such as Apple's Pages or MarinerWrite (MarinerSoftware.com). Although TextEdit can't do all the fancy things a big word processor can, it's excellent for many projects.

You'll find TextEdit in your Applications folder. If you use it regularly, drag its icon to the Dock.

If you've never used a word processor before and you don't know how to enter text, select text for formatting, cut/copy and paste, etc., please read *The Little Mac Book* first! This chapter assumes you know the basics of working in a word processor.

Read Microsoft Word Files

Do you work with people who send you **Microsoft Word files,** but you prefer to keep a Microsoft-free environment on your own computer? TextEdit can open Word files and save as Word files. Some of the advanced features will be missing, but this works great for basic text documents, including those with simple tables or numbered/bulleted lists.

If you don't have Microsoft Word installed on your Mac, file names ending with .doc (which are usually Word files) **automatically open** in TextEdit when you double-click them.

To force a Word document to open in TextEdit (if it's not your default), drag the file and drop it on the TextEdit icon.

(If the TextEdit icon is not in your Dock, it's in the Applications folder. If you want TextEdit in the Dock, drag it from the Applications folder and drop it in the Dock.)

Change the default application to open Word files

If you own Microsoft Word and want your **.doc files to open in Word,** not TextEdit, you can **change the default application**:

1 Control-click (or right-click) on the Word file icon to get its contextual menu.

2 While the menu is visible, also hold down the Option key. This changes the "Open With" command to "Always Open With."

3 Choose "Always Open With." If Microsoft Word is on your Mac, you'll see it listed in the top part of the pop-out menu. Select it, and your .doc files will now automatically open in Microsoft Word.

I don't own Microsoft Word, so it doesn't appear in my list of options. But if you own it and it's installed on your Mac, you'll see the option here to always open with Word.

Save TextEdit files as Word docs

You can save any TextEdit file as a Microsoft Word document to send to people who insist on that format.

To save a TextEdit file as a Word document:

1   Go to the File menu and choose "Save As...."

2   In the File Format menu at the bottom of the Save As dialog box, choose "Word 2007 Format (docx)." This automatically adds the Word extension, .docx, to the end of your file name.

As you can see in that Format menu, you can also save your files in several other formats. Keep these other formats in mind!

If you don't see the extension at the end of the file name—and you want to—make sure there is no checkmark next to "Hide Extension," circled below.

If you don't see the entire panel, as shown here, single-click this disclosure triangle.

Find and Replace Words or Phrases

Did you write your entire novel using your sweetheart's name, Peter, as the hero? And now Peter's abandoned you and you want to **change** the hero's name to Heathcliff? No problem:

1   Go to the Edit menu, slide down to "Find," then from the pop-out menu, choose "Find...," *or* skip all that and press Command F.

2   Find "Peter" and replace with "Heathcliff."

If you create a lot of text in TextEdit, it will be worth your time to experiment with the options you see in the Find dialog box, as described below.

To replace:

Only the *currently selected occurrence* of the text, click "Replace."

All occurrences of the text in the document, click "Replace All."

All occurrences of the text *in a block of selected text,* hold down the Option key and click "In Selection" (it appears when the Option key is down).

To simultaneously select (but not replace):

All occurrences of the text, hold down the Control key; "Replace All" changes to "Select All."

All occurrences *in a block of selected text,* hold down both the Control key *and* the Option key; "Replace All" changes to "In Selection."

Paste Text to Match the Existing Text

This is one of my favorite features. Let's say you're writing a term paper and you copy a quote from a web page to add to your paper (properly cited, of course). Typically the copied text pastes in with the typeface, style, size, and color that were originally applied to it. But to add this quotation to your term paper, you want it to look like the rest of your page. Use this great feature instead of the regular paste:

> From the Edit menu, choose **Paste and Match Style,**
> *or* use the keyboard shortcut, Shift Option Command V.

The pasted text will pick up all the formatting *from the character to the left of the flashing insertion point.* This technique works in Mail as well.

Use your Favorite Text Styles Easily

TextEdit doesn't have the powerful style sheets of a full-blown word processor, but it does make your writing life much easier by letting you create **favorite styles** of basic type features so you can apply them quickly. A "style" contains all of the formatting information, such as typeface, size, color, indents, etc., so you can apply everything to selected text with one click of a button.

These styles are saved with TextEdit, not with an individual document, so you can use the same styles in different documents.

To create your own favorite style:

1   Type some text, any text, and set up the typeface, size, color, linespace, and the ruler the way you want it.

2   Click anywhere in that formatted text.

3   From the "Styles" menu in the toolbar, choose "Other..."

4   Click the button, "Add To Favorites."

5   Name your new favorite style and choose your options. Click "Add."

To apply a style, select the characters, then choose the style name from the Styles menu. All of the formatting that you saved with that style will be automatically applied with the click of that button.

Complete your Word Automatically

The **Complete** command in the Edit menu pops up a menu of possible completions for an unfinished word, as shown below. The list learns new words—type a word once, then next time you start to type it, that word appears in the list. Frequently used words appear at the top.

1   Start to type a word that you're not sure how to spell or one that is long and you don't want to type the whole thing.

2   From the Edit menu, choose "Complete," *or* press Option Escape (the **esc** key in the upper-left of the keyboard). A menu like the one shown below will appear.

3   If the word you want is already highlighted at the top of the list, just hit Return. If not, use the Down arrow key to select a word and then hit Return, *or* double-click on the word you want.

Typographer's Quotes!

At last, in the year 2007, TextEdit finally gets automatic typographer's quotes, or **smart quotes.** Smart quotes (and apostrophes) are the curly ones, not the lame, straight, typewriter quotes. Nothing will make your work look as amateurish as typewriter quotes.

typewriter quotes

It's "Baby Doll."

smart quotes

It's "Baby Doll."

There are two places where you can turn "Smart Quotes" on or off. In the TextEdit preferences (explained below), you can turn them on or off *for the application.* But you can also *override* this application setting in individual documents.

To turn on Smart Quotes for every new TextEdit document:

1   From the TextEdit menu, choose "Preferences...."

2   Click the "New Document" tab, if it isn't already blue.

3   Check the box for "Smart quotes."

To turn Smart Quotes off or on for an individual document:

1   From the Edit menu, slide down to "Substitutions."

2   In the sub-menu, click "Smart Quotes." A checkmark means they're on, and no checkmark means they are off.

Why would you want to turn them off? So you can type the feet and inch marks without looking dumb. For instance, I am 5′8″ tall, *not* 5′8″ tall.

Tabs and Indents

The tab and indent markers in TextEdit function as in any word processor. Drag tab markers from the Tab box to the ruler; drag them off the ruler to remove them. Drag the indent markers shown below to indent either just the first line of text or both the left and right edges.

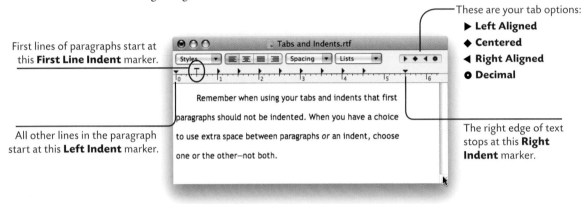

First lines of paragraphs start at this **First Line Indent** marker.

These are your tab options:
▶ **Left Aligned**
◆ **Centered**
◀ **Right Aligned**
● **Decimal**

All other lines in the paragraph start at this **Left Indent** marker.

The right edge of text stops at this **Right Indent** marker.

Remember when using your tabs and indents that first paragraphs should not be indented. When you have a choice to use extra space between paragraphs *or* an indent, choose one or the other—not both.

Examples of tab and indent settings

Below are some examples of how to set up your tabs and indents to create certain effects. Remember, for a tab, first set the marker, then hit the Tab key *before* you type the text. Once you've got tabs set up, you can move the tab and the text will follow; *just make sure you select the text before you move the tab!*

Follow the directions as explained in each window below to achieve the look you see in the window. *The tab applies only to the selected paragraphs.* Because of the way paragraphs work on the Mac, you need only click inside a paragraph to select the whole thing. To select more than one paragraph, press and drag to highlight several characters in each paragraph.

This is a common setup. It might seem a little tricky at first, but once you get it, you'll love knowing how to do it.

1. This is a list of numbers in which the text aligns with the text, not the number. Set the tabs as you see above. Then make sure you hit the Tab key *before* you type a number.

2. At the end of the number (after the period), hit the Tab key again to make sure all the text will align.

3. Notice there is a **Left Aligned** tab *sitting directly on top of* the **Left Indent** marker.

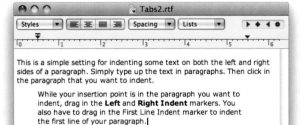

This is a simple setting for indenting some text on both the left and right sides of a paragraph. Simply type up the text in paragraphs. Then click in the paragraph that you want to indent.

While your insertion point is in the paragraph you want to indent, drag in the **Left** and **Right Indent** markers. You also have to drag in the First Line Indent marker to indent the first line of your paragraph.

All paragraphs follow those three Indent markers! Play with them!

This is an example of an individual paragraph indented on both sides.

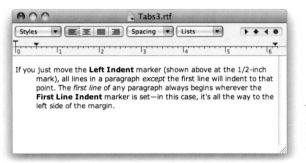

If you just move the **Left Indent** marker (shown above at the 1/2-inch mark), all lines in a paragraph *except* the first line will indent to that point. The *first line* of any paragraph always begins wherever the **First Line Indent** marker is set—in this case, it's all the way to the left side of the margin.

You can call this an outdent, where the first line is outdented further than the other lines.

To make **columns of information,** set up the tabs and then make sure you hit a Tab *before* each column, then type. You can always adjust the columns later. Just make sure you select every line that you want to adjust *before* you move the tabs and indents!

Ryan Williams	**Jimmy Williams**	**Scarlett Williams**
30 years old	26 years old	22 years old
Navy SEAL	Artist	Adventurer
San Diego	Portland	Portland

Columns are easy to create. Just remember to hit ONE tab to get to the next column.

Create Lists that Number Themselves

If you have a list of items, TextEdit can number them for you with numbers, capital or lowercase letters, or other options. When you add or delete items from the list, TextEdit automatically updates the numbering.

When you click on the Lists menu (circled above) and choose a numbering option, the numbers apply to **either** of the following:

> If you **selected text** on the page before you went to the Lists menu, your choice of list numbering will apply to the selected text. Each time you hit a Return, TextEdit considers that line to be the next item in the list.

> If there is no selected text, the flashing **insertion point** is "filled" with the list specifications, and everything you type from that point on will be in the list format. This is a good way to start a new list: Just make sure your insertion point is flashing where you want the list to begin, *then* go to the List menu and choose your numbering system, *then* start typing.

Choose "Other..." in the Lists menu to set up the specifications of your choice.

To end the sequencing of numbers in a list, hit the Return key twice at the end of the last item.

To delete the list numbers, single-click anywhere in the list. Open the Lists menu and choose "None."

Create Tables

You can create simple tables in TextEdit. This table feature also helps ensure that tables created in a Word document will open in some form in TextEdit.

To create a table in TextEdit:

1   Position your insertion point where you want the table to begin.

2   Go to the Format menu, slide down to "Text," then choose "Table...."

3   The Table palette appears, as shown below. Choose how many rows and columns you want in the table. You can determine how the text is aligned vertically as well as horizontally in each cell (use the "Alignment" icons), and more. Spend a few minutes to familiarize yourself with the tools.

If you don't want any border, enter **0** (zero) in the "Cell Border" field.

Click on the color well to get the Colors panel.

To activate this color well, first choose "Color Fill" from the menu to its left.

As you **type in a cell,** the cell expands downward to fit the text.

Change the formatting of the text as you do on a regular TextEdit page: select the text first, then choose formatting from the menus or palettes.

4   **To resize rows and columns,** position your pointer over the edge of a cell. The pointer turns into a two-headed arrow. With that two-headed arrow, press-and-drag on a cell edge to resize it.

Create Live Web Links and Email Links

It's easy to create web links and email links on a TextEdit page. If you send someone the TextEdit file, that person can click on a web link; her browser will open and go to the page you specify. An email link in the document opens her email program, pre-addressed to whomever you specified.

If you make a PDF of your document (see page 71), the links will still work in the PDF.

Create links as you type web addresses:

1   Simply go to the Edit menu and slide down to "Substitutions."

2   In the pop-out menu, choose "Smart Links." If there is a checkmark next to "Smart Links," it's already on!

3   On your TextEdit page, just type the web address. It needs the *www* part of the web address. If your address doesn't have *www,* then be sure to include the *http://* in the address on the page. You'll know if it's working or not because the text will turn into an underlined link.

Sometimes the text on the page is not the actual address, but you do want the *link* to go to the address. For instance, perhaps you wrote, "Please visit our Mary Sidney web site," and you want the link attached to "Mary Sidney" to go to MarySidney.com. Or you want to say, Email me! as a link to your actual email address. In either case, use the manual process.

To manually create a web link on a TextEdit page:

1   Type the text that you want to apply a web link to. *This text can be anything— it doesn't have to be the web address itself!*

2   Select the text to which you want to apply the link.

3   From the Format menu, slide down to "Text," then choose "Link...."

4   Enter the web page address. Make sure you include this code at the beginning of the web address: **http://**

5   Click OK.

To create an email link on a TextEdit page:

1   Type the text to which you want to apply an email link. This text can be anything—it doesn't have to be the email address itself.

2   Select the text you want to apply the link to.

3   From the Format menu, slide down to "Text," then choose "Link...."

4   Type into the field: **mailto:**

5   Immediately after the colon you typed (as shown above), enter the entire email address just as you would address it.   mailto:**name@domain.com**

6   Click OK.

Select Non-Contiguous Text

This is really quite wonderful. "Contiguous" means "sharing a common border." Very few applications allow you to select individual sections of text that are not physically next to each other (text that is *non-contiguous*). This technique lets you apply formatting or copy, cut, or delete separate sections of text all at once.

To select non-contiguous text:

1   Press-and-drag to select a section of text.

2   Hold down the Command key. Press-and-drag to select some other text that is not contiguous!

Print Automatic Page Numbers

You can add page numbers to a *printed* document (the numbers won't appear on the screen). This feature also automatically adds the name of the document in the upper-left corner (including the extension, probably .rtf), the date and time in the upper-right corner, and the words "Page ___ of ___" in the bottom-right corner. That is, in TextEdit you can't choose one or the other of these—they all appear on the page, or none.

To print the page numbers (and everything else), press Command P (or go to the File menu and choose "Print..."). In the Print dialog box, shown below, make sure "TextEdit" is chosen from the menu. Check the box to "Print header and footer."

Extra Tips and Notes

Ruler: If the ruler isn't showing, press Command R. Without the ruler showing, you can't set tabs, indents, or margins.

Formatting: If text won't let you apply formatting, it's probably using "Plain Text." Go to the Format menu and choose "Make Rich Text."

Wrap to Page: If the text is stretching the entire width of the window no matter how wide you open it, you might want to switch to the option where the text wraps according to the page it will be printed on. To do this, go to the Format menu and choose "Wrap to Page."

When the TextEdit page is using "Wrap to Window," your printer will reduce the size of the text on the printed page to match the line lengths on your screen. So **if your text prints really tiny,** follow the step above to "Wrap to Page."

Standard Mac OS X Application Features

Don't forget that TextEdit includes all of the standard Mac features as explained in Lesson 13, such as spell checking and grammar checking, creating shadows for text, applying color, using special characters, previewing before you print, making PDFs, and more.

TextEdit is Integrated With:

Safari: Web address links open in Safari.
Control-click on a word in TextEdit to search for it in Google.

Dictionary: Control-click on a word and choose "Look Up in Dictionary" from the pop-up menu to get that word's definition and thesaurus entry.

Mail: Email address links in TextEdit open a pre-addressed email message in Mail.

Preview: Create a PDF in TextEdit (see below) that opens in Preview. You can also annotate the PDF in Preview (see Lesson 11).

Speech: Have your text read aloud to you. Select the text to read just the selected part, or select nothing and the voice (named Alex) starts at the beginning of the document. Then go to the Edit menu, slide down to "Speech," and choose "Start Speaking." To turn the voice off, you have to go back to the menu and choose "Stop Speaking," or use the contextual menu (Control-click or right-click in the document) and from the contextual menu, choose "Stop Speaking."

Other Relevant Lessons for TextEdit

Search: Besides the search-and-replace feature explained on page 60, you can also do a Spotlight search, as explained on page 350.

PDFs: All TextEdit documents can be turned into PDFs with the click of a button: just go to File and choose "Print...," and in the Print dialog box, click the "PDF" button and choose "Save as PDF...."

Fax: You can fax any TextEdit page with the click of a button. See Lesson 17.

5

GOALS

Mail for Email, Notes, and To Do Lists

Mail is Apple's application for sending and receiving email. If you have more than one email account on more than one server, Mail can check them all at the same time. You can send mail from any of your accounts right through Mail.

A really wonderful feature is "stationery," where you can create fancy HTML email messages with special fonts, images, and design—all with the click of a button.

And take advantage of the Notes and To Do lists in Mail. They even coordinate instantly with your iCal information to expand their usefulness.

New Account Setup Assistant

It's easy to add your email account to Mail if you didn't do it when you first installed Leopard or turned on your new Mac. **If your account is already set up, skip to page 78.**

1   In Mail, go to the File menu and choose "Add Account...."

2   A window, shown below, appears. If you enter your .Mac account name and password, you're done—your Mac will fill in everything else and your email will appear in the viewer window. Skip the rest of these setup instructions (except take a look at the SMTP info on page 76).

   If you have an email account that is not a .Mac account, enter the information required, then click "Continue."

Add Account You'll be guided through the necessary steps to set up an additional mail account. To get started, fill out the following information: Full Name: Robin Williams Email Address: robin@TheShakespearePapers. Password: ••••••••	This is the name that will be visible to the people to whom you send email.

Cancel   Go Back   Continue

3   The next window asks technical details about your account. If you don't know what kind of account it is, call your Internet Service Provider and ask. *Generally speaking,* this is how to choose the type of account:

   Choose POP if you have an email account with your ISP, or if you have a domain name that you paid for and you opted for an email account with it (regardless of whether there are actually web pages for that domain name). **This is the most common.**

   Choose IMAP if your account is the kind that you can use on different computers and always see your mail. This is usually with a paid service or a large company intranet (although most POPs can be set up as IMAP if you ask your provider).

Choose Exchange if your company uses the Microsoft Exchange server and the administrator has configured it for IMAP access. See your system administrator for details.

This is what will appear in the Mail sidebar so you know which account it is.

See below.

See below.

Each account type has slightly different information to enter.

For instance, if you choose a POP account, Mail wants to know the **Incoming Mail Server.** It's usually something like *pop.domain.com* or *mail.domain.com.* The "domain," of course, is to be replaced with the domain name of your email. For instance, I use *mail.TheShakespearePapers.com* for my mail that comes from that web site. If you're not sure, check your email host's web site or call and ask for the "incoming mail server."

If you use a **webmail** account, such as Hotmail, GMail, AOL, Yahoo, etc., it's a wee bit trickier to set up Mail. It's not difficult at all, but you have to know certain information. Because this information changes all the time, check this great web site: www.EmailAddressManager.com. Go to the "Email Tips" and from there find the information about incoming and outgoing mail servers and ports for your particular kind of account.

The **User Name** for a POP account might be different from your email name, or it might be your entire email address (most often) or it might be something different altogether. If your email address doesn't work, ask your provider.

Enter your password as provided by your provider or set up by you when you opted for the email account.

Click "Continue."

—continued

4   The **Outgoing Mail Server,** or **SMTP,** has a couple of options. For instance, your .Mac account will be automatically set up with a .Mac SMTP. However, I've found that the most reliable SMTP is the one provided by your Internet service provider. For instance, if you use Comcast, your best SMTP is "smtp. comcast.net." That is, *your most reliable outgoing mail server is going to be the company that you pay to connect you to the Internet.*

Some providers, like Qwest here in the West, have a cheesy low-end broadband option that does not allow you to have an outgoing mail server. You are forced to go to Microsoft's web page to check and send your mail. If that's your situation and you don't like it, call them and upgrade your service so you can get an SMTP (or change providers).

The **Description** field is just for you to name this SMTP so you can choose it from menus. Enter something that will make it clear to you.

Unless your provider insists, you usually don't have to enter a user name and password for authentication, so for now you can leave those blank.

5   Successful creation of a new account is announced as soon as you click "Continue."

To add another account or edit an existing account:

At any time you can add another account or edit an existing one by using the Mail preferences.

1   Go to the Mail menu and choose "Preferences...."

2   Click the "Accounts" icon in the toolbar.

3   **To add a new account,** single-click the **+** sign at the bottom of the Accounts pane. Fill in the information on the right.

 To edit an existing account, single-click the account name in the pane, then use the pane on the right to edit.

4   When finished, just close the preferences or click on another icon. A message will appear asking if you want to save these changes.

Check your Dock Icon

When email is received, your Mail icon in the **Dock** displays a little red tag telling how many messages are unread.

Single-click on this Mail icon to bring the Mail window to the front. You don't have to quit Mail when you're finished working in it.

Or press (don't click) on the Dock icon to pop up a menu with options to get new mail and to create a new message (among other things).

Read and Send Email

The default in Mail is to automatically check your mail every five minutes. This, of course, assumes you use a full-time broadband connection. If you use a dial-up connection, go to the Mail preferences (from the Mail menu), click the "General" tab, and change it to "Manually."

As mentioned on the previous page, when you have messages in Mail that are yet unread, the Dock icon puts the number in red so you always know.

To read mail that has arrived:

1   If you have more than one account, your "Inbox" will have a disclosure triangle next to it. Click on the triangle to see the individual accounts (shown below).

2   On the left, single-click on the account you want to see. The messages are displayed in the message pane to the right. Unread messages have a **blue orb** next to them.

3   **To read a message,** single-click on it and the message will be displayed in the lower pane. **Or** double-click on a message and it will open into a new window.

Click "New Message" to compose and send a message.
Enter the recipient's email address, plus a subject.

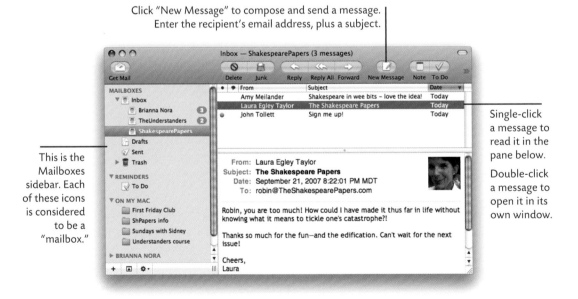

This is the Mailboxes sidebar. Each of these icons is considered to be a "mailbox."

Single-click a message to read it in the pane below.

Double-click a message to open it in its own window.

To send an email message:

1   Click the "New Message" button in the toolbar, or press Command N.

2   Enter an email address in the "To" field.

> **Or** if you have an address in your Address Book or if you've sent a message to this person before, as soon as you start typing, the rest of the email address appears. If there is more than one person with those beginning letters, you'll get a list of possibilities. You can use the arrow keys to go up or down the list and select the addressee you want; hit Return to put that address in the field.

> **Or** click the "Address" icon in the toolbar to bring up the Address Book pane, a limited version of your Address Book. Double-click on anyone's name to add it to the "To" field.

3   Enter a subject in the "Subject" field. Do not type something that might be construed as junk mail! For instance, don't type "Hi" or "Thought you might like to know" or "About last night" or "I've got a great opportunity for you—all I need is your bank account number." Be specific so the recipient will actually open your message instead of immediately deleting it because it sounds like spam.

4   In the message pane, type your message. Mail will automatically check your spelling and display suspect words with a red dotted underline. You can change the font, the color, the size, the alignment, and more—use the Format menu. You can use the Font panel, Colors panel, Spelling Checker, and all the other Mac OS features—see Lesson 13 for details.

5   If you want to send a file of some sort, just drag it into the message window and drop it (see pages 100–103 for more details).

6   When you're ready, hit the "Send" button. **Or** click the "Save As Draft" button in the toolbar to save it for later. To open that letter later, go to the Drafts folder in the sidebar.

TIP —— If you can't do format the text in a message, such as color it or even make words bold, go to the Format menu and choose "Make Rich Text." If it says "Make Plain Text" in that menu instead of rich text, that means you're already working in rich text. If you still can't make bold or italic text, then the font you chose does not have bold or italic versions. Check the Fonts panel (press Command T; see pages 234–235 for details).

Customize the Message Window

It's easy to customize the message headers, the toolbar, and to add or delete various columns of information.

To add or delete columns of information in the message pane:

1   Make sure the Mail viewer window (the main window) is open in front of you.

2   Go to the View menu, slide to the first item, called "Columns," and slide out to the right. Choose the information that you want to see from that list.

To customize the toolbar:

1   From the View menu, choose "Customize Toolbar...."

2   Drag anything into the toolbar from that pane. While the pane is open, drag anything *out* of the toolbar that you don't want—drag it off the toolbar and drop it on the Desktop. Drag icons left or right to rearrange them.

To reorganize the existing items in the toolbar at any time, hold down the Command key and drag icons to different positions in the toolbar, or drag them completely out of it.

To customize the message headers:

1   Open any new message (click the "New" button in the Mail toolbar).

2   Click the Action button (shown circled, below), and choose "Customize..." to get the pane shown below.

3   Check the boxes of the items you want to see in your messages. Click OK when you're done.

Signatures,
see pages 86–87.

Priority,
see page 104.

Do Not Display Junk Mail!

Some junk mail sends an invisible message back to its sender as soon as you open it, telling the despicable junk mailing scum that this is a working email address. To prevent opening and displaying that mail at all, get rid of the message pane, as shown below. Then when you click on a message to delete it, it doesn't automatically appear in that pane. **When you want to read a message,** double-click on it and it will open in a separate window.

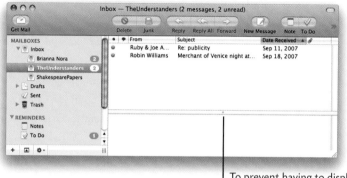

To prevent having to display junk mail before you throw it away, drag this bar all the way to the bottom.

Delete Junk Mail Without Ever Seeing It!

Mail has a **junk mail filter** that can toss your spam automatically. Actually, while in "training," it will put spam in a special brown "Junk" folder where you can check to make sure messages really are garbage before you toss them. Once you are confident it's doing a good job, use the rules described on page 85 to delete junk mail immediately.

To turn on Junk Mail filtering, go to the Preferences pane (in the Mail menu), click the "Junk Mail" icon, and check the box to "Enable junk mail filtering." Carefully read the other choices in the pane and choose your options.

Use Stationery to Send Fancy Mail

It's actually called "HTML" mail, not "fancy" mail. HTML just means it has HTML code written into the message for you that creates the layout, the space for photos, the fonts, etc. *You* don't have to write one single piece of code. All you do is choose the stationery template, type your message, and drag photos to replace the existing ones.

To create an email with stationery:

1   Open a new email message (Command N).

2   Single-click the button on the right side of the message toolbar called "Show Stationery." (If you don't see that button, open the message window wider, or click on the arrow you see where the button should be—that will pop out a menu with "Show Stationery" on it.)

3   A row of stationery templates appears, as shown below. Single-click on a category on the left to show the template options on the right.

4 **To replace the text,** click on it and it automatically selects all the text in that section. Whatever you type will replace that text, but will retain the font.

5 **To add photos,** you can do several things.

> Click the "Photo Browser" button in the toolbar. This opens the Photo Browser and displays all the photos you have in iPhoto, Aperture, or Photo Booth. Just drag an image from the Photo Browser and drop it directly on top of the image you want to replace.

> Drag an image from anywhere on your Mac and drop it on an existing image.

> Open iPhoto and drag an image directly from iPhoto onto an existing image.

6 **To resize photos,** double-click on an image and a little slider bar appears, as shown on the previous page. Drag the slider right or left to enlarge or reduce the image.

7 **To reposition the image within the frame,** double-click on the image (as above). Then press-and-drag on the image to reposition it within its frame (you can't reposition the frame itself).

You can **change templates at any point—**if there are fewer photos in the new template, some of them will disappear. Your text will reappear in the new template.

Click the "Hide Stationery" button to put the row of templates away so you have more room in which to write.

Save as stationery

You can save your own designs as stationery. You can't use the templates that Apple provides, but you can set up an email message with the fonts you like to use, as well as colors, links, and images that you want to appear in the message. When you've got it the way you want it, go to the File menu and choose "Save as Stationery."

A new category appears in the list of stationery, called "Custom." Click on that new category and you'll see your own stationery.

To delete stationery you made, position your mouse over it and a little **X** appears in the upper-left corner. Click the **X** to delete the stationery.

Create Mailboxes to Organize your Mail

Organize your mail with mailboxes in the same way that you make folders in a Finder window to organize all the files on your Mac. (In fact, most of the mailboxes look just like folders.) Use the "Mailbox" menu to create new ones, or Control-click in the Mailboxes sidebar. If you Control-click directly on an icon in the sidebar, the new mailbox will be a subset of that icon.

Once you've got your mailboxes set up, use the filters (called Rules; see the next page) to automatically send incoming mail to the different folders/mailboxes. Also check out pages 89–91 about Smart Mailboxes.

You can see here that I've got:

- Three email accounts in my Inbox.

- Folders that Mail has created for Drafts, Sent messages, and Trash.

- A Reminders folder for my To Do lists and Notes.

- Mailboxes that I created so I can store messages on my Mac (instead of on an email server somewhere else).

- Mailboxes that .Mac has created for my .Mac account.

- An RSS folder that was created when I chose the option to receive RSS feeds in Mail (see Lesson 7 on Safari).

Filter your Incoming Mail with Rules

Create rules, or filters, to **sort incoming mail** into the appropriate mailbox. First, create the mailboxes you want for organizing (see opposite page). Then:

1 From the Mail menu, choose "Preferences…."

2 Single-click on the "Rules" icon. Single-click "Add Rule."

3 Choose your parameters for the type of mail coming in and what to do with it. (If you forgot to make a special mailbox for something, you can actually do it while the Rules pane is open on your screen; use the Mailbox menu. The new mailbox will immediately appear in the drop-down menu.)

> In the example below, I first made a new mailbox called "NancyD" (although you *can* make one while this dialog box is open).
>
> Then I created a new rule to find any incoming mail from my editor, Nancy Davis.
>
> When found, I want that message to move straight into the "NancyD" folder and play a little sound so I know it arrived.

Add Signatures to your Messages

An **email signature** is the little blurb you can automatically add to the bottom of your messages. A signature might include your contact information, promotion for your upcoming art show or book publication, your favorite quote, or even a small graphic. You can make more than one signature, then choose which one you want for an individual email message, as a default signature that automatically appears, or you can let Mail randomly choose one for you.

This is a signature. —

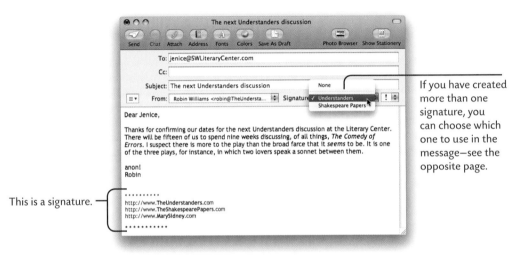

If you have created more than one signature, you can choose which one to use in the message—see the opposite page.

To create a signature:

1 From the Mail menu, choose "Preferences...."

2 Single-click the "Signatures" icon. You'll see the window shown on the opposite page.

3 At the top of the left-hand pane, single-click on "All Signatures."

4 In the middle pane, single-click the plus sign (+). The new one is probably called "Signature #1." Double-click on it to name it something more relevant.

5 Single-click in the right-hand pane and type your signature. You can use the formatting menus at the top of your screen to choose a font, size, style, alignment, and color. You can use Returns and Tab keys.

Don't choose a font that you have bought or acquired along the way because most of your recipients probably won't have that same font installed. Use one of the fonts that came with your Mac.

6 If you want an **image** to appear in this signature, drag the image from the Finder and drop it into the right-hand pane. Keep in mind that this should be a very small image, both in file size and in visual size!

If you like, drag an image from the Finder and drop it in this pane.

7 Drag a signature from the middle column and drop it on the account name in the left column to add it to that email account. You can have lots of signatures, yet have only certain ones available for different email accounts.

8 Each email account can have its own **default signature** that automatically appears in each email message you write: First select the account in the left-hand pane, then use the "Choose Signature" menu circled above.

To use a signature, put the "Signature" menu in your message window:

1 Open a new message as if you're going to write a letter.

2 Single-click on the Action button to get its menu; choose "Customize...."

3 Put a checkmark in the box next to "Signature."

4 Click OK. Now you will see the Signature menu in every new mail message, as shown below. Choose the one you want to use for each individual message.

Action button.

You won't see an option to add signatures if you haven't made any yet!

87

Search your Mail

In Mail, Spotlight searches very thoroughly. It's very simple.

1 If you want to limit the search to a particular mailbox or to Notes, select that mailbox or the Notes mailbox. Or click the "Inbox" to search all mail.

2 Enter a word or phrase in the search field; results immediately appear.

3 A new bar also appears, as shown below. In this bar you can choose which account to search, and choose which part of the email to search.

Choose "All Mailboxes" or click on one in the sidebar, then choose it here in this header.

"Entire Message" includes not only the message, but the From, To, and Subject lines as well.

4 **To display all your messages again,** click the gray **X** in the search field. As long as there is even one character in the search field, you will see the search results instead of your mail.

Smart Mailboxes

You can create **Smart Mailboxes** that will hold all the email messages that meet certain search criteria. If you are familiar with the Rules (filters), as explained on page 85, you'll notice there are a couple of differences between Rules and Smart Mailboxes.

- A Rule is an *action* that is applied to incoming messages, such as filtering certain email into a certain folder. The *original* email is *moved* into the folder.

- A Smart Mailbox contains messages that match search criteria. No action is taken on the messages.

- A Smart Mailbox does not contain the *original* message, thus the same message can be "stored" in a number of Smart Mailboxes.

- A Smart Mailbox automatically updates itself as messages come in or are deleted.

- A Smart Mailbox applies the search rules to mail that is already in your box, not just on future incoming mail.

Below you see an example of several Smart Mailboxes in the sidebar. The ones named "Understanders" and "The Shakespeare Papers" are actually Smart **Folders** that each contain Smart **Mailboxes.** The folder is just for organizational purposes. Both are explained on the following page.

This **Smart Mailbox** is one that Apple provided.

These two folders are **Smart Mailboxes** that I created.

A **Smart Folder** has a disclosure triangle to its left, indicating it holds other mailboxes.

Create Smart Mailboxes

There are several ways to **create a Smart Mailbox.** One is from the Mailbox menu (below) and another is with the Save button, as shown on the opposite page.

To create a Smart Mailbox from the Mailbox menu:

1 If you go to the Mailbox menu, you'll see there are two similar options, "New Smart Mailbox Folder..." and "New Smart Mailbox...."

The **Smart Mailbox Folder** creates a folder with no search parameters; it is simply for organizing other **Smart Mailboxes** inside (as shown on the previous page). If you choose to make a Smart Mailbox, you will only be asked to name the folder and click OK.

If you want your Smart Mailbox to be *inside* of an existing Smart Folder, first select that folder in the Mailboxes sidebar; if not, make sure that folder is *not* selected.

2 When you choose "New Smart Mailbox...," the search box shown below appears. Choose your parameters and click OK.

3 If you need to edit the parameters of your new Smart Mailbox, select it, then either Control-click, right-click, or go to the Mailbox menu and choose "Edit Smart Mailbox...."

To create a Smart Mailbox from the Save button:

1 Do a search as usual, as explained on the previous pages.

2 If the search gives you what you need and you think you'll want to use the same search again, click the "Save" button.

3 The saved search is automatically named with the search phrase you just used. You can refine your search in the edit box, if you like. When ready, click OK.

4 If you need to edit the parameters of your new Smart Mailbox, select it, then either Control-click, right-click, or go to the Mailbox menu and choose "Edit Smart Mailbox...."

TIP ———— If the command to make a Smart Folder is gray, it's probably because something is selected in the sidebar and Mail can't put a Smart Folder inside of whatever is selected. Click on an empty space in the sidebar, and the option to create a Smart Folder will become available.

To Do Items

Mail is no longer just an email program—it's the message center for your digital lifestyle. When you use Mail to create To Do lists and Notes, you stay organized and can find all your information quickly and easily. Mail keeps track of everything and even integrates with iCal to make sure you never miss a date.

To create a To Do item from text in an email message:

All you do is select the text in a message you've received, then click the "To Do" button in Mail's toolbar (or Command-click and choose "New To Do"). You can create as many To Dos from one message as you like.

This blue selected text becomes the To Do item.

Your To Do items also appear in Mail's sidebar, and they have their own viewer pane with their own **columns of information.** Control-click on any column header to see the other columns you can add.

Click this arrow to open the "To Do Options" menu. The due date gets inserted into your To Do text.

Click the **X** to delete the item.

Check the box when the To Do is completed.

Click this arrow to show the original email message.

To create a To Do item related to an email message:

Control-click in a blank area of the message. From the pop-up menu that appears, choose "New To Do." A To Do graphic slides down from the top of the window. Type a brief note.

To create a To Do item without using an email message:

Just click the "To Do" icon in the toolbar. Type your message in the field provided. Control-click on the message to get options for setting priorities, due date, etc. This To Do item will be associated either with the last email account you made a To Do in, or the one you choose in the Mail preference, in the Composing pane.

To Do items in Mail's sidebar

To Do items are in their own section of the sidebar, as shown below. If you have more than one .Mac account, the To Dos are sub-categorized into the different accounts. All non-.Mac mail accounts go into a category called "On My Mac."

You won't see those categories in your sidebar until you make a To Do item, and then they appear automatically.

The title bar tells you how many
To Do items are incomplete.

You can add or delete columns of
information: Control-click on any
column header to see the options.

The numbers indicate how
many To Dos are incomplete.

Click the gray circle/
arrow to open the
original message.

If there is no gray circle/arrow,
you created this To Do without
selecting text from an email
message (as explained on the
previous page).

TIP ——— The Mail To Dos are intimately connected with iCal (another Apple application on your Mac). Dates will be inserted as events on the appropriate day, and you can send email invitations out from iCal. Please see Lesson 8 for details.

Automatic date detection for events

This is amazing. If you hover your mouse over a day or date in an email message, it highlights with a gray dotted outline and adds a menu button. If you click the menu button, you can choose to immediately open iCal and see what's going on for that date, or choose "Create New iCal Event…." Notice this is not creating a To Do item, but an *event* in iCal.

A dialog box opens in which you set all the information, then click "Add to iCal." In this example, even though a numerical date was not available (just the word "Monday"), iCal automatically assumed the message meant the next Monday following the date of the email.

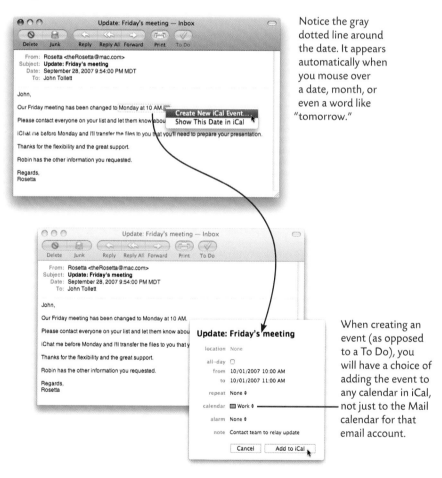

Notice the gray dotted line around the date. It appears automatically when you mouse over a date, month, or even a word like "tomorrow."

When creating an event (as opposed to a To Do), you will have a choice of adding the event to any calendar in iCal, not just to the Mail calendar for that email account.

About the calendars

To Do items and events are automatically sent to iCal. If you have already set up iCal with a number of calendars, you can send events and certain To Dos to any of those pre-existing calendars.

If your email account is a .Mac account, Mail/iCal makes a special Mail group for you in iCal with a default calendar in it cleverly called "calendar." You can rename it, of course. Any To Do item you create from your .Mac email account will be assigned to a calendar in this Mail group *only;* you cannot assign a To Do item to any of your other calendars. Any To Do items in this Mail calendar will be available to you automatically anywhere in the world through your .Mac account online.

To Do items from any other email message or in any other email account besides a .Mac account can be assigned to any calendar in the Calendars group.

These are the calendars I made in iCal. They're in the **Calendar group.**

The instant you make your first To Do item in Mail in a .Mac email account, this **.Mac group** is created for you.

Events (as opposed to To Do items) that you create in Mail can be assigned to any calendar, regardless of which email account it originated from.

From within Mail, you can create new calendars; these calendars instantly and automatically appear in iCal.

- If you make a new calendar from a **.Mac account,** the calendar goes into the **.Mac group,** as shown above.

- If you make a new calendar from **any email account that is not .Mac,** that new calendar goes into the **Calendars group,** as shown above.

To make a new calendar in Mail, Control-click on a To Do account in the sidebar.

Use the columns to assign options

Take advantage of the information you can display and change in the columns of the
To Do items. Control-click in the column header area and you'll get a list of possible
columns you can add, or you can delete ones you don't need. You can also use the
View menu (the "Columns" sub-menu) as long as you are showing the To Do pane
when you go to the View menu. (That is, if you're looking at email messages, the
Columns sub-menu shows you column headings for email, not To Dos.)

To set a due date for items that don't have one, move your pointer over the "Date
Due" column; a small triangle appears. Click that triangle to get the pop-up menu
shown below. To set a specific date, click "Other…."

You can also **assign a calendar** to a particular To Do item from the Calendar
column, or switch the item to a different calendar. Just click in the Calendar column
for that To Do item. A little menu pops up with the calendars available to that
particular email account, as explained on the opposite page.

The little menu arrows
appear when your mouse
hovers over the column.

Notes

While the To Do items are great for tracking things that need to get done, Notes are a handy place to store ideas, thoughts, or any other information you want to keep track of. Mail becomes a central location for information—messages, Notes, and To Do lists.

Create a new Note

To create a new Note, click the "Note" button in Mail's toolbar. (This button is only available when you're in the main viewer window, *not when an email message is open and active.* To Do items can be created from email messages, but not Notes.)

A "New Note" window opens in which you can type a brief or lengthy note. Mail uses the first line of text as the subject of the note (keep that in mind as you write the note), and shows the first line in Mail's list of Notes.

If you want an automatically bulleted or numbered list, go to the Format menu, down to "Lists," and choose the type of list you want. Type your list, hitting a Return after each item. To stop the list so you can type regular text, hit the Return key twice.

When finished, click "Done."

If multiple Mail accounts are active, the note is added to the Mail account that was selected in the Mailboxes category in the sidebar, unless you have specified otherwise in the Composing pane in the Mail preferences.

Format and add attachments to a Note

You can format the text in a Note just as you do in an email message, and you can add attachments and To Do items. Just click the appropriate buttons in the Note toolbar. When you choose to "Send" a Note, an email window opens with this note inside the message area.

These buttons work just as they do in your email messages.

View Notes in Mail

The Mail window includes a Notes mailbox in the sidebar, which displays all your notes, as shown below. But you'll also see the Notes appear in your list of email messages when viewing an inbox. Notes are identified by an icon in the "Message Status" column on the far left, as you can see below.

Attachments

One of the greatest things about email is the ability to send files and photos back and forth. Mail has some great features for attachments, making it easier than ever to share files.

To send an attachment:

1   Open a new message window and type your subject, message, etc.

2   To attach a file or photograph, single-click the "Attach" icon.

This opens the standard Open dialog box. Find your file, select it, and click "Choose File." You can hold down the Command key to click on and select more than one file to attach.

Or drag a file or photo from a window on your Desktop and drop it directly into the message window.

3   A file icon appears in your window. If it's a one-page PDF or a photo, the actual image will probably appear, as shown below, instead of a file icon.

4   If the file in the window appears as the actual image, you can change it into an icon if you like (you don't have to): Control-click (or right-click) on the image. From the menu that pops up, choose "View as Icon." This does *not* determine how the person who *receives* the file will view it.

If the photograph is too large, you can choose to send a smaller version right here.

5   Send your email.

To receive and download an attachment:

1   An attachment appears in someone's Mail message, or yours, as an actual image or as a file icon, shown below.

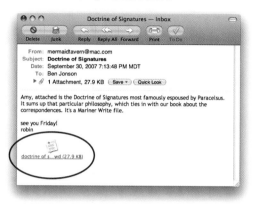

2   There are several ways to deal with this file:

If it's a photograph and you can see it in the window, then you see it and maybe that's all you want to do with it. So you're done. Or . . .

If it's **one file or photograph,** you can do any of several things:

Either drag the file to the Desktop or directly into any window or folder on your Mac.

Or single-click the "Save" button in the header information at the top of the message; the files are instantly added to the Downloads folder; see page 103.

Or save the image directly into **iPhoto** (if you have iPhoto installed): *Press* (don't click) on the "Save" button and choose "Add to iPhoto" (shown on the following page).

Or Control-click (or right-click) on the photo or file icon and choose any of several options, shown below.

—*continued*

If you have a **series of photographs** in your email message, you have even more options. You can do everything mentioned above, plus:

Save only one file from the collection. *Press* (don't *click*) on the "Save" button and a menu appears, as shown below. Choose the file you want to save.

You can view a **full-screen slideshow** of the photos. Simply click the "Quick Look" button in the header information.

This is the Quick Look button. Check it out!

Downloads Folder

When you click the "Save" button in an email to save the files that someone sent you, the files are automatically stored in the **Downloads folder** in your Home folder; a copy of this Downloads folder is in the Dock. Open either folder to get to the files. These folders in the Dock are also called "stacks" because of the way their contents sprays out into a stack, as shown below.

You can see that the files in the Downloads folder above are exactly the same as the ones in the Downloads folder in the Dock.

The picture on the folder in the Dock changes all the time, depending on what's in it.

Single-click on this Dock icon to display the files, as shown to the left.

Single-click on any image to display it in an application.

Single-click the arrow at the top to open the Downloads folder in a Finder window, as shown above.

Priority Options

You can set one of three **priority** options in Mail messages so your recipient understands how urgent (or not) a particular message is—provided the recipient's email program can display the priority marker. If someone sends you a message marked as high or low priority, Mail will mark it as such.

To set a priority:

With an email compose window open, go to the Message menu in the menu bar, slide down to "Mark," and choose the priority option you want for this message.

If you would like to have the priority options handy, put this tiny menu in the message window. See page 80.

To check the priority of an incoming message:

If the Flag column is visible in Mail (if it isn't, see page 80), you will see two exclamation marks to denote a message that has been labeled **High Priority.** A dash indicates **Low Priority.** (One exclamation point means the message is **Normal Priority,** but you won't see any symbol for this kind of message.)

Use the Standard Application Features

Mail includes all of the **standard Mac features** as explained in Lesson 13, such as spell checking, text with shadows, text in color, special characters, creating PDFs, previewing before you print, reading text aloud, and more.

The "Complete" feature, as explained on page 62, can be used in email messages. Any styles you created in TextEdit, as described on page 61, are also available in Mail messages—from the Format menu, slide down to "Style," then out to "Styles…."

Mail is Integrated With:

Parental controls: See Lesson 18 to make another "user" for your child or children and have full control over their email access.

Address Book: Click the "Address" icon to bring up a minimalized Address Panel. See page 79.

iChat: A green dot in a column in your Viewer window indicates an iChat Buddy is online and available. If you don't see that column, go to the View menu, select "Columns," then choose "Buddy Availability."

iCal: Email announcements to all attendees of an event. All To Do items can go straight to iCal. Calendars created in Mail appear instantly in iCal.

.Mac Sync: Synchronize your .Mac account with the .Mac mail web site so you have access to your mail on any computer in the world.

TextEdit: Click an email link in TextEdit to open Mail and automatically address the email.

Safari: Safari will email complete web pages or just the links, as well as send email from email links.

6

GOALS

Make and edit
contact cards

Add photos
to your contacts

Designate your own card
for automatic fill-in
on web pages

Create mailing lists (Groups)
and Smart Groups

Search your Address Book

Share your contacts
with .Mac members

Print envelopes, a list
of contacts, and more

Address Book for Contact Info

The **Address Book** is a great **contact list** integrated with so many other parts of your Mac. It's much more complete than its simple appearance might lead you to believe—take the time to explore its possibilities!

How you'll Use your Address Book

Before I explain how to do specific tasks, such as create new address cards, add a photo to a person's card, send email, etc., first let me briefly describe how you can use this great application.

You can customize individual cards and/or add new *fields* (those places where you type in information) to all of them. For instance, you can add a "birthday" field or a nickname field. You can change the labels, add a photo or image, and customize the address for another country.

You can create Groups of addresses to make a mailing list so you can mail everyone in the Group with one click.

In Mail, all the contacts you put in your Address Book will be available via the Address Pane (see page 79). (In the Address Pane in Mail, you can't add or edit or delete or group addresses—you can just access them for emailing.)

While in Mail (not Address Book) **you can automatically add an address from an email you receive:** open the email in Mail and press Command Shift Y.

Your iPhone will synchronize with all the addresses or with certain Groups that you specify. As you add contacts to your iPhone, they will automatically be added to your Address Book on your Mac next time you connect and sync your phone.

Make and Edit New Cards

To make a new card, (sometimes called a vCard), click the **+** sign at the bottom of the "Name" pane, which displays the new card in the right pane, ready for you to add information.

If you don't see three columns, click this button.

● Click the green button to **add another field** for that particular type of information, like another phone or email address. You won't see this green button until you have filled in the blank area and are ready for another one.

● Click the red button to **delete** that field.

♦ Click these tiny double triangles to **change the existing field labels.**

To edit an existing card, select the card in the "Name" column, then click the "Edit" button (circled above). Edit the card to your heart's delight. When you're finished, click "Edit" again.

> **TIP** —— Only the fields that contain information will be visible on the card.
>
> Also, be sure to check out the preferences for Address Book (under the Address Book application menu). Use the "Phone" preferences to automatically format phone numbers, and use the "General" preferences to customize your contacts and several other features.

Add a photo to a card

You can add a photo to any contact card. That photo will appear in email that you receive from that person; it will be transferred to your iPhone so you can see his handsome face when he calls; and you can print it with his contact info.

To add a photo to a contact card:

1 Go to that card in your Address Book and click the "Edit" button (if it isn't already).

2 Double-click the empty photo space to the left of the name. A sheet appears:

The empty photo space on the card looks like this, a ghost.

Effects button.

3 Drag any type of image into the pane, **or** click "Choose..." to find a photo on your hard disk, **or** click the camera icon to take a picture of someone, even someone you are iChatting with. (If there is no camera attached to your computer, your camera icon is gray.)

4 Drag the blue slider bubble to the right or left to enlarge or reduce the image. Press on the image to drag it around inside the space.

Click the effects button to choose from different weird effects.

5 Click "Set" when you like it.

Add photos via your iPhone

If you have an iPhone, next time you are with someone whose contact information is in your Address Book (or whose contact info you are adding into your iPhone), edit her contact info in your phone and take her photo. The next time you sync your iPhone to your Mac, this photo will automatically apppear in your Address Book and when you get email from this person, it will include her photo in the upper-right corner of the message.

Designate your Own Card

In your Address Book, you can designate the card with your contact information on it as "My Card." Other applications, Safari and iChat in particular, will use that information in various ways, such as filling in forms online, accessing your email address, displaying your photo.

Your card name has a little human silhouette next to the name.

Enter a **card** for yourself in the Address Book (Apple might have done that for you already). Then go to the Card menu and choose, "Make This My Card." (Apple might have already done that for you too).

To keep some of the information private so it won't show up if you send your vCard (virtual card) to someone else (as explained on page 122):

1 Go to the Address Book preferences (under the "Address Book" menu).

2 Click the "vCard" icon in the toolbar.

3 Check the box to "Enable private me card." Close the preferences.

4 Go to your own card and click the "Edit" button. You'll see a blue checkbox for each item on your card; the checkmark means it is public information. **Uncheck** the boxes that you want to be private.

Customize One Card or All Cards

The fields for data only appear on the card if there is data in them; otherwise the fields disappear, which is kind of nice. Select a card and click the "Edit" button to see what fields you might have on a card that are not filled in.

You can add a number of other fields to an individual card or to all cards.

To add a field to ONE card:

1 Select that card.

2 From the Card menu in the menu bar across the top of your screen, slide down to "Add Field," and make a choice from the pop-out menu.

To add a field to EVERY card:

1 From the Card menu, slide down to "Add Field" and then choose "Edit Template...."

   Or go to the Address Book menu and choose "Preferences...." From that toolbar, click on the "Template" button.

2 Click the "Add Field" button to display its menu. All the field names in gray are already on the card template. Choose any field name that is in black and it will be added to *all* of your cards. Until you enter information into that field, you'll only see it when you click the "Edit" button on individual cards.

Check Out the Options

There are lots of hidden options in the Address Book. Single-click or Control-click on the small labels to the left of the fields on a card. You'll get little menus, depending on which key you're holding down and what you click on. Check them out! Below you see where I chose the option "Large Type" to display a fax number. (This option only shows up on phone or fax numbers, but you could put a love note instead of a phone number to surprise your sweetheart.) You can send text messages to cell phones, dial numbers with your Bluetooth-enabled cell phone, send email, chat, and more. If you have Skype installed, even more options will appear.

Map It

You can instantly get a Google map of any address in your Address Book. (You must be connected to the Internet, of course.)

Click on the label to the left of an address in Address Book. A little menu pops up where you can choose "Map Of." Safari opens to Google Maps and displays the location of that address. Freaky.

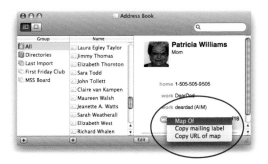

Create Group Mailing Lists

After you've made a Group mailing list, you can **send email to the name of that Group** and your message will go to everyone in the Group.

To make a new group:

1 Click the **+** sign at the bottom of the "Group" column.

2 Change the existing name of the Group to something you'll recognize.

3 Click the "All" group.

4 Drag names from the "Name" column of the "All" group and drop them on the Group name. You can put the same name in many different Groups.

To email a message to a Group:

■ **In the Address Book,** Control-click (or right-click if you have a two-button mouse) on the Group name and choose "Send Email to Group."

■ **OR in the Mail application,** type the name of the Group in the "To" field of an email message.

To prevent all the addresses from appearing in everyone else's email:

1 Open Mail (not Address Book).

2 From the Mail menu, choose "Preferences...."

3 Click the "Composing" icon.

4 Uncheck the box, "When sending to a group, show all member addresses."

TIP ——— Option-click on a person's name to highlight all the Groups he is included in.

Create Smart Groups in Address Book

A Smart Group is a list of contacts that automatically updates itself as contacts meet its criteria. For instance, you might want a Smart Group that automatically adds people who work for a certain company or who are part of your literary salon. You can create a Smart Group that tells you when someone's birthday or anniversary is approaching. Or you might want to gather a list of everyone in a particular city without having to find them all in your Address Book—a Smart Group will find existing contacts and automatically collect them.

Most of these searches require, of course, that you have a particular field on your card and that it has data in it. For instance, you can't have a Smart Group that tells you when a birthday is coming up if you don't have the Birthday field on your cards. For directions on how to **add new fields** to individual cards or to all cards, please see page 112.

To create a Smart Group:

1 From the File menu across the top of the screen, choose "New Smart Group...."

2 In the sheet that drops down, as shown below, choose your parameters.

3 If you need more parameters to narrow down or open up the possible items in the Group, click the **+** sign (circled above).

4 If you want to see a visual clue when a new item has been added to the Smart Group, be sure to check the box to "Highlight group when updated." Then when a new item is automatically added, the Smart Group will change color to let you know someone's been added to it.

Search your Address Book

You can do a standard, simple search for anyone or any information in your collection of contacts. And you can do a Spotlight search of anyone in your Address Book that searches your entire hard disk for everything related to that person.

To search your Address Book for a contact:

1 **To search for a contact within a Group,** single-click the Group name you want to search.

  To search your entire database of contacts, click the "All" group, as shown below.

2 Single-click in the search field.

3 Type the first couple of letters of the name of the person you want to find, either first or last name or the business name. As you type, results will appear in the center "Name" pane.

4 Type more letters to narrow your search, or single-click one of the contacts in the "Name" pane.

Click this **X** to delete everything in the search field.

If there is even one character in this field, you won't see all of your contacts.

5 **To display all of your contacts again,** click the **X** in the search field, and single-click on the "All" group.

To search for a person or business in Spotlight:

1   Find the person you want to Spotlight, as explained on the previous page.

2   Control-click (or right-click) on the person's name; from the pop-up menu that appears, choose "Spotlight *'This Person'*" (where *'This Person'* is the name of the contact you just searched for; that name automatically appears in the menu). See the illustration below.

3   You will get the Spotlight window (a Finder window), as explained in Lesson 19. It will show you every file on your computer that is connected with this person, such as email she's sent, files she's mentioned within, documents she has created and sent to you, images of her, and more.

Share your Address Book Contact List

If you are a .Mac member (see www.Apple.com/dotmac), you can **share your entire contact list** with other .Mac members. This can be useful for families, teens and their friends, organizations, businesses, and others. And you can **subscribe** to someone else's shared Address Book, provided that person has already put you on their shared list.

Remember, you must have a .Mac account to share, and the only people who can share your Address Book are other .Mac members running Tiger (Mac OS 10.4) or Leopard. The people you want to share with must already be in your Address Book as contacts, so if they're not there yet, add them before you follow these steps!

1   From the Address Book menu, choose "Preferences...."

2   Single-click the "Sharing" icon.

3   In the window that appears, check the box to "Share your address book."

4   You must choose who is allowed to access and share your Address Book: Single-click the **+** sign at the bottom of the window.

5   This drops down a sheet displaying the people who are in your Address Book, as shown at the top of the next page. Select the names you want to share with; hold down the Command key to select more than one name.

6 Click OK. After you add names, you can send an email inviting someone to share your Address Book: Single-click a name (or Command-click several names), then click "Send Invitation."

Subscribe to someone's Address Book

You can only subscribe to an Address Book that someone else has already set up as shared, as explained above. And that person must have already chosen you as someone who is allowed to access her Address Book. Once that's done:

1 In your own Address Book, go to the File menu and choose "Subscribe to Address Book…."

2 Enter the .Mac account name of the person whose Address Book you want access to. After you enter the account, click OK.

Print in a Variety of Ways

From Address Book you can **print** mailing labels, envelopes, customized lists, and even pages that fit into a standard pocket address book.

1   First, in Address Book, select the names or the Group that you want to print.

2   Press Command P to get the Print dialog box. If you don't see the full window as shown below, click the small blue triangle to the right of the "Printer" pop-up menu.

You can save the job as a PDF and then send that PDF to someone else to print.

3   From the "Style" pop-up menu, choose what you wish to print—lists, envelopes, mailing labels, or pocket address book pages. Each "style" has different parameters to experiment with. Whatever you choose will be displayed in the preview window.

Spend some time poking around this dialog box so you know what all your options are. As you can see below, you can add an image to your return address, choose different fonts and colors for the text, choose different envelope sizes, and so much more that it's just amazing.

The Address Book automatically uses your "Me" card for the return address. If you want it to use another card, go back to the Address Book, choose that other card, go to the Card menu, and choose "Make This My Card." You can switch it back when you're done printing. Of course, you can uncheck the box so it doesn't print any return address at all.

To add an image to your return address, click the "Label" tab above.
You'll have options to change fonts, colors, add an image, and more.

Backup your Entire Digital Database

There are few things more annoying than losing your entire Address Book that you have carefully created over the past year or two. You have a couple of options for backing up your entire Address Book.

- One way is to select everyone in the Name column (or just select the important names), then drag that block of names to the Desktop. This creates a vCard file, shown below, that you can then store on another disk for safekeeping.

Andrew Aguecheek
and 69 others.vcf

  You can send this vCard to someone else on a Mac; she double-clicks on it and the addresses get automatically entered in her Address Book.

- **Or** go to the File menu and choose "Export," then "Address Book Archive…." Your Mac will make a file for you and ask you where to store it. When you want to restore your Address Book, double-click this file or use the Import option in the File menu.

Address Book
2008–…8.abbu

Remember, a backup is only useful if it's not in the same place as the original. That is, don't keep it on your hard disk—if your hard disk goes bad, it will take both the original and the backup! Copy the file onto a disk, upload it to your iDisk if you have a .Mac account, or email it to a colleague for safekeeping.

Address Book is Integrated With:

Dashboard: Pop up a mini-version of your Address Book for quick and easy access. See Lesson 16.

Safari: Put your Address Book in the Bookmarks Bar and you have instant access to any web sites listed in the Address Book. To do this, open Safari, and in the Safari preferences, in the Bookmarks pane, check the box to "Include Address Book."

The AutoFill feature in Safari uses the data you enter in your "Me" card.

iCal: iCal can create a Birthday calendar from your Address Book so everyone's birthday is automatically placed on its appropriate day; see page 152.

Mail: Send email to a selected contact email address with a contextual menu. The photos you put in the Address Book will appear in other Mac users email messages when they send you mail.

To automatically add someone's email address to your Address Book, select a message in Mail, then press Command Shift Y.

iChat: iChat will pick up the data and picture you add in Address Book. And when a Buddy is online and available, his address card displays a green dot.

With a camera connected, you can add a photograph of someone you are chatting with through iChat.

.Mac: Synchronize your other Macs and your .Mac account so you have your entire Address Book accessible on the web, anywhere in the world.

Spotlight: Send your Address Book search out to your entire computer through Spotlight. See page 117.

Bluetooth: Beam a contact card to a mobile device with one click.

iPod: Transfer your entire contact list to your iPod using iSync.

iPhone: Transfer your entire contact list or selected Groups to your iPhone using iTunes.

7

GOALS

Safari for Web Browsing and News

Safari is Apple's beautiful web browser for viewing web pages on the Internet. You've probably already used it, but you might be surprised at the tips and tricks it offers that you haven't taken advantage of yet.

Safari also includes its own "news reader" that brings in RSS feeds. RSS stands for Really Simple Syndication. It's an Internet technology that "feeds" you news and information of your choice from a huge variety of sources. Safari can gather the RSS feeds you are interested in and display the headlines from many sources in one place—a web page. You'll have access to them with one click of a button, and you can organize the information, filter the feeds, automatically update them, and more.

Safari Web Browser

Below is a brief overview of the main features of the Safari window. Although it looks simple, it holds a lot of power in subtle ways.

Customize what you see in the toolbar; use the command from the View menu **or** Control-click.

Enter a web address here, then hit the Return or Enter key to go to that page. You do NOT need to type **http://**.

Enter a Google search right here!

This is the Bookmarks Bar.

Status Bar. If you don't see this in your browser, go to the View menu and choose "Show Status Bar."

Drag this corner to resize the window.

Enter a new web address quickly

This is one of my favorite features in Safari: If you double-click between www and .com, it selects *just* the domain so you can change it. This means you don't have to drag the mouse across tiny little letters when you want to change the address. Try it.

And don't forget you never need to type "http://." If it's a .com address, all you need to type is the main word. For instance, to go to www.apple.com, just select everything in the location bar, type *apple,* then hit Return.

Find a Word or Phrase on the Current Page

To find a word or phrase on the *page* you are looking at (as opposed to searching the Internet for it), press **Command F**. Then just type—Safari knows to put the search term in the search field.

To make it easy for you to see the found word or phrase, Safari dims out the rest of the page and highlights every instance of what you're looking for, as you can see below. Just click on the page to un-dim it.

To make Safari put the strong yellow highlight on successive results, press **Command G**. Each time you hit that shortcut, Safari puts the yellow highlight on the next result.

Safari holds onto that search. You can go to another page and hit **Command G** again—Safari will search for the last word or phrase you requested. In fact, you can close or even quit Safari and the next time you open it, Command G will find results of the last word or phrase you were looking for.

This field appears when you press Command F to find something.

It will stay there until you click the "Done" button.

Fill in Forms and Passwords Automatically

This is wonderful. Safari will **fill in online forms** with the information you have entered into your Address Book; it takes the data from the card you have designated as "My Card" (use the Card menu in Address Book to do that; see page 111). You can also tell Safari to remember your **user ID and password** for specific sites, which is great if no one else uses your Mac or if you have set up different users.

To enable Safari to fill in forms and passwords, go to the Safari Preferences and click the "AutoFill" icon. Check the appropriate boxes.

Notice the "edit" buttons. You can delete the information from any web page that was hanging on to your info or passwords.

Next time you start to fill in a form, Safari will fill it in for you. Next time you go to a page that needs an **ID and password,** go ahead and fill them in, then Safari will ask if you want to save that information. Try it on your .Mac page.

To delete saved user names, passwords, or forms, go back to the AutoFill preferences. Click the "Edit…" button. Select and remove items.

AutoFill is turned off when you turn on private browsing, as explained on page 136.

Block Pop-Up Windows!

Go to the Safari menu and choose "Block Pop-Up Windows." Woo hoo! Only pop-up windows that you click on will appear—none of those obnoxious ads.

Occasionally, however, this can cause a problem. You might run across a web site where you click on a link for extra information and nothing happens. This might be because the extra information appears in a pop-up window. If so, go back to the Safari menu and choose "Block Pop-Up Windows" again to take the checkmark off.

⊙ SnapBack to a Results Page or Other Page

Do you see those little **orange arrows** in the location field and the Google search field below? Those indicate "SnapBack" pages.

When you do a search in Google, either at Google.com or through the Google search field in the upper-right corner of Safari, you get a page of results. As soon as you click on a link on that page, the SnapBack arrow appears. Wherever you surf, you can always click the SnapBack arrow **to return to the original results page.**

You can **mark any page** you want as a SnapBack page: Go to the History menu and choose "Mark Page for SnapBack." As soon as you leave that page, the arrow appears in the location field, ready for you to click to return. You'll also see the SnapBack arrow anytime you type in a web address yourself (as opposed to getting there from a link or bookmark).

Quickly Enlarge or Reduce Text

Make the **text on a web page** larger or smaller with Command **+** (larger) or Command **−** (smaller). You don't have to select anything first.

Tabbed Browsing

When you click on a link, of course, Safari takes you to another page and thus you lose track of the one you were on. Besides taking advantage of the SnapBack feature described on the previous page, you can also choose to open web pages in **tabs**.

Instead of losing your original page, a tabbed page gets loaded and displays as a tab, as shown below. **To open any link into a tabbed page,** Command-click the link (hold down the Command key and click on the link).

Command-click on lots of links and they will all load themselves into individual tabs. Then when you're ready, click any tab to display that page, while leaving your original page still available.

Tabs.

Click a tab to display that page.

Click the **X** to close that page.

Option-click the **X** to close all the open tabs.

To use tabbed browsing, go to the Safari preferences and click the "Tabs" icon. Take a few minutes to check out the options. For instance, if you check the second box, shown below, the tabbed window will immediately come to the front instead of lining up behind the current page.

Also see pages 140 and 144 about displaying all bookmarks in a folder as individual tabs, all at once.

Bookmarks

The bookmarks in Safari are powerful and easy to use.

Choose this to display
the Bookmarks Library.

The **Bookmarks Menu,** shown above, is what drops down from the menu bar across the top of your screen.

The **Bookmarks Bar** is that strip in the browser window, just below the address field, as shown on the opposite page. To show it (if it isn't already showing), go to the View menu and choose "Show Bookmarks Bar."

The **Bookmarks Library** and the various **Collections** you create let you organize hundreds of bookmarks, but you don't have to put them all in the Bookmarks Menu, which would make your list a yard long. Click the "Show all bookmarks" button ( ) at the far-left of the Bookmarks Bar when you want to open the Bookmarks Library and make new folders for **organizing your bookmarks.**

When you hit Command D to **create a bookmark,** a little sheet drops down and asks you where you want to store it. You can rename the bookmark at that point and choose to store it in any folder *you have already made* in the Bookmarks Library.

Organize your bookmarks with folders

You can organize all your bookmarks in the Bookmarks Library.

1   From the Bookmarks menu, choose "Show All Bookmarks," or click the bookmarks icon on the far left of the Bookmarks Bar.

2   In the bottom-left of the window, click the **+** sign. This puts a new bookmark folder, called a Collection, in the left-hand pane.

When you make bookmarks, as mentioned above, you can choose this folder in which to store the bookmark.

3   To put this folder in the Bookmarks Menu so you can access it in that menu, first click on the "Bookmarks Menu" item in the Library. Now drag the folder from the left pane and drop it into the large right pane, which is the list that will appear in the Bookmarks Menu. You can drag the items into the order you want them listed. You can also drag folders or bookmarks directly into the Bookmarks Bar.

Email the Contents of or a Link to a Web Page

Safari makes it especially easy to **email an entire web page** to anyone, complete with images and links.

1   Open the web page in Safari.

2   From the File menu, choose "Mail Contents of This Page."

3   The Mail application opens with the name of the web page as the subject. The entire web page is in the body of the email. All you have to do is add the recipient's address and click the "Send" button.

Or you can **email just the link.** Follow the steps above, but choose "Mail Link to This Page."

View PDF Documents

To view a PDF document right in Safari, just drag the PDF file and drop it into *the middle* of any Safari page.

To enlarge or reduce the size of the PDF on the screen, Control-click (or right-click) anywhere on the PDF page. From the menu that appears, choose "Zoom In" to enlarge or "Zoom Out" to reduce.

If the PDF has **more than one page,** but all you see in Safari is one page, Control-click (or right-click) and choose "Continuous."

Save a Page and Everything on It

Safari lets you save a web page and all the images and links and text on the page. It creates one file, an archive, that you can open at any time; all the links will work (as long as the destination pages haven't changed). This is particularly handy for pages that you know aren't going to last long, such as online newspaper articles or purchase receipts. Keep in mind that some web pages can prevent you from saving items on the page.

1   Open the web page you want to save.

2   From the File menu, choose "Save As...."

3   In the Format menu in the dialog box, choose "Web Archive," as shown.

4   Choose the folder you want to save into, then click "Save."

You can also save a page as "Page Source," which saves the source code. This is handy if you want to study that code or use it in a web page of your own.

To save a frame of a web page, Control-click (or right-click) on the frame. From the menu that pops up, chose "Save Frame As...."

Make a Web Clip Widget

This is pretty cool. There's a button in the Safari toolbar that lets you make a Dashboard widget of any section of any web page. Any buttons, fields, or links that are captured in that widget will work in Dashboard. If you delete this widget, you'll have to remake it from scratch to get it back.

To make a web clip widget:

1 Go to any web page in Safari.

2 Click the Web Clip Widget button in the toolbar. (If you happen to have removed the button, right-click on the toolbar and choose "Customize Toolbar" so you can drag it back in.)

3 The page grays out, except for a clear box that follows your mouse around. Click in the area that you want to capture as a widget. Immediately eight handles appear on the clear box. You can drag any of these handles to reshape the box. Press and drag inside the box to move it.

4 When you like where it's positioned, click the "Add" button in the upper-right.

5 Immediately Dashboard opens up, displaying the new widget.

   Click the tiny *i* that appears in a bottom corner to flip it over and add a fancy border, if you like.

The selected area above became this Dashboard widget. The links work.

With this Wikipedia clip, I can go to Dashboard, enter a search term, click Go, and I'm there.

Print Web Pages

You can see a preview of how your web page will print. You can tell the background not to print, and you can make sure the web address and date appear on the page.

To print a web page:

1   Just go to the web page you want to print, then press Command P to get the Print dialog box, as shown below (or go to the File menu and choose "Print…").

2   If you don't see the expanded box shown below, click the blue disclosure button.

3   Make sure the "Safari" option is chosen in the menu in the middle of the pane, shown below. You'll see the preview on the left.

4   Check or uncheck the boxes to print the background or the headers and footers, shown below.

5   If the web page needs more than one piece of paper to print, the preview will show you every page; use the arrows to go back and forth.

6   Click "Print."

Click this disclosure button to show or hide the large pane you see here.

Private Browsing

You may have noticed that Safari keeps track of where you've been and what you've entered into search fields and what web pages you've asked to see. Safari's AutoFill feature even keeps track of user names and contact information you've entered on sites, as well as passwords and credit card numbers. If there are other people who use your computer, or if you are using Safari on someone else's Mac or at a school or an Internet cafe, you probably don't want Safari keeping track of all that information. That's where **private browsing** comes in handy.

When you turn on private browsing:

- None of the information you enter on any page is saved.
- Any searches you do will not be added to the pop-up menu in the Google search field.
- Web pages you visit are not added to the History menu. However, you can still go back and forward to pages you've viewed.
- If you downloaded anything, those items are automatically removed from the Download window when you quit Safari or turn off private browsing.
- Cookies are automatically deleted when you turn off private browsing or quit Safari.

To turn ON private browsing, go to the Safari menu, choose "Private Browsing."

To turn OFF private browsing, first close all Safari windows. Then go to the Safari menu and choose "Private Browsing" again to remove the checkmark.

When you **quit Safari,** private browsing is automatically **turned off,** even if you left it on before you quit. So each time you open Safari, you need to turn private browsing on again if you want to use it.

To further secure your privacy, when you are finished go to the Safari menu and choose "Reset Safari…." You can eliminate any trace of your whereabouts from the options you see listed here. This, however, will remove *every-thing* from that feature in Safari, not just the ones you used today!

Parental Controls

If you have a young child (or anyone acting like a young child), you can set up some serious parental controls to limit access to web sites. It involves multiple users, which are explained in detail in Lesson 18. You'll need an admin user (you) to set up another user for the child. The child will be able to view only web sites you have placed in the Bookmarks Bar. He won't be able to enter web addresses in the Address field, modify any bookmarks, or use the Google search field in the toolbar.

To limit web access to a young user:

1   Using the Account preferences, set up another user (details in Lesson 18). In the "New Accounts" menu, choose "Managed with Parental Controls."

2   In the next pane, click the button to "Open Parental Controls...."

3   Choose the account to which you want to add parental controls.

4   Click the tab labeled "Content."

5   Click the button to "Allow access to only these websites."

6   Select any site listed in that pane and delete it with the – button.
    Click the + button to type in web addresses of your choice.

7   Log in to that users account, open Safari, and make sure it's what you expect. Safari puts the web sites chosen in Step 6 into the Bookmarks Bar, as shown below, and the user will not be allowed to go anywhere else.

Bookmarks Bar.

Note: This does not prevent the user from surfing the web with any other browser. If you want to limit the *applications* this user can use, do so in the Parental Controls, as above.

So What is RSS?

All major news organizations, as well as thousands of personal web logs (blogs) and individual web sites, offer article summaries and headlines in the form of RSS feeds. Below is a sample of what an RSS feed from Apple looks like in Safari.

You can drag the "Article Length" slider (shown below, on the right) to display more or less of an article. Use the categories to organize the information.

At any time you can add more feeds to Safari, delete ones you don't want to view, search through feeds for particular information, and even bookmark searches to which you want to return.

You can separate the various feeds into your own folders so with the click of a button you can view all the headlines from each particular area of your life. For instance, you might want to see just the technology headlines or just the screenwriting headlines or just the personal blog headlines.

View the existing feeds in Safari

Apple has provided an RSS feed to get you started. Experiment with it for a while and then start building your own collection of RSS bookmarks, as described on the following pages.

To see the RSS feed/s:

1   Open Safari, your web browser.

2   If the Bookmarks Bar is not showing, press Command Shift B,
    or go to the View menu and choose "Show Bookmarks Bar."

3   Open the Bookmarks Library: Single-click on the little book icon
    at the far-left end of the Bookmarks Bar (circled, below).

4   In the Collections pane, which appears on the left side of the Bookmarks
    Library, single-click on "All RSS Feeds." The list will appear on the right.
    You'll see the blue **RSS** icon for each web site that has a feed.

This is the Bookmarks Bar.

This entire window is the Bookmarks Library.

Notice that a large news site might have separate RSS feeds for different sections of the news.

5   Double-click any link to open its feed page.

View the RSS Collections Apple has made for you

Apple has placed a number of folders, or Collections, of bookmarks in the Bookmarks Bar for you, including an rss "News" folder, as shown below.

If you click on a folder in the Bookmarks Bar and choose **View All RSS Articles** from the menu that appears, as shown below, every headline from every feed in this folder appears on the page. You can organize the information as explained on the next page.

If you choose **Open in Tabs,** each bookmark in the list will open as a separate tab (see page 144) and each page will display just the headlines for that source.

The number tells you the total number of new headlines in this Collection.

Customize the information display

Once you display an RSS feed page, you can adjust how information is shown. Use the options on the right side of the window to sort the headlines by date or by title, by the source of the headline, or whether it's unread. You can view headlines by relative time; for instance, you can view all articles from yesterday or from last month.

In the illustration below, notice that the "Article Length" slider is almost all the way to the left so only the main headline for each article is shown.

To display an entire article, single-click on any headline.

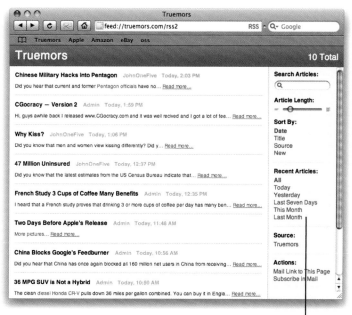

Click these links to sort the headlines.

Find other feeds

When you come across a web site that has an RSS feed, Safari will display an RSS icon in the address field, as shown below.

To view the actual RSS feed, click the icon in the address field.

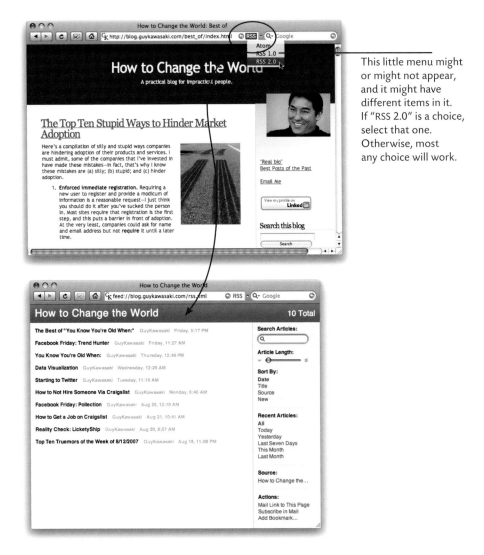

This little menu might or might not appear, and it might have different items in it. If "RSS 2.0" is a choice, select that one. Otherwise, most any choice will work.

To find a directory of RSS feeds, go to your favorite search tool, such as Google.com. Search for **directory RSS feeds** or **directory XML feeds.**

Bookmark your favorite feeds

There are at least three ways to bookmark a feed you want to keep track of.

If you plan to categorize your bookmarks, first make folders in the Collections pane in the Bookmarks Library (click the plus sign at the bottom of the pane, then rename the folder). You can create a folder for an eclectic collection of headlines in a number of your favorite interests so you will have your own customized "newspaper."

To bookmark a feed, do one of the following:

- Click the RSS icon in the address field, as shown on the opposite page. This takes you to the news feed page. *Bookmark that page;* in the little sheet that drops down, choose the folder (one you previously created in the Bookmarks Library) in which to save the bookmark *or* choose "Bookmarks Bar" to put that RSS feed bookmark directly into the Bookmarks Bar.

- Look on the web site for a little **RSS** or **XML** logo, icon, or note (or also check for "Atom"). Single-click it, which takes you to the news feed page. Bookmark that page and choose the folder in which to save the bookmark.

- If you find a link to **RSS** or **XML** on a web page, Control-click on it (or right-click). From the menu that appears, choose "Add Link to Bookmarks…." Be sure to give it a name that will describe what it is.

Auto-Click to view all pages or feeds in tabs

Safari has a nifty little feature called "Auto-Click" that lets you load all the pages in a Collection into different tabs with the click of a button. Instead of going to each individual page one at a time and then losing the previous page, you can peruse them all while they are all open, each in its own tab.

To view all pages in tabs automatically:

1 In the Bookmarks Library, single-click on "Bookmarks Bar" in the Collections pane, as circled below.

2 Put a check in one of the "Auto-Click" checkboxes that you see next to each folder. (Of course, if there are no folders, you won't see any checkboxes!)

3 As soon as you check the "Auto-Click" box, you'll notice that the tiny triangle in the Bookmarks Bar has changed to a tiny square.

Click this button to open or close the Bookmarks Library.

Note the visual clues:

A triangle gives you a menu.

A square opens all pages into tabs.

A number in parentheses means you have new RSS feeds.

4 When you click on a folder in the Bookmarks Bar that has the tiny square, every page in that folder opens, each with a different tab (which indicates a different page), as shown below. Single-click a tab to go to that page.

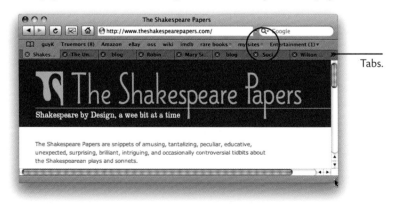

Tabs.

View RSS feeds in Mail

To make it even easier to get your info fix, you can send the RSS feeds directly to Mail so whenever you check your email, you can see if you have news waiting. **To send the RSS feeds to Mail,** make a bookmark (press Command D) of an RSS feed and in the sheet that drops down, check the box to add the bookmark to "Mail."

Change the RSS preferences

In the Safari preferences, you can tell Safari RSS how often to check for updates, what color to highlight new articles, when to get rid of old articles, and more.

To open the RSS preferences, go to the Safari menu and choose "Preferences...." Then click the "RSS" tab to get the RSS options.

If you choose to "Automatically update articles," Safari will put a number after the feed or folder of feeds to tell you how many new and unread articles there are. You can see that number in the Safari illustrations on the previous pages.

Send an RSS feed to a friend

If you want to share a feed with someone, simply open that RSS feed page in Safari. On the right-hand side of the Safari window, at the bottom of the pane, is a link called "Mail Link to This Page." Click on it, and your Mail program will open with the link to the page already in the message area and a subject line already written. Just add an address and send.

Use RSS Feeds as a screen saver

Ha! This is very clever. You can let the current headlines from your favorite RSS feed become your screen saver. It's sexier than it sounds.

1   From the Apple menu, choose "System Preferences...."

2   Click on "Desktop & Screen Saver," then click the "Screen Saver" tab.

3   In the left-hand pane, choose "RSS Visualizer."

4   Click the "Options..." button to choose your favorite feed. After you have made all the setting changes, close the pane.

Safari is Integrated With:

Address Book: Put your Address Book in the Bookmarks Bar and go to the web site of any contact in your Address Book. In the Safari preferences, in the Bookmarks pane, check the box to "Include Address Book."

The AutoFill feature uses the Address Book contact you have designated as "My Card."

Mail: Email a web page or just the contents to someone; see page 132.

Email links open a pre-addressed message in Mail.

RSS feeds can show up in Mail.

TextEdit: Web links on a TextEdit page will open in Safari; see page 68.

iCal: Web addresses in events open in Safari.

Dock: Drag the tiny icon that you see to the left of a web address and drop it on the far right side of the Dock to create a web location. No matter which application you're in or which Space, you can click that icon in the Dock and Safari instantly opens to your favorite page.

8

GOALS

Create calendars

Add events and
create To Do lists

Send email notifications
of events

Publish your calendar and
subscribe to others

Print data in useful ways

iCal for Organizing your Life

iCal is a calendar program that keeps track of events, creates a digital To Do list, and pops up reminders to you, among other things. You can publish your calendar over the Internet for other iCal users (publicly or privately), and they can subscribe to it and get automatic updates. Or publish it to a web page and anyone on any computer can view it.

iCal is a great tool for keeping track of family activities or for coordinating corporate events. And you can do it all in one application because you can create separate calendars for separate parts of your life.

If you have an iPhone, iCal syncs selected calendars to it so you always know what's going on.

The iCal Window

The iCal window is in a familiar calendar format, but because it's digital you can switch to different views with the click of a button. View a month at a time, a week, or a day; go back in time or forward into the future. Set recurring events to happen every first Friday or every three months. Create To Do lists that are attached to certain calendars. Turn calendars on or off so you can view just individual ones, or view several at a time to see how they overlap.

Every calendar has its own events and To Do list.

Choose the view from these buttons.

Uncheck a calendar to hide its events and To Do lists.

These are called Mail calendars. They are created when you first make a To Do item in Mail for a .Mac account. You cannot add events to these calendars, just To Dos.

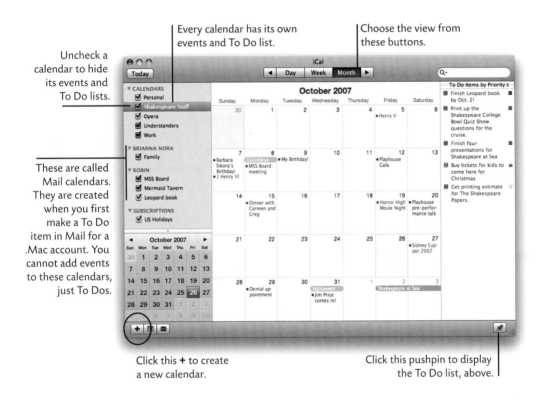

Click this **+** to create a new calendar.

Click this pushpin to display the To Do list, above.

Create Calendars

To create a new calendar, go to the bottom-left corner of the iCal window, click the **+** sign, then name the calendar.

You can have lots of different calendars. The checkmark next to a calendar name indicates those events are displayed. Thus you can have a calendar for each one of your kids' activities, plus your work calendar, and choose to see all the events at once or just selected ones. You'll have a visual display of just how crazy your life is.

To change the color of the calendar or to give it a description, Command-click (or right-click) on the calendar name. You'll see the pane below where you can change the color or add information.

Click this color box to choose another color or to make up one of your own.

Create a Group of Calendars

Create calendar **groups** to organize related calendars. You might want to group together the calendars that all have to do with your children. Or perhaps a particular project has several different calendars associated with it.

To make a group, go to the File menu and choose "New Calendar Group." *Or* Shift-click on the **+** sign in the bottom-left corner of the iCal window.

Name the new group, then drag other calendars into it.

I made this Group calendar.

Click the disclosure triangle to the left of a Group calendar to tidy up your list.

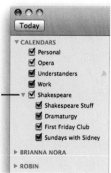

Automatic Birthdays Calendar

iCal can work with your Address Book to create a Birthdays calendar that automatically updates itself.

1 First you must add the Birthday field to your Address Book, as explained on page 112.

2 Then, in iCal, go to the iCal menu and choose "Preferences…."

3 Click the "General" icon.

4 Check the box to "Show Birthdays calendar." The calendar will appear in the "Subscriptions" group. If you don't have a Subscriptions group in your calendar list, iCal will put it there now.

Double-click any birthdate showing in the calendar to open its Info pane. There you can click the link to go straight to that person's contact information in Address Book, from which you can send a birthday email.

You can't make any changes to the Birthdays calendar in iCal; in fact, you can't even add alarms to notify you of upcoming birthdays.

Create Events

An event is what you'd expect it to be—something that happens on a particular day. You can **create events** in a variety of ways.

First select the calendar in which you want the event to appear. Then:

- In the "Month" view, double-click on a day to create a new event. A little tag appears on that day and you can add your information. Double-click on the tag to get the Info pane where you can add more information; click anywhere outside the Info pane to put it away. iCal arranges multiple events on one day according to the times you enter.

- In the "Week" or "Day" views, press-and-drag over the times for your event. Double-click the event to open the Info pane and add information; click anywhere outside the Info pane to put it away.

- To stretch the event out across multiple days, be sure to click the "all-day" button in the Info pane.

- To create a recurring event, use the "repeat" feature in the Info pane. iCal automatically repeats the event at a time interval you specify. For instance, the Shakespeare readings I hold repeat the first Friday of each month.

You can press Command I to open the Info pane for a selected event. Press Commend E to open it ready to edit.

These little icons indicate there is a file associated with this event, plus there is a list of attendees who have not all responded yet.

Double-click the event to show the Info pane with the information about that event.

Create To Do Lists

Each calendar can have its own **To Do list.** As you check and uncheck the calendar checkboxes, their attendant To Do lists show and hide accordingly.

To create a To Do item:

1   If the To Do pane isn't showing on the right side of iCal, click the pushpin button in the bottom-right corner.

2   Select a calendar from the calendar pane on the left.

3   In the To Do pane on the right, double-click in a blank space. *Or* Control-click (or right-click) and choose "New To Do" from the contextual menu.

4   Double-click directly on a To Do item to open its Info pane.
    You can **prioritize** your item, add a note, give it a due date, change the calendar, and more.

5   When the item has been **completed,** check the tiny box to its left.

Email a To Do item

You can email a To Do item, and if that person has a Mac, she can choose to click the link in the email to add the To Do item to her iCal.

To email the To Do from iCal:

1   Control-click the item in the To Do pane, and from the menu that pops up, choose "Mail To Do."

2   The Mail application opens with the To Do included as an attachment. Address the email form and click Send.

You can also email To Do items from Mail and they will be added to iCal.

3   The recipient of the email clicks the link and the To Do is added to the calendar of his choice.

Email Notifications

You can send someone an email invitation to an event, and she can send one to you. Mail automatically puts a notification in iCal and adds the new event to the calendar.

To send an invitation/notification:

Command-click (or right-click) on an event in a calendar. From the pop-up menu that appears, choose "Mail Event." Address the message and send it.

To respond to an email notification:

1   When you get an email message from someone inviting you to an iCal event, the Notifications box appears in the bottom-left corner of iCal.

   If the box isn't showing and you want to see it, single-click the Notifications button, as shown below.

2   When an invitation comes in, the Notifications button displays a red arrow. In the Notifications box, shown below, click the button to indicate your response. An email message is immediately sent to the person who notified you.

3   If you accept the notification, that event is added to your calendar on the appropriate day.

Notifications button.

Link Events and To Dos

To turn an Event into a To Do item, drag the Event from the calendar grid to the To Do pane. The event stays put, but now you also have a To Do item relating to it.

To turn a To Do item into an Event, drag a To Do item to a date in the calendar grid. The To Do item stays put, but now you also have an event attached to it.

Sort (organize) your Information

Automatically sort your To Do list by due date, title, calendar, or priority. Just click on tiny arrows in the heading of the To Do list and choose your option.

No matter how you've chosen to automatically sort items, once you manually drag an item into a different position (which you can do at any time), the sort order returns to "Manually" and is no longer an automatic arrangement.

Backup the Entire Calendar of Information

To make sure you don't lose the valuable information you have entered into your calendar, go to the File menu and choose "Back up iCal...." You will be asked where to save the file. If you have a lot of information you don't want to lose, you should save that file onto a CD and store it in a safe place.

Publish your Calendar

If you have a .Mac account (or a private server), you can **publish** your calendar of events, including the alarms and To Do list if you choose, to a web page and anyone in the world on any computer can view it. It's really remarkable.

To publish, just select the calendar in the list, then go to the Calendar menu and choose "Publish…." A little dialog box (shown below) drops down. Make your choices, then click "Publish."

A message appears telling you the web address and asking if you want to email people with the address.

To notify other people at any time, select the calendar, go to the Calendar menu, and choose "Send Publish Email…."

Subscribe to Calendars

There are many public calendars you can subscribe to, such as calendars for the PGA tours, NASCAR races, musician's tour dates, and many more.

To subscribe to a public calendar, go to the Calendar menu and choose "Find Shared Calendars…." This takes you to an Apple web site with dozens of public calendars (mostly sports).

To subscribe to a private calendar, go to the Calendar menu in iCal and choose "Subscribe…." Enter the web address you have been given.

Print in a Variety of Ways

Check out the great features in the Print dialog box. Each "View" (Month, Day, Week, or List) you choose changes the options, so spend a few minutes here exploring the possibilities for each view. You can choose to print the data from as many or as few calendars as you like. They are all color-coded, so just as in iCal itself, you can see how different events overlap.

Change the view here; the preview
will immediately change.

Turn
calendars
on or off
here.

Slide this bubble to
resize the preview.

iCal is Integrated With:

Address Book: Use the cards and groups to invite people to events.

Any birthdays you enter in Address Book can automatically appear in iCal (go to the iCal preferences and check "Show Birthdays calendar").

When you enter attendees names in the Info pane, iCal picks up their email addresses from the Address Book.

Open the Address panel from the Window menu. Quickly add people to the attendee list—drag them to the "attendee" button.

Mail: iCal will mail invitations and notifications of calendar updates, and Mail can automatically send notifications to iCal.

You can create iCal calendars in Mail and add events to them from Mail.

To Do items you create in Mail can be automatically added to the To Do list in iCal.

iPhone: Sync your iCal information to your iPhone.

iSync: Synchronize the calendar on one computer with all the other computers in your office, as well as with your .Mac account.

9

GOALS

iChat for Text, Audio, and Video Messaging

Using iChat you can communicate with others around the world using text messages, audio chatting, or video conferencing—free. You can text-chat with one other person or with a group of people, exchange files, and save printable copies of your chats. With a fast Mac and iChat, you can have audio chats with up to ten people at a time. You can have video conferences with up to three other people. You can even have one-way video chats where someone can see you but you can't see her (or vice versa). Amazing.

Set up iChat

When you first open iChat, it will ask you to fill in certain information to get started. You need a chat account of some sort.

> If you already have a .Mac account, that will be your "screen name" or "buddy name." Include the **@mac.com** part of your name when you tell others your buddy name.

> In the setup process, you can click the button labeled "Get an iChat Account...." This takes you to Mac.com where you can get a **FREE** iChat buddy name with a 60-day .Mac trial account, and you can keep the buddy name after the free trial is over even if you cancel the trial account.

> Or go to www.AIM.com and sign up for a free AIM account; you can use that as your buddy name. This buddy name does *not* include @aim.com.

> If you already have a Jabber account, you can use that name as well.

> You can get a free Google Talk account at www.Google.com/talk. This is also a Jabber account. Include **@gmail.com** in your Buddy name in the iChat setup.

If you skipped the initial set up the first time it asked, just open iChat (single-click its icon in the Dock) and it will ask you again to set it up. Follow the simple instructions.

A sample Buddy List and chat

So you'll know what to expect after you've gone through the process, below you see a typical Buddy List and text chat.

This is a Buddy List. Double-click a buddy name to open a text chat. The people whose names are grey are not available at the moment.

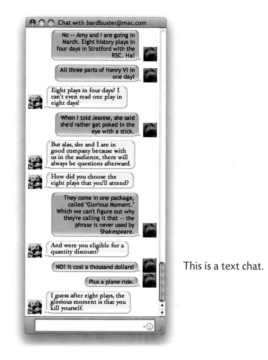

This is a text chat.

Customize your chat view through iChat preferences (from the iChat menu); use the "Messages" pane.

Create a Buddy List

To iChat with people, first set up a **Buddy List** of names. If you're using a Google Talk account or other Jabber account, your Buddy List is called **Jabber List.**

1   If you don't see the Buddy List when you open iChat, go to the Window menu and choose "Buddy List."

   If the title bar of the Buddy List says you are "Offline," click on the tiny triangle and choose "Available."

2   To add a new buddy, single-click the **+** sign at the bottom of the list and choose "Add Buddy."

3   In the dialog box that appears, enter the person's screen name or buddy name in the "Account Name" field. Choose whether it's an AIM account or a .Mac account. If you choose .Mac, it will enter the @mac.com part for you.

   Or click the disclosure button to display your Address Book, then choose a buddy from your list of contacts.

Click this disclosure button to display your Address Book contacts, as shown here.

4   Choose a Group in which to organize this buddy. Apple has provided several groups for you, and you can create your own.

5   Click the "Add" button.

   This account is automatically entered in the Address Book for you, if s/he wasn't already there.

Chat with One Other Person

To have a **text chat** with someone around the office or around the world, simply open your Buddy List and double-click the name of the person you want to chat with. Double-click on the person's name or icon, *not on any camera or phone icon that might be visible.* A chat window opens. Type a message, then hit Return. *Or* select a buddy name, then single-click the "A" at the bottom of the Buddy List.

Chat with a Group of People

You can text chat with at least twenty-three different people around the world in one Chat Room.

1   From the File menu, choose "Go to Chat Room."

2   In the window that appears, type a name that will become the name of this chat room. Make it something distinctive because if anyone else around the world types the same word, they'll end up in your chat room.

3   A Participants drawer pops out to the side of the chat room window. Click on the **+** sign and invite someone.

4   Click the **+** sign again and again to invite as many people as you like.

Or tell people ahead of time to all meet in a chat room called, say, "dogfood," at a certain time. At the prescribed time, tell everyone to do this:

1   Open iChat and go to the File menu; choose "Go to Chat Room…."

2   Enter the chat room name (in this case, dogfood) and click "Go." Everyone around the world who does so will end up in the room together. Remarkable.

Here I've started a Chat Room and invited my sweetheart, John, and my mother, Pat.

Audio Chat with One or More

Talk, **literally talk,** with other people. Make sure you have a microphone built in or connected to your Mac, or an iSight or other video camera attached. Newer iMacs and laptops, of course, have built-in cameras. Your buddies will display little telephone icons next to their pictures if they are able to audio chat back to you.

To audio chat with someone, she has to be in your Buddy List (see pages 163–164). In the list, as shown below, you can have a one-on-one audio chat with anyone who displays a telephone icon next to her name.

If a buddy shows *multiple* telephone icons, like "jtratz" and "roadrat," below, that means you can invite him to an audio chat that involves more than one person.

To audio chat, double-click directly on that person's phone icon. Or single-click his name and then click the phone icon at the bottom of the Buddy List.

If your Buddy doesn't have a microphone to chat back with you, select his name, then go to the Buddies menu and choose "Invite to One-Way Audio Chat." Your friend will hear you, but will have to send typed instant messages back.

This Mac has no camera attached, nor does it have a microphone. We can only text chat with each other.

TIP —— iChat picks up your photo from the Address Book; you can change the photo there.

TIP —— To add a photo to a buddy, select any buddy name and press Command I to get the Info window (or Control-click on a buddy name and choose "Show Info" from the menu that pops up). Drag any image into the image well.

Open an audio chat and invite others to join you

To *initiate* an audio conference with more than one other person, you need a more powerful machine than you do to *join* an audio chat. Any machine purchased within the last couple of years is powerful enough to initiate an audio chat.

1   Single-click a buddy name that displays multiple phones, then single-click the phone icon at the bottom of the Buddy List (**or** just double-click directly on the phone icon next to the buddy's name).

2   That person hears a little phone ringing and sees a message on his computer; he clicks the message to see who it is, then clicks "Accept." This begins the chat. Your window looks like this:

3   Now click the **+** button to get a little menu that lists the other people in your Buddy List who are capable of joining an audio conference. Select a person, then add others in the same way.

Although it says "with 2 People," there are really **three** people in this chat—I'm the third person.

Click the microphone icon to **mute** the session. The green bar and the microphone will turn orange as visual clues that the sound is muted.

4   **To delete someone** from the audio conference, move your pointer up towards his icon. A red **x** appears; click it and that person is gone.

5   **To terminate an audio session,** click the red close button in the upper-left of the little window.

Video Chat with up to Three Other People

See other people on your screen while you talk (not type) with them. To video chat, of course you must have a video camera attached to your Mac. All of the newer iMacs and laptops have built-in video cameras. You can use Apple's cute little iSight camera if you already have one (they're not sold anymore), or you can attach any FireWire video camera to your Mac, or one of the new USB2 cameras.

With whom can you video conference?

A video conference with more than one person takes a powerful Mac and a good broadband connection. If you are able to *participate* in a video conference with more than one person, the camera icon in your Buddy name shows multiple cameras. If someone in your Buddy List is able to participate, she shows multiple cameras, as well. And it takes a very powerful Mac to *initiate* a video conference with up to four people.

I can do a multiple video chat with two of my buddies, the two with multiple camera icons.

iChat AV preferences

You can make some minor adjustments in the Audio/Video pane of the iChat preferences. You might try changing the "Bandwidth Limit" to see if it affects your video chat one way or another. Depending on your Internet connection and how many other people use it, a different setting can work better (or worse).

Open a video chat and invite others to join you

To *initiate* a video conference with more than one other person, you need a more powerful machine than you do to *join* a video conference.

1 Single-click on a buddy name that shows multiple video camera icons. That person hears a little phone ringing and gets a message on her screen inviting her to a video chat. When she clicks "Accept," she appears in your video window instead of you.

2 To add two more people to your video conference, click the **+** sign; a menu drops down with the names of the people in your Buddy List *who are capable of joining you.*

This machine doesn't have a camera attached, but that person joined the audio portion of the video chat.

If your Buddy doesn't have a camera with which to video chat with you, select her name, then go to the Buddies menu and choose, "Invite to One-Way Video Chat." Your friend will see you, but will have to send instant messages back.

169

iChat Effects

iChat Effects are useless but grand fun. You can distort your image, add artistic touches, and even add new backgrounds so it looks like you're somewhere else.

To preview the various effects:

1 Go to the Video menu and choose "Video Preview."

2 Now from the same menu choose "Show Video Effects."

3 Select an effect from the palette (shown below) to see what it will do.

To apply an effect during a video chat:

1 During a video chat, click the "Effects" button in the bottom-left corner of the chat window. This opens the "Video Effects" palette shown above.

2 The original, non-effect version appears in the middle of the palette. Click an effect to apply it as you chat.

3 To return to the original, non-effect image, click the "Original" image in the center of the palette.

Add backgrounds

In addition to distorting your video image with various effects, you can add a photo or a movie to replace the existing background that's really behind you. This background replacement feature works best if you have a simple, uncluttered, single-color background. We got the best results (but not perfect) by using a background wall that was smooth and almost white. Although you can do this in the middle of chatting, you might want to get it all set up before you call someone on a video chat and surprise them.

1 In the Video Effects palette, click the right arrow button until you get to the palette of background images. They're photos, not your picture.

   To add your own background photos or movies, click through the effects until you find an empty well. Drag your image or movie into that well.

2 Click on a background image to select it. A text prompt appears and asks you to move yourself out of the video frame. The prompt notifies you a few seconds later with a "Background Detected" message.

3 Move back into the picture. iChat replaces the original background with the photo or movie you selected and puts you in front of it.

   If you want to change to another background, iChat will *not* ask you to step out again—it will just replace the existing one.

John's holding his nose, you see, because he's under water.

iChat Theater

Once you've initiated a video chat, you can use iChat Theater to show files, photos, slideshows, or movies while you continue your chat. This is amazing.

To share a file with iChat Theater:

1   Start a video chat with a buddy.

2   From the File menu, choose "Share a File With iChat Theater...."

3   In the Finder window that opens, select a file, photo, or movie you want to share, then click "Share."

Or simply drag any file, photo, or movie from your hard disk and drop it onto the video chat window.

When you drag a file to the video chat window, the buddy's image minimizes to the bottom-left corner to make room for an image of the file. Your buddy sees you as a thumbnail video and sees the same file image that you see.

iChat Theater also opens a *file window* on your screen (shown below). It allows you to scroll through a shared multi-page document as your buddy watches, play or pause a movie, or show previous or next files in the chat window.

Click here to end an iChat Theater session.

This is the file window for a PDF in iChat Theater.

If the shared file is a movie, the file window displays a Play/Pause button and a scrub bar to drag the clip backward or forward.

To share *multiple* files of the same or different types, Command-click to select the files on your hard drive, then drag the files to the video chat window. The files play as a slideshow.

iChat Theater movie.

The file window for multiple files.

Share iPhoto with iChat Theater

You can also share entire iPhoto albums as a slideshow.

1   Start a video chat with a buddy.

2   From the File menu, choose "Share iPhoto With iChat Theater...."

3   In the iPhoto window that opens, select an album, then click "Share."

Select an album or select multiple photos to show as a slideshow in the video chat window.

iChat Theater opens this file window so you can control the slideshow.

Bonjour on your Local Network

Bonjour is an integrated component of **iChat**. If you have two or more Macs connected through a local area network (an Ethernet network, wireless network, or a combination of both), Bonjour automatically detects and connects all of the computers on the network. You can send Instant Messages or files to Bonjour buddies on your local network. You can have audio or video chats with others on the local network (if a microphone or digital video camera is connected to your computer, of course). And you can use Screen Sharing to share your computer with others or to see another buddy's computer (see the following pages).

You don't have to have a .Mac account or AIM account or any other kind of special account—just computers that are connected in some way.

To set up Bonjour:

1   Open iChat, then from the iChat application menu, choose "Preferences."

2   Click the "Accounts" button, then click "Bonjour" in the Accounts pane on the left side of the window.

Turn Bonjour on or off.

If you select "Send text as I type," the recipient of your message will see the text as you type it. If you leave this unchecked, the recipient sees an empty little message cloud until you finish your message and hit Return.

Or you can just open iChat, go to the Window menu and choose "Bonjour List." It will give you a button to login to Bonjour.

The Bonjour List looks just like a Buddy List—except it's labeled Bonjour List. Your chat windows look similar too.

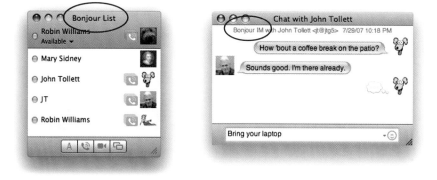

Bonjour automatically detects a local network and connects you to it. If you're in a public space, such as an Internet cafe, you should quit iChat and turn off Bonjour when you're not using it to ensure privacy and security.

To send a file to anyone on the Bonjour List, just drop the file on a buddy's name. Your buddy will get a message asking if he wants to accept the file.

Or drag a file into the message field where you type to chat. Hit Return and off it goes. If the file is an image, the image itself will appear in the chat window, and your buddy can drag it to his Desktop.

TIP —— If you're interested in sharing files on your network or sharing computer screens (where you can actually manipulate the other person's monitor wherever she is in the world), please see Lesson 21 on connecting and sharing files.

Record Chats

When an audio or video Chat is in progress, you can record the chat. Recorded video iChat files require a lot of storage space, approximately one megabyte for every five seconds of video.

1 Start an audio or video chat with a buddy.

2 From the Video menu at the top of the screen, choose "Record Chat."

3 The buddy's audio or video chat window reveals a "Recording Request" sheet (below-left). When the buddy clicks "Allow," the chat begins.

4 A red Record light alerts both participants that recording is in progress.

To stop a video recording, from the Video menu choose "Stop Recording."

To stop an audio recording, click the red Record button.

A red Record button means the audio chat is being recorded.

Find recorded chats

To locate a video or audio chat file, go to the Home folder, open the Documents folder, then look in the iChats folder.

The files are also found in iTunes. Look in your iTunes sidebar for a playlist named "iChat Chats." Click that playlist to show any recorded iChats.

iChat is Integrated With:

Address Book: The photo you put in Address Book appears in your Buddy and Bonjour List, and the photo you put in the Buddy or Bonjour List appears in the Address Book.

When an iChat buddy is online, a green dot appears on her card.

Mail: You can send email to a buddy through your Buddy List—Control-click (or right-click) on a buddy name, then choose "Send Email...." And when a buddy in your list is online, a green dot appears in the "Buddy Availability" column in Mail.

iTunes: Let others know what music you are listening to; in the Buddy List, click on the word right beneath your name (it's a menu). Choose the option "Current iTunes Song."

iSight camera, built-in camera, attached video camera:

You video conference with this camera, of course, but you can also click a button to take a picture of the person on the other end to use for his buddy image ("Show Info" on a buddy, and drop a new photo in the well).

Drop a photo or graphic image in this well. If you want this image to override the one your buddy uses, check the box to "Always use this picture."

10

GOALS

Buy music, movies,
music videos,
or television shows.

Create Playlists and
Smart Playlists of
selected music.

Burn your own CDs
of music.

Watch movies or shows
right in iTunes.

Listen to radio from
around the world.

Print covers
for your own CDs.

iTunes for your Listening Pleasure

Import music into iTunes, create Playlists of your favorite songs, copy the Playlists to CDs so you have your own discs of customized music, or stream your music from your office down the hallway to hear it in the kitchen. You can buy music directly through the iTunes Store with the click of a button and download it right to your computer.

If you have an iPhone, your phone automatically opens iTunes to sync music and data to it. And of course your iPod gets its life from iTunes.

The iTunes Window

Below is an overview of the iTunes window. This short chapter is only an overview; if you want an entire manual about iTunes, please see John Tollett's book called *Cool Mac Apps* (which contains entire manuals about all the other cool apps that are available from Apple). There is so much to iTunes! I encourage you to explore the menus and all the buttons.

All of your songs, books, shows, etc., are imported into the **Library.**

Click the Play button and all the *checked* songs in the window will play.

Click these view buttons to display your collection in various ways.

The **Playlists** help you organize all the music in the Library.

Apple has made a number of **Smart Playlists** for you (see pages 182–183 about Smart Playlists).

Click this arrow to send this album to someone as a gift or to post your Playlist to iTunes.

Click one of these arrows to find more of this artist's songs in the iTunes Store.

You only see these arrows on items that you have selected (single-click to select).

Buy Music, Movies, or Television Shows

To buy music, movies, or television shows, click on "iTunes Store" in the sidebar. You can search for music: use the search field in the upper-right.

The first time you click a "Buy" button, you will be asked to set up an account. If you have a .Mac account or email address, use that. You'll be asked for a credit card number and contact info. After you've got an account, you can buy and download music, movies, and television shows with the click of a button. To watch a show or movie, see the next page.

Download Album Art

When you buy music through iTunes, you automatically get the **album art** with it. If the art is not showing at the bottom of the sidebar when you select a purchased song, click the artwork and video-viewer button (shown to the left, circled below).

You can add your own art to this well—select a song, then drag any graphic into this spot.

Create a Playlist

A Playlist is a **collection of songs** from your iTunes music Library. You might create one Playlist of your favorite jazz, another of Scottish folk songs, and another of a particular artist. The same song can be in any number of Playlists. You can take two songs from this CD, one from that CD, etc., to create your own personal collection, then burn that collection to a CD of your own.

1 Playlists are made from songs in your iTunes Library, so first import songs from CDs (see the following page) or buy songs at the iTunes Store (see the previous page).

2 Then click the **+** sign at the bottom of the sidebar. A new, untitled Playlist label appears in the sidebar.

3 Name this new Playlist.

4 Single-click on the Music collection in the Library section of the sidebar.

5 Drag songs from the Library window to the Playlist name.

The purple Playlists that you see already in your sidebar are ones that Apple has created for you. They display the songs their labels describe—the recently played songs, the 25 you play most often, etc. These are purple and have a different icon because they are Smart Playlists, which are Playlists that automatically add items to themselves based on chosen parameters; see the next page.

Create a Smart Playlist

A regular Playlist holds the songs or music videos that you add to it by dragging items into it. A Smart Playlist **automatically adds certain music all by itself.** It's really great. Remember, buy the songs or import the songs to iTunes first.

1   Hold down the Option key; the **+** sign at the bottom of the sidebar turns into a gear wheel; click the gear wheel. **Or** go to the File menu and choose "New Smart Playlist…."

2   In the dialog box that appears, click the menus from left to right and make your choices. Click the **+** sign to add more parameters. Click OK.

3   The Smart Playlist appears in the sidebar, waiting for you to rename it.

Import Songs from a CD

Put an **audio CD** in your drive and iTunes automatically opens. If you're online, iTunes goes to an online database and (if it can find the CD in the database) gets the artist, album title, song names, times, and more, and displays that information in the iTunes window.

Single-click the checkboxes to check or uncheck songs—checked songs are the ones that will be imported. (Command-click to check or uncheck all boxes.)

A button in the bottom-right appears called "Import CD." Click that button, and the *checked* songs will import into the Music library.

Share the Wealth

Share your Library of music with other computers in your office. Open the iTunes preferences. Click the "Sharing" tab, and then check "Share my library on my local network."

To find music that other computers are willing to share with you, check the box to "Look for shared music."

Adjust the Sound

Use the powerful **equalizer** for sound quality. From the Window menu, choose "Equalizer." Experiment with the controls.

Watch Movies in iTunes

You can buy movies or television shows and watch them directly in iTunes. If you buy an Apple TV device and have a wireless system and widescreen TV in your home, you can stream the movies and shows from your computer to your television. (To do so, you'll have to read the directions that come with the Apple TV!)

To watch a movie in iTunes:

1   Go to the iTunes Store and buy a movie or television show. After it's downloaded, it will appear in the "Movies" or "TV Shows" list.

2   Select "Movies" in the Library section of the sidebar, then double-click on the name of the movie or show. The film immediately opens in the iTunes window, as shown below.

Tune in to Visual Effects

To see **visual effects** that change depending on the music you're playing, go to the View menu and choose "Turn on Visualizer,"

Or press Command T to turn on the visualizer.

Press Command F to view the effects full screen.

Press the letter R to randomly change the effects.

Press the Escape key (esc) to turn off the visualizer.

Below are samples of the variety of visual effects that iTunes produces, based on the music playing and the effect.

Add a Ringtone to your iPhone

If you have an iPhone, you can buy ringtones and add them to your phone. You must first buy the song, and the ringtone costs another 99¢.

Add the "Ringtone" column to your window: Control-click (or right-click) on any column header; from the pop-up menu that appears, choose "Ringtone."

Any song that is authorized for ringtones has a little bell in that column. Single-click on the bell and you get an option to select whatever section of that song you want as a ringtone, up to 30 seconds. Drag either end of the blue clip, then click the "Preview" button to hear it. You can choose how long of a gap you want to hear before the sound repeats (loops). Keep repeating that until you get exactly the clip you want, then click the "Buy" button. Plug in your iPhone and the ringtones are automatically synced to your phone.

Burn a CD of your own Collection

To burn a CD of your own collection, first import the songs and make a Playlist, as described on the previous pages. You can't just select songs in the music library to burn to a CD—you must make a Playlist. Then:

1   Insert a blank CD-R (newer Macs can also burn to CD+R discs).

2   In iTunes, select a Playlist. You can only burn one Playlist onto a CD, so make sure it's got everything you want in it. You can burn about 600 MB onto one regular CD, so add as many songs from as many different artists and albums as you like. Check the status bar at the bottom of iTunes to know how many megabytes are in the selected Playlist.

3   Click the "Burn Disc" button in the lower-right of iTunes (this button only appears when there is a burnable disc loaded in your Mac). iTunes immediately begins the process of burning the songs to disc.

4   When it's finished, you'll see the name of the CD in the sidebar, along with an eject symbol. Eject the CD and enjoy!

> **TIP** ——— You can make a huge Playlist that holds many more songs than will fit on one CD. When you put in the first disc and click the "Burn Disc" button, iTunes will warn you that it will take more than one disc. You click OK and iTunes will tell you when the first disc is full, will eject that completed disc, and ask you to insert another one.

Listen to Radio from around the World

This never ceases to amaze me. You can listen to radio from around the world—all you do is click a button.

In the sidebar, click the "Radio" icon, as shown circled below. Then double-click on a category to see the variety of stations available in that genre, and double-click on the radio you want to listen to. Amazing.

Once you've got the radio on, click the green minimize button in the upper-left of the iTunes window. That will reduce iTunes to just a tiny little window so it's out of your way, but the radio will continue playing. (Click the green button again to enlarge iTunes to its full size.)

With this small frame, I can see what I'm listening to at the moment, start and stop the music, and change the volume.

Print a CD Cover Insert

You can print in a variety of ways from iTunes.

1 Select a Playlist.

2 Hit Command P to **print.**

3 Experiment with the options. Choose different "Print" options and then choose different "themes" within that print option. For instance:

To print a cover with the original album art that slips into your CD case, choose "CD jewel case insert," then choose the theme "Single cover."

The option to print a "Mosaic" theme will print a song list and a collage of all the album covers that belong to songs in your Playlist.

iTunes is Integrated With:

iPhoto   Choose a song from your iTunes collection to play during a slideshow.

iChat   iChat Buddy List and Bonjour List windows can display the songs you're listening to: In either window, click the tiny triangle under your name in the title bar; choose "Current iTunes Track."

Screensaver   Your screen saver can display album art you've downloaded. Go to the System Preferences, click on "Desktop & Screen Saver." Click the "Screen Saver" tab, and then select "iTunes Artwork."

iPod   Transfer all your songs to your iPod.

iPhone   Use iTunes to synchronize all your songs, contact information, and other data from your Mac to your phone and back again.

Wireless connections

The AirPort Express wireless device includes built-in AirTunes software. Plug the AirPort Express brick into any electrical outlet in your house and you can stream iTunes from your Mac to that other room. Way cool. Of course, your Mac has to be connected to a wireless network or have a wireless card inside.

.Mac account   Use your .Mac account to purchase music with one click.

Dashboard   Display a small controller; see page 286.

11

GOALS

Learn to crop, color adjust,
and resize images

Learn how to annotate
and mark up a PDF

Search PDFs and create
bookmarks for easy
retrieval

Copy text from a PDF
to paste into another
document as editable text

Fill in PDF forms

Make screenshots

Print images
or documents in a
variety of ways

Save files into other
formats

Preview for Viewing Images and PDFs

The small picture-viewing application called Preview does a great deal more than merely display photographs for you. It's actually quite a powerful program in which you can open and annotate PDFs, change file formats, crop images, adjust the color, make screen shots of what you see on your screen, and more. Take a few moments to explore the possibilities.

Open an Image or Folder of Images

If you haven't changed the settings, you can just double-click on images or PDFs and they open in Preview. Preview is in your Dock (if it isn't, see page 20 to put it there).

Click this button to show or hide the sidebar.

Sidebar.

Enlarge or reduce the size of the images in the sidebar.

To open an image or multiple images in Preview, do any of the following:

- Double-click the file.

- Drag-and-drop an image or PDF onto the Preview icon in the Dock.
  You can drag an **entire folder** of images to the Preview icon and they will all open and display themselves in the sidebar, as shown above.

- Drag an image or a collection of images from your Desktop or a window and drop it in the Preview sidebar.

- Control-click on an image, select "Open With," and choose "Preview."

Be sure to check the Preview preferences (under the Preview menu) for options on displaying your images.

Sort the Images or Email Them

To sort the images (arrange them in a particular order), use the Action button, as shown above. You don't have to select anything first. You can also **email** a selected image from this menu, as you can see above (or use the File menu).

Rotate, Reduce, or Enlarge the View

If an image appears sideways, press Command L to **rotate** it to the left, or Command R to **rotate** it to the right. Or use the commands in the Tools menu. From the Tools menu you can also **flip an image horizontally or vertically.** If you want to keep it that way, **save** the image (go to the File menu and choose "Save").

If an image looks bitmapped, blurry, and too large, reduce its view: click on the **−** sign in the Zoom button. Enlarge an image, of course, with the **+** sign.

View a Slideshow

This is a fun feature: Drag a selection of images and drop them on the Preview icon in the Dock. This opens all of them at once in Preview. Then click the "Slideshow" button in the toolbar. Each image appears for three seconds, then switches to the next image. If you don't see the control bar in the slideshow, click in the middle of your screen. To stop, press Command Period or click the **x** in the control bar.

Display Facing Pages or Continuous Pages

You can display facing pages of documents, as in a book (the first page will always display alone, like the first page of a chapter). This works whether or not the person who created the PDF saved the file in the "Spreads" format (which combines facing pages in the PDF). In fact, if someone *did* create the PDF pages in spreads, you can view them in Preview as individual pages. This comes in very handy when you need to print the document because otherwise the entire spread would print on one page.

To switch back and forth from single pages to facing pages, go to the View menu, slide down to "PDF Display," then choose your option.

Continuous means the pages run continuously in the viewer pane, rather than as individual pages. Scroll up and down to see your entire file.

Crop a Photograph or Other Image

You can crop any photograph or image very easily in Preview. Keep in mind that when you crop an image, the part you get rid of *is gone from the original image forever.* You might want to make a copy of the file before you crop. (Cropping a **PDF,** however, is "non-destructive"; see the following pages.)

To crop a photograph or other image:

1   Open the image in Preview.

2   Choose a cropping tool from the "Select" button in the toolbar (you have to *press* on that menu to see the options; a *click* selects the option you see in the button). You can crop into a circle, oval, rectangle, or use the Lasso tool to draw a shape.

3   **To resize** the cropped area, press on any of the tiny square "handles" that you see around the edges. Drag any handle to resize.

4   **To move the cropped area** to a different part of the image, press in the middle of the cropping box and drag.

5   When you are ready to crop, go to the Tools menu and choose "Crop." *Or* press Command K.

This is a handle. If you look carefully, you'll see eight of them. Drag any handle to resize the cropping area in that direction.

Crop a PDF

You can crop any part of a PDF. When you crop it, Preview actually keeps track of the part of the document you deleted and hangs on to it in case you want to uncrop the file, even after you've saved it.

To crop a PDF:

1 Open the PDF in Preview.

2 Single-click on the "Select" tool, circled above. If the little tools are not visible in the toolbar, drag the bottom-right corner of Preview to widen the window. *Or* go to the Tools menu and choose "Select Tool."

3 Starting in an upper corner, drag diagonally downward across the PDF to select the part of it you want to save. The light area is the part you're going to keep.

4 If you need to resize the cropped area, position the mouse directly over one of the eight "handles" you see on the corners and edges of the cropped area (see the previous page). Drag a handle to resize.

5 If you need to move the cropped area to another part of the page, position the pointer in the middle of the crop box. You'll notice the pointer turns into a gloved hand. Press the hand in the middle of the crop box and drag.

6   If you have a multi-page document, it looks like the cropping will apply to every page. But don't worry—you'll have a choice about that in a minute. When you have the cropped area finalized, go to the Tools menu and choose "Crop," *or* press Command K.

7   You will be asked if you want to crop just the current page or all pages. Click the button of your choice.

To switch between displays of the full page or the cropped page:

▪ **Display the entire contents of the PDF:** Go to the View menu, choose "PDF Display," and choose to see the "Media Box" (as shown below).

▪ **Display the cropped image:** Go to the View menu, choose "PDF Display," and then choose to see the "Crop Box."

View	
Sidebar	⇧⌘D
PDF Display	▶
✓ Automatically Resize	⇧⌘R
Show Image Background	⌥⌘B
Actual Size	⌘0
Zoom To Fit	
Zoom In	⌘+
Zoom Out	⌘−
Zoom to Selection	⌘*
Hide Toolbar	⌘B
Customize Toolbar...	
Show Notes	
Slideshow	⇧⌘F

PDF Display submenu:
✓ Single Page
Single Page Continuous
Two Pages
Two Pages Continuous

Crop Box
✓ Media Box

When you **re-open a cropped file,** it might open in the uncropped version. Just use the technique above to view the cropping again.

Search a PDF

The search feature in Preview is quite amazing. Use the standard keyboard shortcut for "Find," Command F. Once you have found an instance on the page, press Command G to find the next instance. These are the same shortcuts you've probably used in Safari to find text on a web page or in TextEdit to find text in your document.

To search a PDF:

1 With the PDF document open in front of you, press Command F.
   Or go to the Edit menu, slide down to "Find," then choose "Find...."

2 A search drawer appears on the side of the document window, as shown below. Type your search word or phrase into the search field.

3 As you type, Preview starts finding words that match. The more you type, the narrower the search becomes and the fewer words it finds.

4 In the list of results, double-click any one to go directly to that result. Preview will outline the word briefly, and then the outline fades to a highlight so you can see the word.

5 To find the next occurrence of the word or phrase, press Command G, or double-click any other result in the list.

Single-click the **X** to delete everything in the search field.

Create Bookmarks

The bookmarks in Preview are not stored in the document itself. A bookmark puts the name of a file in the Bookmarks menu of Preview so you can open the document or photograph immediately without having to go look for it—just open Preview and choose the bookmark and the file opens from your hard disk and displays that particular page. It's like having a list of bookmarks in your web browser so you can instantly go to a favorite web page.

To make a bookmark for an open document or image, press Command D (the same shortcut as in Safari). You will be asked to name the bookmark. Give it a name that you'll recognize in a list.

> If the PDF is a **multi-page document,** you can make several bookmarks for the same document, each one to a different page. Just make sure you are viewing the page you want to bookmark before you press Command D.

To open a bookmarked file, open Preview, go to the Bookmarks menu, and choose the file from the list in the menu.

To edit the name or to remove a bookmark, go to the Bookmarks menu and choose "Edit Bookmarks…." In the dialog box that appears:

> **To delete a file,** single-click the file name, then click the "Remove" button.

> **To edit the file name,** double-click on its name, then edit.

Annotate a PDF

You can add comments, highlights, shapes, and more to PDFs to call out items for other readers. The note symbol completely obscures the text and cannot be moved once the PDF is saved; the note itself will be in a sidebar. They print in exactly the same places as they appear on the screen, so be judicious about where you place your notes!

There are **two sets of tools** available for annotations. By default, they are not in the toolbar but only accessible through the Tools menu. If you find you use them regularly, **put them in the toolbar:** Go to the View menu, choose "Customize Toolbar...," and drag them into the toolbar.

Press on a toolbox to make the little menu appear so you can choose other tools. (A click will not open the toolbox; you need to press and hold it down.)

To create a text note on a PDF:

1 In an open PDF, go to the Tools menu, slide down to "Annotate," and choose "Add Note." If you have added the annotation tools to your toolbar, as above, then select "Add Note" from the "Annotate" toolbox button.

2 Click anywhere on the page. Preview creates a tiny note marker on the page and immediately opens an area to the side with the actual note.

3 **To type the note,** just start typing and the text will appear in the note on the side. The preferences (from the Preview menu) tell it to also add your name. If you want to **add more to that note later,** double-click on it.

4   **To move a note symbol,** double-click on the note symbol on the page. Then press-and-drag. The note itself (on the side) will move along with the symbol.

5   **To delete a note,** double-click on the symbol to select it. Hit Delete.

To draw a red oval or an orange rectangle annotation:

1   In an open PDF, go to the Tools menu, slide down to "Annotate," and choose "Add Oval." (**Or** if you added the annotation tools to your toolbar, as on the opposite page, select "Oval" from the "Annotate" toolbox button.) You can add an explanatory note next to the oval (see the opposite page).

Of course, if you want an orange rectangle, choose "Add Rectangle."

2   With the tool, press-and-drag anywhere on the page **to create a shape.**

3   **To resize a shape,** single-click on the "Text" tool in the toolbar. Then double-click on the shape and you'll see a grey box in the bottom-right corner. Drag that dark corner to resize.

4   **To move a shape,** single-click on the "Text" tool in the toolbar. Then double-click on the shape. Press inside of it and drag.

5   **To delete an oval,** single-click on the "Text" tool in the toolbar. Then double-click on the shape to select it. Hit Delete.

To highlight, underline, or strike through text:

1   Choose the "Text" tool from the toolbar.

2   Press-and-drag over the text you want to annotate.

3   Go to the Tools menu, slide down to "Mark Up," and choose your annotation method. (**Or** if you added the annotation tools to your toolbar, as on the opposite page, then select the method from the "Mark Up" toolbox button.)

To delete all or part of a mark up, press-and-drag over the text whose mark up you want to delete. Then select that method again from the menu or toolbox button (that is, if you want to remove a highlight, select the text with the Text tool and then choose "Highlight" from the "Mark Up" toolbox menu).

TIP —— Once you have chosen a tool from the Annotate or Mark Up toolbox buttons, it becomes the default. When you want to use that tool again, just single-click on the button (it should be showing your tool of choice), then drag on the PDF page.

Create a link on an exisiting PDF

You can create a workable link on any PDF. Send the PDF on to someone else and the link still works. The link can go to any web page, in which case clicking on it opens Safari to that page. Or the link can go to another page in the same document. For instance, you might have a report with a table of contents. If there are no links from the table of contents to the actual pages in the existing PDF, you can add them.

To create a link:

1   In an open PDF, click on the Text tool in the toolbar.

2   Press-and-drag over the existing text to which you want to apply a link. What the text says on the page has nothing to do with what you will enter as a link.

3   Go to the Tools menu, slide down to "Annotate," and choose "Add Link."

   Or if you have added the annotation tools to your toolbar, as on the previous pages, you can select "Link" from the "Annotate" toolbox button *instead* of using the menu.

4   The "Inspector" (shown below) automatically opens up to the "Annotations" pane, as shown below. (If it doesn't show up, go to the Tools menu and choose "Inspector.")

   If you don't see the same pane shown below, click the red oval to display the "Annotations" pane.

5   In the little "Action" menu inside this pane, you have a choice of linking
    to a "URL" on the web or to a "Link within PDF."

    If you choose to link to a URL, type in the entire web address including
    http://. Click the "Set URL" button.

    If you choose to link to another page in the PDF, you'll get a list of pages
    to choose from. Choose the page and click the "Set Destination" button
    that appears.

6   On the page, the link appears as a gray-lined box, as shown below.
    Mouse over it to see a tool tip appear with the name of the link.
    You can click on the link in Preview to make sure the link works.

or mail: The Mary Sidney Society
           7 Sweet Swan Lane
           Santa Fe, New Mexico 87506

           http://www.MarySidneySociety.org

Copy Text from a PDF to Paste Elsewhere

You can copy text from a PDF file (as long as the person sending it to you hasn't locked it) and paste it into any other document as **editable text.** Or you can copy a section of text as a **graphic** and paste it into another document as a graphic image that can be resized as a unit.

To copy text:

1   Select the Text tool, shown circled below, *or* press Command 2.

2   Press-and-drag over the text you want to select.

   To select just a vertical portion of text, as in one column, hold down the Option key before you start to drag, and keep it held down as you drag.

3   From the Edit menu, choose "Copy," *or* press Command C. Open your other document and paste it in (Command V).

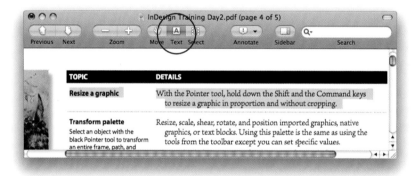

To copy any part of a PDF as a graphic, see page 195 to select a cropping area. Then, instead of cropping, go to the Edit menu and choose "Copy."

Now you can go to any document in any application and paste that graphic in. To paste it once you open the other document, press Command V, *or* go to the Edit menu and choose "Paste."

Edit a Graphic

You can do some editing in graphic images such as photos. You can crop, as explained on page 195, resize, and resample (change the pixels per inch). And you have some pretty powerful color adjustments available. The only way to learn how to use them is to experiment! Always save a copy of the original photo before you start messing with it.

To adjust the color of an image:

1   Open an image in Preview.

2   From the Tools menu, choose "Adjust Color." You'll see the panel shown below-right.

3   Move the sliders left and right to see what all the options do. The image will immediately change as you adjust the sliders. You can always click the button, circled below, to "Reset All" and restore the image to the way it looked in the first place.

4   If you like the changes at any point, press Command S to save. Then you can carry on with more changes that you can choose to save or not.

Above-left is the original image.

Straight above you can see where I randomly adjusted the sliders until I got an image that looks like what I remembered when Laura took the shot, shown to the left.

205

Fill in PDF Forms

If you download forms from the web, you can actually fill them in by typing. *Then* you can print the fully completed forms, instead of printing them first and filling them in by hand. The PDF must have been created and saved in such a way that it has fields ready for you to enter data. That is, you just can't start entering data into any old PDF—it must be an actual form format.

After you save a form that you have filled in, you cannot edit any of the information you entered! You might want to save a clean copy of the file *before* you fill in the form.

To fill in a PDF form:

1 Open an appropriate PDF form in Preview. The example below is a tax form downloaded from the IRS site.

2 Click on the Text tool, as shown circled below.

3 Click in the area where you are supposed to enter data. An insertion point appears and the field displays a border, as shown below.

4 Type! Be sure to save regularly (or don't save in case you want to edit later).

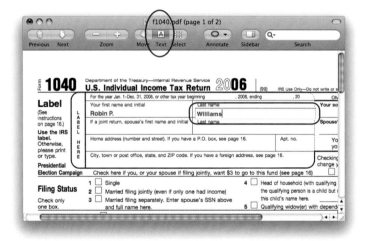

Make Screenshots using Preview

A screenshot is a picture of what your screen looks like at that moment. It's useful to send to someone who's trying to help you or to show someone something cool that's only on your Mac. Preview uses the Grab utility to take pictures of items on your screen.

To make a screenshot:

1   Open Preview. You don't have to have any window open.

2   Go to the File menu, slide down to "Grab," then choose either:

   Selection: A crosshair icon appears. Press-and-drag around an area to take a screenshot of just that area. When you let go, it makes the shot.

   Window: A camera icon appears, shown below. As you move the camera icon on top of different windows on your screen, it highlights each one. When the window you want is highlighted, single-click. It takes a picture of the entire window, whether or not you can see the whole thing.

   Timed Screen: Preview gives you ten seconds to get your screen set up the way you want it for a screenshot. For instance, you might want a picture of a particular menu and submenu. After ten seconds, Preview snaps a screenshot of the entire screen.

A file icon whose name begins with "Snapshot" appears on your Desktop, and it immediately and automatically opens in Preview.

Also see page 431 to learn how to take screenshots with keyboard shortcuts.

Print or Fax from Preview

You can print any image or document from Preview, of course. But you can also print groups of photos or entire folders of images.

If you have multiple images open in Preview, select the ones you want to print: choose them from the sidebar. Then press Command P to print. You'll get the dialog box shown below. Be sure to spend a few minutes looking through all the options.

Above you see a preview of what the page will look like when printed with the specifications chosen in the dialog box.

To the left, you see a preview of what the printed page will look like with the option of "Fill Entire Paper" selected.

To fax an image or selected images:

Not all computers today have an internal modem installed, and you can't fax without one. You must have a phone cable connected to a telephone outlet—you can't fax from your Mac over the Internet or through your broadband connection.

If your Mac has a modem that is connected to a phone line, it is automatically configured to send faxes. If you use your dial-up modem to connect to the Internet, your Mac will wait until you log off, then send the fax.

1   From the File menu, choose "Print...."

2   Click the button in the bottom-left corner named "PDF."

3   Choose "Fax PDF...."

4   Enter the fax number you want to send this to. Make your choices in this dialog box, similar to your choices when printing (as explained above).

5   Click the "Fax" button.

Also see Lesson 17 on printing and faxing.

Save as Another Format

If you know you need a particular image in another **file type,** go to the File menu and choose "Save As...." Click the "Format" menu, as shown below, and make a choice. Each choice will give you different specifications for that particular file format.

12

GOALS

Use the Burn Folder to collect files for burning to CD or DVD

Create clips and bookmarks in DVDs

Create a PDF from any file

Use Font Book to install and preview fonts

Keep track of your life with Stickies

Learn to use PhotoBooth to take still shots and movies of yourself

Miscellaneous Tools on your Mac

Your Mac has a number of great tools in the form of small applications, some of which get overlooked. This lesson introduces you to some features and possibilities that you might not be taking advantage of yet.

Burn a CD or DVD with a Burn Folder

You'll want to burn backups of your important work. Be sure to burn backups of any applications or fonts or other files that you download straight from the Internet.

The steps below describe how to burn data files (as opposed to music or movies) onto a disc. A CD holds about 650 megabytes; a DVD holds about 4.3 gigabytes, even though the package might tell you it holds 4.7. (To burn a music CD, see page 186.)

The **Burn Folder** is the easiest way to burn a CD or DVD. Drag items into this special folder, and when you're ready, burn the contents to a disc. Your Mac automatically creates **aliases** of those files (see page 430 for details on aliases). This means that after you burn the disc, you can throw away the entire Burn Folder without destroying any original files.

The wonderful thing is that you can collect items you want to burn without having to actually burn the disc at that moment—you can collect files over the period of a project and when finished, you have a folder ready to back up onto a disc.

To create a Burn Folder, put files inside, and burn it:

1   Open a Finder window and select the window in which you want the Burn Folder to appear. For instance, single-click on your Home icon in the Sidebar, or single-click the Documents folder icon. Or click on the Desktop, if you want the folder to appear there. (You can always move the Burn Folder to wherever you like, of course.)

2   From the File menu, choose "New Burn Folder."

3   A folder with the "Burn" icon on it appears in the selected window.

Burn Folder

I put this Burn Folder in my Home folder. Then I dragged it into my Sidebar so it's always available to me.

4   **To put a file in the folder** so you can burn it later, just drag the original file and drop it into the Burn Folder. Your Mac will put an *alias* of the file into the Burn Folder and the original will stay right where it was, safe and sound.

5   **To burn the folder onto a CD,** first insert a blank CD-R or DVD.

6   **Then** single-click the Burn Folder; a bar across the top of the window appears with a "Burn" button, as shown on the opposite page.

  You will be asked to name the disc, which of course you should do.

  Click the "Burn" button in the dialog box.

TIP —— If you drag the Burn Folder into the Sidebar, it displays a burn icon next to it. You can just single-click that burn icon to start the process.

TIP —— You can make as many Burn Folders as you want. Rename them as you do any other folder. This makes it easy to have a separate Burn Folder for each project.

To check the amount of storage space used in the folder:

1   Single-click the Burn Folder icon.

2   Press Command I to display the Info window.

3   Click the disclosure triangle next to "Burning."

4   Click the "Calculate" button to see how much you have collected in the folder.

It says there is no device available, even if there is one ready to burn.

TIP —— If you change your mind and want to take an unburned disc out of the Mac, Control-click (or right-click) on the disc icon and choose "Eject '_____ CD.'"

DVD Player

DVD Player

Besides playing your DVDs and allowing you to control things as you do on your television, the DVD Player has several special tricks.

Display the thumbnail bar and controls

A video starts playing automatically in full screen.

> **To see the controls,** push your mouse down to the bottom of the screen and they appear.

> **To see the thumbnail bar** that displays chapter markers, bookmarks, and video clips, push your mouse toward the top of the screen.

> **To show the DVD application menu bar,** push your mouse all the way to the top of the screen.

Create bookmarks to find specific points in the video

A bookmark lets you skip immediately to certain points in the video that you choose. That is, you are not limited to the chapter markers that were created when the DVD was made.

To create a bookmark:

1   Play a DVD. Then . . .

2   Go to the Window menu and choose "Bookmarks." A palette appears. When you get to the point in the DVD where you want to insert a bookmark, click the **+** sign at the bottom of the Bookmarks palette.

> **Or** when you get to the point in the DVD where you want to insert a bookmark, press Command = (*or* go to the Controls menu and choose "New Bookmark…").

3   A sheet drops down where you can either leave the time code as shown, or you can rename the bookmark so you know exactly which one this is.

Once you have created bookmarks, you can go to the Go menu and choose to skip straight to any bookmark you made. If you make more than one bookmark, use the Bookmarks palette to choose one of them to be the "default" bookmark. These bookmarks are *not* stored with the DVD; that is, if you loan the DVD to anyone, it will not include your bookmarks. They are stored only on your Mac.

Create your own clips with endpoints

Amazing. You can create individual video clips of selected segments of a DVD and then choose to play just those clips. This feature and the bookmarks feature are terrific for teachers or trainers who want to separate segments or start a scene in a DVD at a particular point. Or maybe there's a specific section of your dance or exercise video that you want to view over and over again—this makes it so easy!

To make a video clip:

1   While viewing the DVD, view until you get to the beginning of the section you want to save as a clip. Then press Command – (hyphen).

2   A special frame appears. Single-click the upper "Set" button, as circled below.

3   Click the triangle button ("Play") under the main picture to continue playing the DVD (or hit the Spacebar to play). When you get to the *end* of the clip that you want to mark, click the lower "Set" button. Click "Save" when you've got it.

The movie continues playing from the beginning of the clip and carries right on, but your clip has been saved. You can find it in the Video Clips window from the Window menu, or from the Go menu, and in the Video Clips pane of the thumbnail bar across the top of the screen.

Make adjustments

To adjust video color, sound, and zoom controls, go to the Window menu. Choose the adjustment you want to make and use the sliders.

Create your own personal disc jacket on the screen

This is great—you can add your own image to the DVD so whenever you stop the DVD, it displays the image of *your* choice.

To add your own disc image:

1 Open a DVD in the DVD Player.

2 Go to the File menu and choose "Get Disc Info."

3 Click the "Jacket Picture" icon in the toolbar, shown circled below.

4 Drag any image from your hard disk and drop it into the well. Click OK. Cool.

Remember, changes like this don't really apply to the actual DVD—they are stored on your Mac. So the disc jacket will only appear if you show this DVD from the computer on which you added it.

Go back to the Finder

Push your mouse to the top of the screen, go to the Go menu, and choose "Switch to Finder." Or press Command Option F.

Create PDF Files

A PDF (Portable Document Format) is a file created in such a way that most people can open and read it, no matter what kind of computer they use. The graphics, the images, the fonts, and all the formatting are held intact in the document. And it's usually compressed into a smaller file size (not physical size) so it can travel through the Internet quickly.

To make a PDF in most applications, have the document open in front of you. From the File menu, choose "Print…," then click the "PDF" button.

Save as PDF Saves a regular PDF that you can share with others. The graphics are at full resolution and the fonts are embedded. When you choose to save as a PDF, you'll get a window with a "Security Options" button where you can choose to require a password to open, copy, or print.

—continued

Save as PostScript

This saves the document as a PostScript Level 2 file in ASCII format, meaning if you open it, you'll see a lot of code. But you can send it directly to a Postscript printer or run it through Acrobat Distiller. Don't choose this option unless you know you need it.

Fax PDF   If you have set up your fax specifications as explained in Lesson 17, then your Mac will make a PDF of the document and open the fax dialog box where you can enter the fax number and a message. Remember, you must have a phone line connected to the Mac.

Mail PDF   This creates a PDF of the file, opens Mail, creates a new message, and puts this PDF in the message ready to send. This is a great time-saver, but I've noticed that people using AOL or PCs often can't read these.

Save as PDF-X

The PDF-X standard from Adobe is designed for high-end printing. I don't suggest you choose this option unless you *know* you need a PDF-X file, and even then it would be best to create it in a high-end application.

Save PDF to iPhoto

Your Mac will turn this document into a PDF, open iPhoto (if you have it installed, of course), ask you which album to put it into (or ask you to create a new one), and then put the PDF in that album.

If you have an iPhone, this is a great way to get PDFs onto it. You might have tried putting a PDF directly into iPhoto and discovered that iPhoto won't accept it, says it's an unacceptable format. But iPhoto *will* take PDFs through the method described above. Next time you sync your iPhone in iTunes, go to the "Photos" tab in the sync pane and choose the album in which you're keeping the PDFs. They're kind of blurry, but if you need the info to take with you, it's an option.

Save PDF to Web Receipts Folder

Web Receipts

I love this. Have you ever bought something on the web and you got that page that says, "This is your receipt"? And you know you should print it but maybe the printer isn't turned on at the moment or it's three pages long and you know they're going to send you an email receipt anyway, but what if they don't send you the email receipt and you need this web page receipt? Well, this is a great solution: The Mac will save this web page as a PDF and it will make you a folder in your Documents folder called "Web Receipts" and it will store this PDF (and all others you make like it) in that folder.

Be careful, though—if you make a web receipt from the same site more than once, it will probably write over itself with the same name. I wish Apple would give me an option to give the file a name I'll remember.

Font Book

Font Book allows you to install new **fonts** you acquire, disable fonts in your font menus that you never use, and view fonts before you install them.

Preview fonts you haven't installed

If you acquire new fonts or if you just have some fonts on a disk and you don't know what they are, simply double-click on the font file. Font Book will open automatically and display the font. If you want to install it, click the "Install Font" button.

Install fonts

You can use the step above to install fonts. You can also:

1 Open Font Book (it's in your Applications folder).

2 In the Collection pane, single-click on "User" (if you want the fonts available only to you as the user) or "Computer" (if you want the fonts available to every user of this particular computer).

3 Go to the File menu and choose "Add Fonts…."

4 Find the font you want to install and double-click it. Font Book *moves* the font from its enclosing folder and puts it in the Library Fonts folder. If the fonts don't appear in your application's Font menu, you might have to quit the application and reboot it so they'll show up.

The default location for installing fonts is determined in the Font Book preferences.

Preview fonts you have installed

Single-click on any typeface name in the Font pane of Font Book. A preview appears on the right. Use the slider to enlarge or reduce the typeface, or type in a point size.

Go to the Preview menu and choose:

"Sample" to display the upper and lowercase letters, as well as the numbers.

"Repertoire" to see every glyph (letter, number, punctuation, etc.) in the font.

"Custom," and then type your own words to see them displayed in this typeface. Use the slider bar on the right to enlarge the font.

To disable an individual font, find it in the Font list. Single-click to select it, then click the little checkmark button at the bottom of the Font list.

Create your own Collections

A **Collection** is simply an easy way to look at fonts you like instead of having to grope through a lengthy font list of typefaces you don't know or want.

To make a new Collection, single-click the **+** sign at the bottom of the Collection pane, then name it. Click the "All Fonts" collection, then drag font names from the Font pane to the new Collection name.

To disable (turn off) an entire Collection, select it in the Collection pane. Then go to the Edit menu and choose, "Disable 'CollectionName.'"

Stickies

Stickies

The **Stickies** application lets you put little Stickie notes all over your screen, just like you'd stick them around the edge of your monitor (my kids tell me my monitor looks like a giant daisy).

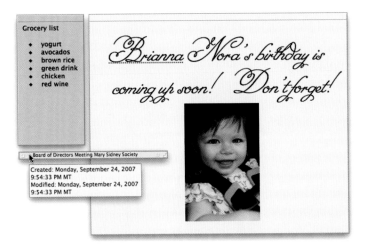

Notice in the examples above you can see these features:

- The grocery note is a **bulleted list.** To make such a list, Command Option–click on the note (or Option-right click) and choose "List..." from the contextual menu that appears. You can choose from a variety of bullets and numbers, plus you can add a prefix and suffix to the bullet. Thus you could create a numbered list that uses **(1)** or **Act 1:** or **•A•** or any other combination. The list options even include Greek characters and Asian characters.

  To start the list, hit Option-Tab *before* you type the first item in the list. To continue the list, just hit a Return after each item. You can hit Option-Tab-Tab to indent an extra level.

  To end the list, hit Return twice.

  You can change the bullet formatting at any time—just use the List options from the contextual menu as explained above.

- You can **change fonts, size, color,** etc., just as in any other Mac application, using the Font dialog box (press Command T). See pages 234–235.

- Double-click in the title bar of any Stickie note to "roll it up" so **just the title bar shows,** as you can see on the opposite page. The first line of type appears in the title bar. Double-click the title bar again to unroll the note.

- Mouse over any note to display a **tool tip** that gives you information about the note, as shown on the opposite page.

- Drag a **graphic** image from anywhere on your Mac and drop it into the Stickie note.

- A note can hold many pages of text and graphics. You won't see **scroll** bars, but you can drag the mouse through the text and it will scroll, or use the arrow keys or the PageUp or PageDown keys. Resize a Stickie note just as you would any other window—drag the bottom-right corner.

- Notice the red dots under the name Brianna. This is a visual clue that the **spell checker** is on and working.

- If you prefer working with a certain font and a certain size and a certain color note, you can **set a default** so all your notes look like that without having to select your favorites specifications for every note. Just set up one note they way you like it, then go to the Note menu and choose "Use as Default."

- If you want your Stickie notes to **automatically open** and appear every time you turn on your computer, add Stickies to the Login Items for your user (see page 321).

In the File menu there are two **print** options:

- "Print Active Note" prints the Stickie that's in front of all the others.
  Be careful! If a Stickie note is rolled up so only its title bar is visible, it still might be the active note. To make sure, click on the note you want to print.

- "Print All Notes" prints all of your Stickie notes one after another. Each one is *not* on a separate piece of paper—they are all run together.

The Thunder's Mouth

O that my tongue were in the thunder's mouth!
Then with a passion would I shake the world.

Said Constance in King John

Photo Booth

Photo Booth

Photo Booth is a convenient and fun way to take snapshots or movies of yourself for use as an iChat buddy picture or as your user account picture. You can email the photos or movie clips to friends, upload them to web pages, open in Preview to save in other formats, or view as a slideshow.

Take a still picture

1 Open Photo Booth (it's in your Applications folder).

2 Click the still picture button (the first button in the row of three).

3 Then click the red camera button.

A red timer replaces the toolbar (right-middle) and starts a countdown, including audible beeps. Your screen flashes when the picture is taken, and a thumbnail version of the picture is placed at the bottom of the window. You can take several pictures and they'll all line up in that thumbnail strip.

4 Click a thumbnail to display it in the main window. As soon as you do this, a new toolbar replaces the first one, as shown below. Click an icon in this toolbar to send the photo in an email message, place it in iPhoto, set it as your user Account photo, or use it as an iChat buddy picture.

To delete a snapshot, click the circled **X** on a thumbnail. Or select a thumbnail, then hit the Delete key.

Make a movie clip

1 Click the movie clip button (the film strip icon, shown to the left).

2 The camera button in the center of the toolbar changes to a red video button (left). Click it to begin recording.

   While recording, the toolbar shows a timer and the red video button changes to a Stop Recording button (below). When you stop recording, a video thumbnail appears at the bottom of the window.

   `00:00:10` ⏹

3 When you've stopped recording, select the movie clip thumbnail that appears in the thumbnail strip, then use the toolbar to choose how to use the movie clip. You have the following options:

   ▪ Click "Email" to attach a QuickTime version of the clip to a message in Mail. Movie files are large, about 1MB per second, so keep your clips short.

   ▪ To save the clip as a QuickTime movie, drag the video thumbnail to your Desktop or to any folder on your computer.

   ▪ To use a single frame of the movie clip for your user Account photo or Buddy photo, select the movie thumbnail. Next, use the scrubber bar under the video (shown below) to select the frame you want, then click "Account Picture" or "Buddy Picture" in the toolbar.

This is the scrubber bar. Drag this diamond back and forth to view individual frames of your movie.

This thumbnail strip holds both still photos and movie clips. The movie clips have a tiny camera icon.

Add effects to snapshots

Photo Booth includes a gallery of special effects that you can apply *as you take a snapshot or record a movie clip.* That is, you can't apply these effects after you've taken the photo—you have to choose an effect before you snap the photo.

1 Click the Effects button to show a pane of effects (below-left). The center image always shows a Normal preview (no effects) that you can select to remove all effects and return the image to normal.

2 Click the arrows on either side of the Effects button to see all of the possibilities.

3 Click on the effect you want. A full-size preview displays in the window (below-right).

4 Click one of the snapshot buttons to choose the type of snapshot you want (still picture, 4-up to make an animation, or movie clip), then click the red camera button. The special effect snapshot appears in the row of thumbnails.

5 Select the image in the thumbnail strip, then use the tools in the toolbar to share it (as explained on the previous pages).

Click one of the four gray squares to jump to another pane of effects.

Or click the arrows on either side of the Effects button to cycle through the panes.

Create a special effects backdrop

In the gallery of special effects (opposite page), the last pane is empty. In the empty spaces on that pane, you can add your own photos or movie clips to be used as a special effects backdrops for other still photos or movie clips.

To take a photo or movie using a special backdrop:

1 In the toolbar, click the extreme-right gray square to show the pane of blank spaces.

2 Drag one of your own photos or movies into a blank space.

3 Select your image to use as a special effects backdrop.

4 When you take a snapshot, a message first instructs you to move out of the view so Photo Booth can patch the special backdrop into the background. So move out of the way.

5 A message appears to tell you the background has been detected and it's okay to move back into the frame. Move back in and click the red camera button to take the photo.

TIP ———— To **preview** all of your snapshots that are lined up in the thumbnail strip, go to the View menu and choose "Start Slideshow." Press the Escape key to exit the slideshow.

13

GOALS

Learn to use the tools
that all Apple
applications share:

Spell checker and
grammar checker

Colors panel

Fonts panel

Special characters

Dictionary

Speech

Common Tools in Mac OS X Applications

Every Apple application that comes on your Mac uses certain tools—the spelling and grammar checker, the Colors panel, the Fonts panel, the Dictionary, and a few others. Rather than tell you how to use each one within a certain application, included here are explanations of how to use each tool regardless of which application you're using it in.

Many applications from other vendors also take advantage of these Apple tools, so look for them—they will make your computing life easier and more fun.

Spell Checker

Options for the spell checker are found at the bottom of the Edit menu in Apple applications. You have several choices, each of which are explained here.

Show Spelling and Grammar

This brings up the dialog box shown below. This spell checker runs through your entire document and gives you options for each word it thinks is misspelled.

If you want the spell checker to also alert you to possible grammar mistakes, check the box to "Check grammar."

You can check spelling in a number of different languages. Choose a different dictionary here.

To replace a misspelled word with an alternative, find the word you think is correct in the lower pane, then double-click on it. *Or* you can type the correct spelling yourself in the top edit box, then click the "Change" button.

Ignore the spelling temporarily. If the spell checker keeps telling you the same word is misspelled, but you like the word spelled the way it is, click the "Ignore" button when that word is highlighted by the spell checker. The spell checker will ignore it for this document, but will correct you again in the next document.

Teach your spell checker new words. Spell checkers typically don't recognize most people's names, as shown below, or jargon specific to different specialities. If you often use a particular word that the spell checker thinks is a mistake (because it's not in the dictionary it's using), click the "Learn" button in the dialog box and the word gets added to the current dictionary. It will never bother you again.

Or if you're not using the spell checker dialog box at the moment, Command-click (or right-click) on a word that the spell checker thinks is a mistake (it probably has little red dots under it). In the contextual menu that pops up, click the "Learn Spelling" option while the word is selected. The spell checker will add that word to its dictionary and not whine about it being misspelled again.

—continued

Check Document Now

Use this keyboard shortcut (Command ;) to skim through the spelling in your document without opening the dialog box. It will stop at each word it thinks is misspelled. Well, the dictionary might think it's misspelled, but it might be your Grandmother's name that you don't want to change.

Check Spelling While Typing

This marks words that are misspelled as you type them—little red dots appear beneath words it thinks are misspelled. Any words not in its dictionary are considered misspelled, such as many names of people or towns and most specialized jargon.

Check Grammar With Spelling

Choosing this option automatically checks the box in the dialog box, "Check grammar." It does what it says it does—applies standard grammatical rules to your text and lets you know if you're breaking any of those rules.

Instead of red dots that indicate a misspelled word, the grammar checker puts green dots under a word or phrase. Mouse over the word, pause to the count of three, and you will see a tool tip appear that tells you what the problem is. It's up to you to fix it.

> He go to the store. What is.
>> The word 'go' may not agree with the rest of the sentence.

To change a misspelled word quickly without bringing up a dialog box:

1 Control-click (or right-click) on a misspelled word (you don't need to highlight the word first).

2 A contextual menu appears, as shown below. At the top of this menu is a short list of alternative spellings for the word you clicked on.

3 Just single-click on the correct spelling in the menu—the word is instantly corrected and the menu automatically disappears.

If the correct word is not offered, you can either type the correction yourself, or slide down to "Spelling and Grammar" in this menu and then choose "Check Document Now" from the sub-menu to run a spell check.

Fonts Panel

Press Command T in any Mac OS X application and the Fonts panel appears, as shown below. If yours doesn't look like the one below, it might be because the Preview or the Effects are not showing.

Preview

- **To display the Preview and/or the Effects** if they're not already visible, single-click on the Action button (circled, below). Choose "Show Preview." Click again on the menu and choose "Show Effects."

Preview. ——————

Effects. ——————

Action menu.

Drag this dot down or up to show or hide the Preview.

Don't forget about the tool tips.

If the window is too narrow, the effects toolbar disappears.

In any Apple application, open this Fonts panel to choose the typeface family, the particular style (called "Typeface," above, hidden beneath the tool tip), and the size of type. Whatever you choose here will change the *selected* characters in your document. Note that you must **first select the text** you want to change, *then* choose the font and size. *Or* position the insertion point (the flashing bar in the text) where you want to start typing, then select the font and size right *before* you start typing.

Preview your own words

Well, for years you have been able to double-click the preview word shown at the top, then type your own words. You could choose a different family, typeface, and size to see how *your* text looks in a different font. In my version of Leopard, it doesn't work anymore. But try it and see if it got fixed. I hope it did.

Effects

You can apply **shadow effects** to selected text with these five controls, as shown below. Select text on the page, click the "Text Shadow" button (the button with the T), then experiment with the sliders on the other four tools.

When this button is blue, that's a visual clue that the *selected* text has a shadow effect applied to it.

Collections

The Fonts panel has a number of **collections,** which are simply sub-groups of fonts from the main list. Making a collection does not disable or enable any fonts, it just makes it easier for you to choose a typeface—you don't have to scroll through a long list of fonts you don't care for.

To create a Collection, single-click the plus sign at the bottom of the Collections pane. Rename the Collection. Drag font families from the "Family" pane into the new collection—drop the family name directly on the collection name.

Favorites

If you find you often use a particular family, typeface, point size, and color, turn that combination into a Favorite and keep it in the Favorites collection for easy access. Just select the text on the page that is formatted as you like it, or choose your favorite combination in the Fonts panel. Then go to the Action button and choose "Add to Favorites."

When you want to use that typeface, single-click on the collection called Favorites to display the combination. Select your text, then choose your favorite.

Action button options

Color: See the following page.
Characters: This displays the Character Palette; see pages 236–237.
Typography: Choose sophisticated options for certain typefaces.
Manage Fonts: This opens the Font Book; see pages 220–221.

Character Palette

Many fonts have a lot of characters you don't know about but might like to use if you did. And different fonts have different sorts of **extra characters.**

For instance, these are the ampersands available in the font Zapfino:

How do you know which characters are available? Use the **Characters palette.**

At the bottom of most Edit menus is an option called "Special Characters…." This displays the Characters palette, as shown on the opposite page.

Add special characters to your document:

1 Open TextEdit (it's in the Applications folder). A new, blank document appears on your screen. You'll see the insertion point flashing—that's where new characters will appear. Type what you need until you get to a point where you want to enter a special character.

2 From the Edit menu, choose "Special Characters…."

3 From the "View" menu on the palette (circled on the opposite page), choose "Glyph."

4 Make sure the "Glyph Catalog" tab is selected.

5 From the two "Font" menus, choose the typeface family and the individual style that you want to look at. In the example on the opposite page, you see the font "Skia." (Later, experiment with Zapfino!)

6 Scroll through the character pane to find the glyph you want. ("Glyph" refers to any individual variation of any character. For instance, above you see seven different *glyphs* for the ampersand *character.*)

7 Double-click the glyph you want to see on your page.

> **TIP** —— To reduce the Character Palette to a tiny box that is out of the way, but accessible, click its green Zoom button.

This box displays
other glyphs for a
selected character,
if there are any.

If you don't see
this portion
of the palette,
single-click
this disclosure
triangle.

Hoefler Text Regular   Hoefler Text Italic   Hoefler Text Ornaments

Colors Panel

When you click on one of the color buttons (as shown directly below) in the Fonts panel or the "Colors" icon in a toolbar, you get a deceptively simple Colors panel. Select text in Mail, TextEdit, and other Apple applications, then choose a color.

Text color | | Paper color behind the text

- Click one of the icons across the top of the panel to choose a color mode.

- Click the magnifying glass and your pointer turns into a magnifying glass. Drag it around the screen and when you find a color you want to "pick up," click on it and that color is added to the panel.

- In the "Color Wheel" mode, drag the dot around the circle to choose a color, and drag the slider up and down to change the tone.

- In the "Image Palettes" mode, shown below-right, click the "Palette" menu, choose "New from File...," then choose a graphic or photo. You can also drag any image from the Finder and drop it on this palette. Move the cursor around the photo to pick up colors you need.

To save a color, drag it from here and drop it in one of the squares at the bottom.

Experiment with the different ways you can select colors.

Speech

In applications where there is typically a lot of text, **your Mac can read selected text to you.** You'll find a command for "Speech…" towards the bottom of the Edit menu in applications such as Mail and TextEdit, and you can use the Services menu option for "Speech" in iChat and Safari. (The Services options are in the application's menu.) Also, you can Control-click (or right-click) on text, and in the contextual menu that appears there is often a command under the "Speech" option to "Start Speaking."

Have your email read out loud

1   Open an email message in Mail.

2   Click in the main body of text.

3   Go to the Edit menu, slide down to "Speech…," and choose "Start Speaking."

4   The entire text message will be read aloud to you.

    If you want just a portion read out loud, select that portion before you go to the Edit menu.

5   The voice that's used is the one selected in the "Speech" preferences.

To use the Services menu, first *select the text* in iChat or on a web page in Safari, then go to the application menu and choose the Speech option.

Preview your Page before Printing

You can **preview** any page that you create or plan to print. Just open the document and choose to print (Command P, or choose "Print" from the File menu).

If the small dialog box appears, as shown below, click the "Preview" button. Your Mac will create a preview of the document, open the application called Preview (see Lesson 11), and display the document. You can then print directly from the Preview application.

If you see the big dialog box (click the disclosure triangle circled below to show it), the Preview button is missing because the expanded dialog box displays the preview right there.

Either click the disclosure triangle or the Preview button to see a preview of the document.

Make a PDF of a Page or Document

Notice in the Print dialog box above, there is a button labeled "PDF." Click that button to see many options for creating a PDF of the open document. For details, please see Lesson 12.

Dictionary Panel

Dictionary

I keep the Dictionary application in my Dock because I use it so often. It's not only a **dictionary,** but also a **thesaurus,** an **Apple** resource, and it links directly to **Wikipedia** (if you're connected to the Internet). The Dictionary is in your Applications folder, and if you want it in your Dock so it's always accessible with the click of a button, just drag its icon from the Applications folder and drop it in the Dock.

But this Dictionary has a special little feature that extends its use out to all other Apple applications. Go to its Preferences (from the Dictionary menu when it's open) and check the button to "Open Dictionary panel" (circled, below-left)

Now in every other Apple application (and those that follow Apple standards), Control-click (or right-click) on a word you want to look up in the Dictionary.

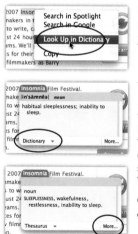

When you Control-click on a word, you'll see this menu.

The Dictionary panel appears right on the document page. You can use the tiny menu (circled, left) to switch to the Thesaurus.

Click "More..." to open the Dictionary.

14

GOALS

Working between Mac OS X Applications

Now that you've had an overview of the main applications that come with Mac OS X and how they are all integrated, let's carry it one step further and work *between* all the applications—pop between windows, drag-and-drop content and files, take advantage of the Spaces feature, use the Services, and more.

Once you realize how easy it is to move data between applications and windows, you'll find more and more uses for it. Plus you'll feel like a Power User.

Work with Multiple Applications at Once

In Mac OS X, you can keep lots of applications and windows open at once so they're always accessible. You can just single-click an application icon in the Dock to switch to it, but there are also a couple of great shortcuts to switch between multiple applications quickly and easily.

Switch between all applications

No matter which application you are currently using, you can bring up a floating palette like the one shown below, then select the application you want to switch to—without ever having to reach for the mouse.

To get the Application Switcher that displays icons for all the *open* applications, press and *hold down* the Command key, then hit the Tab key once. Keep the Command key down. You'll see something like this:

To cycle through the icons from left to right, tap the Tab key (keep the Command key down).

To cycle through the icons in the other direction, right to left, keep the Command key down, but also hold down the Shift key while you tap the Tab key.

Or press Command Tab to display the Application Switcher, then use the mouse to select an icon (you don't have to actually click on the icon—just hover over it to highlight it).

However you choose to select an icon, when the application icon you want is highlighted in the palette, **let go of the keys** and that application will come forward as the active program.

If there is no window open in that particular application, it might look like nothing happened—always check the application menu (explained on pages 4–5) to see which one is currently active! You might need to hit Command N to open a window in that application once it's active.

Switch back and forth between two applications

Most of us probably spend the greater part of our time between our two favorite applications. There's a shortcut that will switch you back and forth between just those two, instead of having to bring up the Application Switcher.

While in one of your favorite applications, switch to another one using the method on the previous page, or just click on its icon in the Dock. Now press Command Tab **to switch between those two applications.** I know it sounds too similar to the shortcut for switching between all applications, but the trick is to hold down the Command key, hit the Tab key *just once,* then let go of both keys right away.

Quit or hide applications

Don't forget that Command H will **hide** all of the windows of the active application, and Command Q will **quit** the active application. Use these shortcuts in combination with the switching shortcuts to quit or hide selected applications.

To hide all other applications except the one you're currently using, press Command Option H.

To switch to another application and hide the windows of the current one, hold down the Option key when you click on the other application icon in the Dock.

Keyboard Shortcuts

Command Tab Tab Tab . . .	Select the open applications
Command Tab	Switch between two open applications
Command H	Hide the currently active application
Command Option H	Hide all the other applications *except* the active one
Command Q	Quit the active application

Spaces

Spaces

And here's yet another way to hide and show different applications if the Command Tab shortcut and Exposé (explained on pages 40–41) aren't enough! Spaces gives you up to sixteen separate Desktops. You can keep all the windows for one project open in one Space, perhaps your Mail application open in another, and iChat and Safari windows in another. This allows you, for instance, to work on a particular project without having to constantly move browser windows and email out of the way—just switch to your project space and everything else disappears. Yet everything is still accessible—you will know if an iChat message comes in even if you're not in the iChat Space at the moment.

Exposé & Spaces

You must first **enable Spaces.** The first time you click the Spaces icon in the Dock it will ask if you want to enable it and will open the "Exposé & Spaces" system preferences, as shown below.

Put a check in "Enable Spaces," and put a check in "Show Spaces in menu bar" so you can keep track of which space you're in at the moment.

Choose a numbered space for each application.

To create or delete spaces, just click the **+** or **−** buttons for "Rows" or "Columns." Even though you can have up to sixteen spaces, you might want to start with just four or six until you get used to working this way.

To assign applications to specific spaces, click the **+** button under the "Application Assignments" pane. This opens your Applications folder. **To select more than one application,** hold down the Command key and click on the ones you want to assign.

To choose the specific space in which you want an application to appear, use the menus on the right side of that pane, as shown on the previous page.

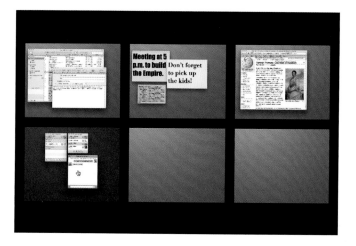

Once you have Spaces set up, it might be a little confusing at first, but you'll find that you get used to it and wonder how you did without it. There are several **shortcuts** for getting back and forth between spaces:

- **To display all your spaces,** as shown above, press F8. (On a laptop, you might need to press fn F8.) Single-click on the space you want to bring forward.

- **To cycle through the actual spaces** (instead of a picture of them all, as above), hold down the Control key and hit the left and right arrow keys.

- **To go directly to a specific space,** press Control *Number,* where *"Number"* is the number of the space you want to go to, such as Control 2.

- If you checked the box to "Show Spaces in menu bar," you'll see a number in the right-hand side of the **menu bar.** Click on this number and you'll get a menu of all the spaces you have set up. Select the one you want.

—continued

You can drag and drop items from one space to another. Even if you can't see the application to which you want to drag something, drag it to the Dock and drop it on that application's icon. That space will appear.

Here I selected the Sticky note text and am dropping it on the Mail icon in the Dock. It will immediately switch to that space, created a new email message, and put that text in the message.

You can drag items from one space to another while viewing all the spaces at once, as shown on the previous page.

And take advantage of the Services options in every application menu to move items from one application to another while they're in different spaces. See page 256 for information about Services.

Simplify your Work with Drag-and-Drop

You probably have lots of applications open on your Mac. Often you'll need to move data from one open application to another. Your Mac makes this so easy with **drag-and-drop:** drag the information you want from one application and drop it into the other application. Below are some examples. Experiment with these, and then try dragging and dropping in all sorts of other ways! If it doesn't work, nothing bad will happen—it just won't work.

Move text around in a document window

In TextEdit or Mail messages, you don't have to cut-and-paste to move text, you can simply drag-and-drop it.

1   First select the text you want to move: with your mouse, press-and-drag over the text so it is highlighted. Let go of the mouse button.

2   Once the text is highlighted, press anywhere in the text and hold it for a second or two, then drag.

3   Watch for the insertion point! It's that thin, flashing, vertical bar. As you move the mouse and pointer, the insertion point moves too. When the insertion point is positioned where you want the new text to appear, let go of the mouse button. *Text will aways drop in or paste in at the flashing insertion point!*

Don't forget to use that great option in the Edit menu to "Paste and Match Style," as explained on page 61.

To move a _copy_ of the selected text to somewhere else in the same document, press the Option key and hold it down while you drag the text.

If you drag text from one document window to another, you don't need to hold down the Option key because it will automatically make a copy.

TIP ——— Often you'll find it works best to select the text or items, then **_press and hold and count to three_** before you drag.

Move text from one application to another

Not only can you drag-and-drop within one application, you can drag text from one application window and drop it in another. Let's say you wrote a nice essay in TextEdit—select it and drag it into an email message in Mail.

This automatically makes a *copy* of the text (instead of deleting it from the first application), so you don't need to hold down the Option key.

Make a text clipping on the Desktop

Have you ever wanted to save a quote from a web page or a statement from an email message? Just select the text, then drag-and-drop it onto the Desktop or into any folder or window. This makes a small file on your Desktop with an extension called ".textClipping" (if your extensions are visible; see pages 44 and 430–431).

The clipping names itself with the first few words of the text.

The lights burn blue.textClipping

Anytime you want to see what the text clipping says, just double-click on it. And you can drag-and-drop that clipping file into most text windows, such as TextEdit or a Mail message, and the actual text will drop onto the page.

Add email addresses to Mail message

Drag a person's name from the Address Book or the Address Panel and drop it into any of the "To" fields in an email message to automatically address a message. You can drag addresses from one field to another.

To add more than one name at a time, select more than one name in the Address Book or Panel: Hold down the Command key and click on the names you want to add. Then let go of the Command key and drag *one* of the names to the email "To" field—*all* of the selected names will come along.

To add a Group name, drag the Group name and drop it into one of the "To" fields.

Send contact information through email

You can send a person's Address Book data (his card information) to anyone who uses Mac OS X. Drag a person's name from the Address Book or Address Panel and drop it into the body of a Mail message. You'll see a "vCard" icon, as shown below.

Denise Kusel.vcf

The recipient can then drag the vCard to her Address Book where it will be added automatically. *Or* she can double-click the icon in the email message and all of the Address Book data will be added to her Address Book.

Make a web location file

In Safari, you can make a web location file that will take you to a specific web page. There is a tiny icon that appears in the location field, directly to the left of the web address, shown circled, below. Drag that tiny icon and drop it in the Dock (on the right side of the dividing bar), onto the Desktop, or into any folder. This creates a web location file, shown below. It has two different appearances, depending on where you drop it.

If you drop the icon in the Dock (shown below), it looks like a spring. You can single-click it to open Safari and that web page.

If you drop the icon in the Finder, it looks like a document file. Double-click the icon, or drag-and-drop it into the middle of any open web page (don't drop it in the location field—drop it in the middle of the open page).

Send a file to a Buddy

Drag a document to a Buddy name in the Buddy List of iChat and drop it. Hit Return or Enter and the file will go straight to that person. This is a great way to quickly send a photo or a document.

You can also use your iChat instant message window—just drag the file into the field where you type your message. Hit Return and both your text message and the file will go to your Buddy. All he needs to do is click the link in the iChat window and the file downloads to his Desktop.

Also send Address Book data this way—to send the information from a person's card, drag his name from your Address Book and drop it on the Buddy List name or in the message field (see the previous page for more Address Book information).

Invite people to an iCal event

Drag a person's name from the Address panel or Address Book (from the Window menu) to an iCal event to automatically add that person as an "attendee." Be sure to drop it in the "attendees" field in the Info pane. You can drag a Group name as well. Once you have the names in here, you can click the "Send" button at the bottom of the Info drawer to send everyone on the list an email update of the event.

Glorious Moment

location	Stratford upon Avon
all-day	☑
from	03/13/2008
to	03/16/2008
repeat	None
calendar	☐ ShPapers
alarm	None
attendees	Amy Meilander / Sarah Maxwell
attachments	☐ To Brianna Nora.rtf / Add File...
url	www.rsc.org.uk
note	8 history plays in 4 days!

Send

Drag addresses or files and drop them into these iCal fields.

Save into a particular folder

When you are saving a file, drag a folder from the Finder and drop it in the window of the Save As dialog box. Your Mac will save the document into that particular folder.

Take advantage of the page proxy

You may not have noticed the tiny page icon that is in the title bar of every document you create (it appears after you save the document). It's called the "page proxy." You can do a lot with this tiny icon.

Make sure the document has been saved recently before you experiment with any of the following techniques. If there is a dark dot in the red button or if the page proxy is gray, that means you need to save the document first.

To create an alias of the document on the Desktop or in any folder or window, drag the page proxy and drop it on the Desktop, on top of any folder icon, or directly into any window. You'll see the telltale sign of an alias's tiny curved arrow as you drag the page proxy. (See page 430 about aliases.)

This tiny arrow indicates this icon is an alias. When you double-click it, it will go open the real file.

Methinks I scent the morning air

To create a copy of the document, hold down the Option key and drag the proxy. Drop it on the Desktop, on top of any folder icon, or directly into any window. You'll see a plus sign as you drag, indicating your Mac is making a *copy* of the document.

To send the document through iChat or Bonjour, drag the page proxy and drop it on a Buddy name in your iChat Buddy List or on any name in your Bonjour list.

Or drag the page proxy into the text field of an iChat instant message. The recipient will get a message with a button to "Save File."

To email the document, drag the page proxy to an email message and drop it anywhere in the body of the message.

To drop the entire document into another application, drag the page proxy and drop it into the window of the other app. For instance, you can drag a Microsoft Word page proxy into a TextEdit page or onto a web page. Remember to watch for the insertion point (well, not on a web page)—that's where the new text will drop in.

Open documents in other applications

Drag documents (or page proxies, as explained above) onto application icons in the Finder or Dock to open those documents in the targeted applications; if an application is capable of opening the document, the application icon will highlight. This is great for when you want to open a document in something that isn't the default.

For instance, **open Microsoft Word files in TextEdit—**just drag and drop the file onto the TextEdit icon, either in the Dock or in the Applications folder.

Or **drag a PDF** and drop it in the middle of a Safari window or directly on the Safari icon and Safari will open and display the PDF.

Take advantage of spring-loaded folders

Combine drag-and-drop with spring-loaded folders to organize the Finder. A spring-loaded folder opens as you hover your mouse over it. You can use this technique to dig down into folders with a file you are dragging: Hover over a folder, its window pops open, hover over the next folder, its window pops open, etc. As soon as you drop the file, all of the previous folder windows close.

You can set the parameters for how long you have to hover the mouse to open a spring-loaded folder—use the Finder preferences (in the Finder menu). Or you can always use the Spacebar instead, even if the option for spring-loaded folders is unchecked: Whenever you want a folder to open instantly, hover over the folder and hit the Spacebar.

Drag content, images, or files between applications

Try dragging anything and everything!

Drag an image from the web onto a TextEdit page or an email message.

Drag a graphic file from the Desktop or a folder and drop it into the text area of your application. This works in lots of other applications, not just the ones from Apple. For instance, I'm using Adobe InDesign to create this book—I dragged the image you see below from the Finder and dropped it on this page (and it's linked):

Mac
Booda
Dakota
Jane
Reilly
Maximus

Drag text content and/or images from any application and drop them into other applications. Not everything will work, or it might work but not quite as you expect, but you will discover some wonderfully useful ways for working in your favorite applications.

You don't even have to open the other application first if you want to drag text from one place into a *new* file in another application. For instance, you can select and drag text from a web page and drop it on the Mail icon in the Dock—Mail will open a new message window with that text pasted in the message area. Or drag text and drop it on the TextEdit icon (which I keep in the Dock)—TextEdit will open a new window with that text in it. Or drag text from Mail and drop it on the Safari icon— Google will immediately do a search on the text and display the results. Amazing.

Take Advantage of System Services

Every application in its application menu has an item called "Services." Exactly which services are available at any moment depend on which application you have open and what you have selected within that application, if anything.

You might find some text in a file that you want to keep in your Sticky Note collection—select the text (and a graphic, if you like) and choose "Make New Sticky Note" from the Services options.

Or you might be viewing a photograph in Preview and decide you want to email it to someone—go to Services, choose "Mail," and then choose "Send To."

Perhaps you are reading the synopsis of a Shakespeare play online and you want to have the synopsis in TextEdit—select the text, go to Services, choose "TextEdit," and then choose "New Window Containing Selection."

Perhaps the synopsis is lengthier than you care to read at the moment, and you'd like to skim it—select the text, go to Services, and choose "Summarize" to open a new window where you can view as much or as little of the summary as you like. Then don't forget about drag-and-drop—drag the selected summary into a TextEdit page.

Keep the Services menu in mind while you work. You'll be surprised how often it comes in handy!

Make it **Your Own Mac**

15

GOALS

Customize your Dock

Set up your Finder
windows to the way
you like to work

Use spring-loaded folders

Color-code your files
with labels

Customize your
Sidebar and Desktop

Learn to use the
System Preferences to
customize many features
of your Mac

Personalize your Mac to Meet your Needs

Now that you've learned all the basics of the various applications and system settings on your Mac, discover how to customize them to suit your particular way of working. Would you prefer to have your Dock on the side of the screen instead of at the bottom? Do you like a brightly colored Desktop? Do you want to customize the insides of certain windows? Color-code your files? Make the icons and text bigger? It's all do-able—and more.

Customize the Dock

When you first turn on your Mac, the **Dock** is sitting along the bottom at a certain size. But like everything else on the Mac, you can customize it to suit yourself. Would you prefer the Dock along the side of your screen? Would you like it to disappear altogether and only appear when you need it? Are the icons too small or too big? You can adjust everything.

There are three ways to customize the Dock: You can use the System Preferences, the Dock options in the Apple menu, or the secret pop-up menu in the Dock itself.

Customize the Dock using the System Preferences

1 Single-click on the System Preferences icon in the Dock, or go to the Apple menu and choose "System Preferences...."

2 Single-click on the Dock icon. You'll get the Dock preferences.

3 Here you can resize the Dock, turn "Magnification" on or off (see the next page), adjust the size of the magnification, reposition the screen, and other options.

Magnification

If you turn on "Magnification," then the icons in the Dock will enlarge as you run your mouse over them, as shown above-right. Just how big they enlarge is up to you—move the slider to "Max," then hover your mouse over the Dock (don't click) and see how big the icons get.

Minimize using

This option has two choices, Genie Effect and Scale Effect. All it does is change how windows float down into the Dock when you click the yellow Minimize button in a window. Choose one of the options, then minimize a window to see the difference. (Hold the Shift key down when you click the yellow button to see the effect in slow motion.)

Animate opening applications

This is what makes the icons in the Dock bounce up and down when you click to open them. You can turn it off.

Automatically hide and show the Dock

Click this and the Dock disappears. It reappears whenever you move your mouse into that edge where it disappeared. As long as your mouse is hovering over the Dock, it stays visible. Move your mouse away, and the Dock hides itself again.

Resize the icons and the whole Dock

■ Press-and-drag on the dividing line. Try it!

Customize the Dock with the Apple menu or Dock menu

■ **From the Apple menu,** select "Dock," then choose your options.

■ **In the Dock itself,** hold down the Control key and single-click on the dividing line, as shown below. A menu pops up; make your choice.

Customize the Finder

There are a number of features you can customize in the **Finder.** You might expect to find these in the System Preferences, but because the Finder is actually an application (it runs the Desktop), its preferences are in the Finder application menu.

Customize the General preferences

1 From the Finder menu, choose "Preferences…." Click the "General" icon.

2 Because your Finder window can display the hard disk icons, removable disc icons, and servers in the top portion of the Sidebar, you can choose that these items do *not* also **show up on the Desktop.** Or if it makes you feel better to see the CD icons on the Desktop, you can choose to show only those. Whatever makes you happy.

3 Every time you open a **new Finder window,** it starts over—that is, it doesn't remember the last window you opened. From this menu, choose the window you want to see whenever you click the Finder icon in the Dock or press Command N to get a new window. For instance, I want to see my Home window every time I open a new Finder window. You might prefer to see your Hard Disk, the Documents folder, or perhaps a project folder.

4 If it bothers you to have only one Finder window open to work in, you can choose to have a **new window open** every time you double-click a folder icon. Usually people who are recently converted from Mac OS 9 like to use this feature for a while, until they get used to working in one window.

Don't forget that you can always open a separate window for any individual folder: Command–double-click on it.

5 If you turn on **spring-loaded folders and windows,** then a folder will automatically pop its window open as you hover a file over that folder. That is, just *hold* the file on top of the folder but don't click ("hover"); the folder will "spring" open. This is great when you are dragging a file somewhere—you don't have to put it down to open the folder. And when you let go of the file to put it in the window, the Mac immediately takes you back to where you started.

The "Delay" refers to how long your mouse has to hover before the folder pops open. If you find folders popping open when you least expect it, make the delay longer.

Even if you turn off spring-loaded folders, you can always hit the Spacebar to make a folder pop open, as long as your mouse is holding a file over that folder.

Create labels for files and folders

Labels are colors that you can apply to any file or folder or application as a tool for organizing and searching.

1 From the Finder menu, choose "Preferences…." Click the "Labels" icon.

2 Change the label names for any color label you want. You don't need to use them all.

3 **To apply the labels,** select a file, then go to the File menu and at the very bottom choose a "Label" color. As you mouse over the color dot, a tool tip appears to tell you the label name.

Or Control-click (or right click) on a file of any sort. From the contextual menu that pops up, choose a color label; choose the **x** to take a label off.

To add the "Label" column to your List View windows, see page 268.

Choose what appears in your Finder window Sidebar

1 From the Finder menu, choose "Preferences...." Click the "Sidebar" icon.

2 Check the items you want to see in the Sidebar of your Finder windows, and uncheck the items you don't want to see. Coordinate this with the "General" Finder preferences shown on page 262—you don't want to eliminate the hard disk icon, for instance, from both the Desktop *and* the Sidebar!

Choose file extensions and turn off the Trash warning

1 From the Finder menu, choose "Preferences...." Click the "Advanced" icon.

2 **File extensions** are those three- or four-letter abbreviations at the ends of file names; see pages 44 and 430–431.

3 If that **warning** you see whenever you **empty the Trash** makes you crazy, turn it off here.

Customize the Inside of Finder Windows

Are the icons too big? The text labels too small? Do you want more columns of information available? Fewer columns? In the List View, would you like to rearrange the columns? In the Column View, do you want to turn off the preview column? You can do anything you want.

Customize the Icon View

1 Open a Finder window. Click the "Icon View" button, as circled below.

2 From the View menu, choose "Show View Options."

Choose this and every window in Icon View will have these specifications.

3 You can choose for *this particular window* to **always open in icon view.**

Notice the title bar of the preferences pane shows you the name of the currently active window, the one to which these changes will apply.

4 Experiment with these options.

Use the sliders to change the **size of the icons** and how far apart they will be spaced (the **grid spacing**).

TIP —— If you hold down the Command key as you move an icon in a window, it will snap to the nearest spot on this grid. Whenever you go to the View menu and choose "Clean up," the icons get arranged according to this grid.

Use the **Text size** menu to change the size of the text that labels each file.

And use **Label position** to put the labels (file titles) to the right side of the icons (they're generally on the "Bottom").

5 **Show item info:** This displays information about some icons. For instance, the window will display how many items are in each folder. It will also display the size (in pixels) of graphic files.

Show icon preview: This displays tiny versions of the actual images for graphic files and photos.

Arrange by: You can choose *two* options from this list. To make every icon in the window snap into that underlying grid, choose "Snap to Grid."

Then, open this menu again and choose an arrangement for all those items. For instance, choose "Name" and any file you drag or save into this window will automatically snap to the underlying grid *and* alphabetize itself. Choose "Kind" and all items will be grouped by what kinds of files they are—applications, folders, text files, etc. "Label" is also an option, but in this case it refers to the colored labels, as explained on page 264, not the labels (titles) mentioned in Step 4!

TIP —— With "Snap to Grid" chosen, you can't reposition icons—they will always jump to the nearest spot in the grid. To override this, hold down the Command key as you drag an icon.

6 **Background:** Click the "Color" button to make a tiny color box appear; click the color box to get the Colors Panel to choose a background color for the window, as shown on the opposite page.

Click the "Picture" button to select a graphic image.

Click "White" to remove all color and images from the window background.

Customize the List View

1   Open a Finder window. Click the "List View" button, as circled below.

2   From the View menu, choose "Show View Options."

Choose this and every window in List View
will have these specifications.

3   Choose whether you want this particular folder (my Home folder, in the
example above) to always open in List View.

4   Choose the **icon size** you want, the **text size** for the labels, and which **columns**
you want visible. This is where you can choose to display the "Label" column if
you like to use labels (see page 264).

See the next page for the option to show "Comments."

5   **Use relative dates:** Under the "Date Modified" and "Date Created" columns,
you will see "Today" or "Yesterday" instead of the actual date.

Calculate all sizes: With NO checkmark in this box, the Size column will
display the file sizes of documents and graphic images, but NOT folders.
Displaying the sizes of folders can take an extra minute.

Add comments and show the Comments column

This is a great feature that not many people take advantage of because they don't know it exists. In the List View options, shown on the opposite page, you see that you can show the Comments column. But where are those comments?

You can add comments to the Info window of any file, as shown below. You might add notes to someone who will be receiving this file, or notes to yourself, or details about the file, or a reminder about what to do with it. This is the same field in which you can add keywords for Spotlight to find, as mentioned on page 341.

To open the Info window and add comments, select a file and press Command I (I for Info). **Or** Control-click or right-click on a file and choose "Get Info" from the contextual menu that appears. Add whatever text you want in the "Spotlight Comments" field, as shown below.

Once you do that, those Comments will appear in the Comments column in the List View, as shown below.

> **TIP** ——— If you want to add comments to more than one file, you don't have to select them one at a time to open their individual Info windows. Do this: Select one file, but instead of pressing Command I to open the Info window, press **Command Option I.** This opens the "Inspector" window. Now when you click on any other file, that file's info automatically appears in the already-open Info/Inspector window.

> **TIP** ——— If you like to use the contextual menus, Control-click on a file, then hold down the Option key; you get the option to "Show Inspector."

Organize the columns in List View

1 **To organize the items in your list** by any column, just click on a column heading to organize everything by that. For instance, if you want all the different sorts of files grouped together so you can clearly see which ones are, say, Photoshop files, organize by the "Kind" column.

The column heading under which everything is organized is the blue one. For example, in the example below, the items are organized by "Name."

2 **To alphabetize, or sort,** the items in the list backwards or forwards, click the heading triangle. That is, perhaps you want the items in the "Name" column to be listed alphabetically backwards: First click on the "Name" column heading. Then single-click the tiny triangle (the "sort" triangle, or arrow) you see on the right side of the column heading.

If you would like your items to be sorted by "Size" in ascending or descending order, first click on the "Size" column heading. Then, if necessary, single-click the tiny sort arrow to reverse the current order.

3 **To horizontally rearrange the order** of the columns (except the "Name" column), *press* on any column heading (except "Name") and drag it to the right or left. You will see the other columns move over to make room. Drop the column (let go of the mouse button) when it's positioned where you want it.

4 **To resize the width of the columns,** just *press* on the dividing line between any column; the pointer changes to a double-headed arrow. Drag the double-headed arrow to the left or right.

Customize the Column View

1   Open a Finder window. Click the "Column View" button, as circled below.

2   From the View menu, choose "Show View Options."

3   Choose the **text size** of the labels.

You can choose **not to show icons at all**—just a nice, clean list of items. Uncheck the box to remove the icons. (But keep in mind that the icon can tell you a lot about a file! If you can't see it, you'll miss its visual clues. This might not matter in a folder that contains nothing but photographs or nothing but text documents.)

If you uncheck **Show preview column,** the last column will NOT display a preview image of the selected file, such as a photograph.

Customize the Cover Flow View

1 Open a Finder window. Click the "Cover Flow View" button, as circled below.

2 From the View menu, choose "Show View Options."

Choose this and every
window in Cover Flow View
will have these specifications.

3 You can't change the actual view of the covers. But you can choose the
text size of the labels.

You can choose **not to show the icon preview** in the list part of the window.
You'll still see icons, but graphic image icons will just display a document icon,
not a preview of the actual image.

Customize the Desktop View

1   Click on a blank spot on the Desktop to make sure no Finder window
    (or any other window or icon) is selected.

2   From the View menu, choose "Show View Options."

These are the same options you have for Finder windows in Icon View; please
see pages 266–267 for details about these options. You can resize the icons or
the text labels, reposition the labels, show extra file information, display an
icon preview, snap the icons to a grid, or always keep the icons arranged by
your chosen criteria, such as alphabetized ("Name"), Kind, Label, etc.

Take Advantage of the System Preferences

The System Preferences control dozens of features on your Mac. Don't like the picture on your Desktop? Do you want your Mac to go to sleep sooner or later or never? Do you need to change the time because you moved? Would you like a whiny voice to yell at you every time you make a mistake? You can customize these and many other things through System Preferences. (Remember, every *application* has its own preferences, as explained on page 53.)

To open System Preferences, click on its icon in the Dock. **Or** go to the Apple menu and choose "System Preferences...."

This is the System Preferences icon.

If you would rather see these preferences in alphabetical order (as shown below) instead of grouped in categories, go to the View menu and choose "Organize Alphabetically."

Global versus user-specific preferences

If you have set up more than one user, as explained in Lesson 18, individual users will discover there are some preferences they can't change because they will affect other users; these preferences are "global" and only the master administrator can change them. Individual users can change the preferences that are "user-specific" because they affect only that one user. So if you run across a System Preference that you can't change, it's probably because you are not the main administrator (please see Lesson 18 for details about users and administrators).

How to use the System Preferences

Once you open the System Preferences pane, single-click an icon to display those particular preferences. Most things are self-explanatory—poke around and see what your options are. We'll look at a couple of examples.

1   Open System Preferences as described on the previous page. Single-click the **Keyboard & Mouse** icon. If the System Preferences is already open to some other preference, click the "Show All" button, and *then* click the "Keyboard & Mouse" icon.

2   What you see in this preferences pane depends on your computer. For instance, a laptop will have a "Trackpad" pane. A Bluetooth-enabled computer will have a "Bluetooth" pane. If a mouse is attached, you'll have a mouse pane, as shown on the next page.

Single-click any tab to see the preferences for that feature.

This is an option for a laptop; you won't see it on a desktop Mac.

See the following page for information about these options.

—continued

3 In the "Keyboard" pane shown on the previous page, you can adjust how fast any **key repeats** across the page as you press it down.

The **Delay Until Repeat** refers to how long your fingers can linger on the keys before they start repeating. If you find you type lots of double letters or spaces, choose a longer delay here. If your fingers are really heavy on the keys, slide the blue slider all the way to "Off" and the keys will never repeat automatically.

4 Click the other tabs to see what preferences you can set for those options.

The "Tracking Speed" refers to how far your mouse travels as you move your hand across the screen. The faster the tracking speed, the less distance you have to move the mouse. Try it.

Check out this pane of keyboard shortcuts.

This is another fun and useful System Preference—use it to **change the color or image on your Desktop.**

Desktop & Screen Saver

1 Open System Preferences as described on page 274. Single-click the "Desktop & Screen Saver" icon. **Or** if the preferences are still open, go to the View menu and choose "Desktop & Screen Saver."

2 Single-click the "Desktop" tab, as circled below.

3 In the list on the left, single-click each folder to see what's in it, displayed in the pane on the right.

4 Single-click any image you see in the pane on the right to immediately view it on your Desktop.

When you choose your own photo, a little menu pops up, as shown below. Use the pop-up menu to adjust the image to your screen. As soon as you choose something, it's displayed on your Desktop.

5 To use your own photo, first put it in the "Pictures" folder that's in your Home window. Then you can choose a photo from the "Pictures Folder" option.

Or click the **+** button, then find the folder where your photos are stored and add that folder. The folder will be placed in the list for easy access.

Correct the **date and time** on your Mac, change it when you go to a different time zone, make a regular clock float on your Desktop, and more.

Date & Time

1   Open System Preferences as described on page 274. Single-click the "Date & Time" icon. **Or** if the preferences are still open, go to the View menu and choose "Date & Time."

2   Click each of the three tabs in the preference pane and see what your options are. You can't hurt anything, so poke around and experiment.

The option to "Set date & time automatically" is useful if you have a full-time broadband connection (don't bother if your connection to the Internet is a dial-up). This keeps your Mac in touch with a satellite so your time is always correct—it will even switch to daylight savings time for you.

Find the right System Preferences for your task

Sometimes you know you need a System Preference to customize a particular Mac feature, but you're not sure which one has the option you need. That's where the Mac's Spotlight feature can help.

Just type what you're hoping to find in the System Preferences search field. As you type, you'll see certain System Preference icons highlight, and you'll see a list of possible options. The more you type, the more specific the results will be.

Try the example shown below. I was looking for all the preferences that give me an option to speak or use sound.

Choose an option in the list, and the appropriate System Preference will slowly flash twice at you and then open.

And don't forget about other features on your Mac that let you customize and personalize your machine! Check out Exposé & Spaces, plus all the individual application preferences. This is *your* Mac!

16

GOALS

Dashboard—Important Information at your Fingertips

Ever want to know what time it is right now in London? Or what the weather is like where you mother lives? Do you need to track the plane your daughter is taking to Istanbul—including whether it's going to leave on time and from what terminal—and then follow the flight path across the world in real time?

These are just a few of the many things you can do with literally the click of one button, using Dashboard. The information appears to you in the form of widgets. Some widgets are already on your Mac, but many others are being created by people and developers. Oh, the things we will see!

Take a Look at Dashboard

Dashboard provides quick access to information customized just for you, displayed in the form of **widgets.** Dashboard pops up in a split second, but only when you want it. With the click of a button, it goes away just as quickly. Below is an example of my **Dashboard,** with the **Widgets Bar** showing (the Widgets Bar doesn't appear until you ask for it; see page 284).

When you activate Dashboard, the widgets instantly appear on top of a greyed-out Desktop, on top of any windows or applications you have open. Do what you need, then click in any blank area to send them all away. Use the Widgets Bar to add and delete items, as explained on page 284.

This is a web clip that I made myself in Safari; see page 134.

Each of these items is a widget.

This is the Dashboard.

Click this **+** or **x** to show or hide the Widget Bar.

This is the Widget Bar.

Single-click the tiny arrow on either end of the Widget Bar to view more widgets that are in the bar.

Single-click any widget in the Widget Bar to make it appear on your screen. You can display more than one of any widget, as shown on page 287.

Discover Different Kinds of Widgets

There are three different kinds of widgets, although they are all so interesting and easy to work with, you won't really care which is which!

- **Information widgets** work with data from the Internet. You can check external events such as the weather anywhere in the world, the flight status of any plane, or current prices of your favorite stocks. You must be connected to the Internet to get the information for these widgets.

- **Application widgets** work with applications on your Mac. They typically provide a small and easy way of displaying the critical features of the main application. For instance, the iTunes widget is a small controller that gives you buttons—start, stop, play songs, and more—to listen to your Playlists or Internet radio without having the iTunes interface take up your whole screen. If the main application requires the Internet to function, so will its widget.

- **Accessory widgets** are self-contained little utilities that provide a variety of features. Widgets such as clocks, calculators, notes, or timers are accessories. Some of these do need Internet access, but they are not dependent on any application on your Mac.

Activate Dashboard and the Widgets

Dashboard is built into your Mac—just single-click the Dashboard icon in your Dock to **make it appear,** or press the F12 key.

If you're using a **laptop,** you might not have an F12 key, or it might be used for something else. You can change Dashboard's keyboard shortcut; see page 288.

Add Widgets to Your Dashboard

To add widgets to your onscreen Dashboard, first open Dashboard and bring up the **Widget Bar:** Single-click on the plus sign you see in the bottom-left of your screen. (The plus sign then turns into an **X** to **close** the Widgets Bar; see page 282.)

To add a widget, single-click on it. The widget appears on your screen.

To see other widgets that are already installed, single-click one of the tiny arrows that appear at either end of the Widgets Bar.

Organize widgets on the screen in any arrangement you like—simply press anywhere in a widget and drag it around. They will stay where you put them, even after you put away Dashboard.

Remove Widgets from Your Dashboard

Hold down the Option key and click the **X** that appears on the upper-left of the widget.

Or remove widgets from the Dashboard when the Widget Bar is visible. So first display the Widget Bar: Single-click the plus sign shown above. Now you see an **X** in the upper-left corner of each widget. **To remove a widget,** click that **X**. It stays in your Widget Bar until you want it again.

Put Dashboard Away

To put Dashboard away, single-click outside of any widget, *or* press your keyboard shortcut again (probably F12). When you reopen Dashboard, your widgets are right where you left them.

Work with Widgets

Different sorts of widgets have different sorts of features. Experiment with them all! For instance, open the Unit Converter and check all the different sorts of conversions you can make.

Many widgets (not all) have a tiny *i* in a corner, the **info button.** It's not in the same corner for all widgets, and it won't even appear until your pointer gets close to it. So hover over the corners of a widget to see if an *i* appears, then click on it—the widget turns over so you can change preferences.

Single-click the *info* button to flip the widget.

On the back side of many widgets are preferences for that particular item. For example, this information tells the Phone Book widget where to look.

Enter information into a field, then be sure to hit the Enter key to enter that data.

Click "Done" to flip the widget back over.

Experiment with Your Widgets!

Lots of different people create widgets and I can't explain here all the different things they will do. So be sure to pay attention to the sometimes-subtle visual clues that are built into widgets.

In the iTunes widget shown below, notice the tiny dot in the outer circle. That's a clue! Drag that tiny dot around to change the volume.

Notice the info button that appears (the *i*)—click on it to flip the widget and see what options are available on the other side. In this case, you can choose which iTunes Playlist to listen to.

In the Dictionary widget below, there are several visual clues, as shown.

The double-arrows are a clue that there is a menu hidden here. Click on it to see the options.

Back and forward arrows indicate you can return to panes you previously viewed.

Now "Thesaurus" is the visible menu option, indicating you are looking at the thesaurus entry.

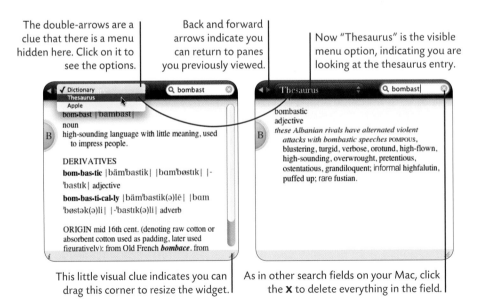

This little visual clue indicates you can drag this corner to resize the widget.

As in other search fields on your Mac, click the **x** to delete everything in the field.

Display More than One of a Widget

You can display multiple copies of any kind of widget. For instance, you might like to know the weather in several different places, view the flight paths of a number of different flights, open several different dictionary widgets to compare words, or view a number of different conversions at the same time.

To display more than one of any kind of widget, open the Widget Bar (when Dashboard is showing, click the **+** sign in the bottom-left corner of your screen). Then just single-click the widget as many times as you want, one for each display on your screen. Each new widget shows up in the center of the screen. Just drag it to any position and it will stay there.

Here I can see at a glance what the weather is like (and whether it's day or night) in the different cities where my kids live.

So now my dog Rosetta is in the puzzle.

TIP ——— To change the picture in the tile puzzle widget, do this: When Dashboard is open, put the tile puzzle on your screen. Close Dashboard.

In the Finder, find the picture you want to use in the tile puzzle. Start dragging it to nowhere in particular. While you are dragging (don't let go of the mouse), press F12 (or whatever your shortcut is, if you've changed it) to open Dashboard. Drop the picture you're dragging onto the tile puzzle.

Change Dashboard's Keyboard Shortcut

If you don't like the default shortcut that opens Dashboard, you can change it.

1   At the Finder, when Dashboard is *not* active, go to the Apple menu and choose "System Preferences...."

Exposé & Spaces

2   Single-click "Exposé & Spaces."

3   In the preferences pane, as shown below, make sure the "Exposé" tab is selected (it will be blue; if not, click on it).

Choose an Fkey from the "Hide and show" menu (circled, below) to use as your shortcut.

To add one or more of the modifier keys to your shortcut, just press that key(s) while the menu is open. The menu will change to reflect the key combination you are pressing. For instance, you might want to use Control F1 to activate Dashboard. So hold down the Control key and click the Dashboard menu, then choose this option in the menu: **^F1** (**^** indicates the Control key).

Options for a two-button mouse.

If you have a **two-button mouse** attached to your Mac, you will see a second column of menus, as shown above, where you can choose to use the middle or right mouse button to activate Dashboard. This is great for a laptop—I can't always use a shortcut like F7 without holding down the fn key also. This means it takes two hands to open Dashboard. But with the middle mouse button assigned to Dashboard, I can click the button once and Dashboard instantly appears. It's great.

Manage your Widgets

If you become a Widget junkie and start collecting lots of them, you'll want some way to get rid of the ones you don't want anymore, or at least remove them from the Widgets Bar. Use the **Widget Manager.** Open it from the Widgets Bar, as shown below, then click on the Widgets you don't want. Hold down the Shift key to select more than one at a time.

The selected widgets will be removed from the Widgets Bar, but they're still hidden away on the Mac somewhere so you can always turn them back on.

Both the button and the icon open the same thing, the Widget Manager, shown to the right.

Hold down the Shift key to select more than one item. Uncheck any widget that you want to turn off.

To get more widgets, click the "More Widgets…" button in the Widget Manager, shown above. This takes you to the Apple web site where you can download lots of free widgets that do cool things.

To make your own Web Clip widgets from Safari web pages, see page 132.

17

GOALS

Set up your printers

Access the special settings
for your printer software

Access the special settings
for your applications

Learn some
troubleshooting tips

Share printers
with other computers
on your network

Fax from your Mac

Receive faxes on your Mac

Set Up Printing and Faxing

Printing gets easier and more reliable with every new operating system. The Mac recognizes and automatically sets up more printers, individual applications can apply so many special parameters to your print jobs, and sharing one printer with many computers gets easier all the time.

Set Up your Printers

If you're already printing to your printer, then skip a couple of pages and go straight to the section about accessing special features of your printer, just in case you're not familiar with what it can do.

If your Print dialog box says, "No Printer Selected," see "Add a printer," below.

Be sure to install the software

If you bought a fancy printer of some sort, meaning it cost more than a hundred dollars, be sure to install the software that it came with. What you particularly need to install is the latest "printer driver." If you don't have the software that was originally shipped with the printer, or if you need an updated printer driver for your older printer, go to the manufacturer's web site. They always have the drivers available to download, free.

You can often print pages without the latest driver, but the more expensive your printer is, the more important it is that you have the proper driver. If not, you will lose some of the most valuable features of the machine. If you have an inexpensive little printer, the drivers that Apple includes will probably work just fine. Try printing and see what happens.

Add a printer

Your Mac automatically finds printers that are directly connected to the computer or that are on your local network. If you've installed the software for your expensive printer or if you have an inexpensive printer, the process is generally really easy.

Try to print something for the first time (press Command P or go to the File menu and choose "Print"). If you see your printer listed in the menu in the Print dialog box, then you're all set up.

Often, however, the first time you try to print, the Print dialog box tells you there is "No Printer Selected," as shown below. Your Mac just needs to be told to go find the printer and add it to its list. So:

1 Make sure the printer is connected to your Mac, that all the cables are secure, and that the printer is turned on.

2 Press on that menu that says "No Printer Selected" and choose "Add Printer...."

3 This brings up a window listing all printers your Mac can find, shown below. If everything is connected properly and the printer is on, you should see the name of the printer in the pane. Single-click on its name.

4 When the name of the printer appears in the bottom portion of the pane, all is well. Click the "Add" button. The Print dialog box, shown above, reappears and you can carry on.

Use the Print & Fax Preferences

Usually the steps on the previous pages to add a printer work just fine. But sometimes you might want to set up printers here in the Print & Fax system preferences before you begin or use this to troubleshoot printing problems.

1   Make sure your printer is turned on and tightly connected to your Mac with the proper cables.

2   Go to the Apple menu and choose "System Preferences...."

3   Single-click on the "Print & Fax" icon to get the pane shown below.

Print & Fax

If you choose the name of a specific printer here, that printer becomes the default.

4   If you don't see the name of your printer in the list on the left, click the **+** button. (Also check again to make sure the cable between the Mac and the printer is snug on both ends, and that the printer is turned on.)

When you click the **+**, it opens an unnamed window, a printer browser, shown on the opposite page, that lists every printer that is turned on or that your Mac is aware of.

If you see your printer listed, single-click its name to select it, then click the "Add" button.

If you *don't* see your printer listed, it has most likely lost its connection. If you're sure it's plugged in properly, then you might want to try a different cable—they can go bad all by themselves.

Laser printers (as opposed to inkjet printers) usually want AppleTalk turned on. If your printer is connected through an Ethernet port (as opposed to the USB or FireWire port), it probably wants AppleTalk. If so, the Mac will usually turn on AppleTalk for you, with your permission; if it doesn't, you can do it yourself **(if you don't have a real laser printer, skip this!)**:

    a. Close this window by clicking the red button in the top left.

    b. Click the "Show All" button.

    c. Click the "Network" icon.

    d. Click the "Ethernet" option on the left, then click the "Advanced" button on the bottom-right.

    e. Click the "AppleTalk" tab.

    f. Check the box to "Make AppleTalk Active." Click OK.

    g. Close the preferences and try printing again.

5 After you click the "Add" button in Step 4, the "Print & Fax" preferences pane reappears. Close it, then try to print.

If you did not see your printer listed in the "Printer Browser," maybe you didn't install the printer software that came with the printer. Install it now, then try these steps again.

Not all printers *must* have the software installed. Generally, the more expensive the printer, the more likely your Mac needs the software and the more likely it has special features that you'll want to access through its own driver.

Access the Special Features of your Printer

If you installed the software that came with your printer, then you probably have special features that allow you to choose the correct paper, the quality settings, adjust the colors, and more. The difference in output between a setting for inkjet paper as opposed to glossy photo paper is quite amazing.

To access the specific printer settings:

1   Start to print the job (press Command P).

2   If you see a small Print dialog box as shown on page 293, click the blue disclosure button (see below).

3   In the expanded Print dialog box, click on the menu circled below.

   Depending on the printer you have selected, you'll see such labels as "Print Settings" or "Image Quality." Here you will have lots of options, different options for each printer you choose, and for some printers you can select specific paper/media (of course, you should have that particular paper loaded in your printer).

Click this disclosure triangle to see the options.

The printer selected above determines what the options are for that printer. Check carefully.

Access the Special Features of your Software

Not only does your printer offer special printing features, but most software applications also have special features.

In the Print dialog box, be sure to check the menu (circled below and on the opposite page) to see if there is an option for the particular software you're using.

Below you see the print settings for Keynote, which is software from Apple for creating multimedia presentations.

Applications often have specialized features.

Buy ink cartridges for your printer

Apple makes it very easy to buy new ink cartridges for most printers and to buy them from Apple. Just single-click on the "Supplies…" button you see at the bottom of the Print dialog box (shown above). This takes you to an Apple web site where you can buy the cartridges for your specific printer.

You can do the same thing in the "Print & Fax" preferences pane shown on page 294: Single-click the button called "Options & Supplies…."

Having Trouble Printing?

Print & Fax

1 If the printer has been chosen but isn't responding when you try to print, open the "Print & Fax" pane: Go to the Apple menu, choose "System Preferences…," then single-click the "Print & Fax" icon.

2 Make sure you choose the correct printer to print to; its name should be highlighted on the left.

3 On the right side of the pane, click the button to "Open Print Queue…." This brings up the list of jobs waiting to be printed, as shown below. These are the jobs that are lined up to print to that particular printer.

	Robin's Printer @ Robin's Office Mac (1 Job)	
Delete Hold Resume Pause Printer Info		Supply Levels

Printing 'Orpheus' lute.rtf'.

Status	Name	User	When	Completed
Printing	Orpheus' lute.rtf	Robin Williams	9/19/07 10:33 AM	

You can also get to this print queue by clicking on the printer's icon that appears in the Dock when you print. I like to keep that icon in my Dock at all times.

4 Check to make sure the jobs are not on hold or paused. The buttons should look like the ones above: "Hold" should be clear (not gray), "Resume" should be gray, and the green button should say "Pause Printer," not "Resume Printer."

If either of the "resume" buttons are available, that means a job is on hold. Select a job in the list and click "Resume" or "Resume Printer" to start the printing process. *Or* select a job and click "Delete" to get rid of it.

TIP —— If you send a job to print and nothing happens, often your initial reaction is to send it again. And again. And again. Then when you remember to look at the Print Queue, you notice there are a dozen copies of the same job lined up waiting to print because the printer's been on hold. So just remember, if you send a job to print and it doesn't come out, do not send it again! Go to the Print Queue and see what the problem is! If you have a dozen of the same jobs lined up to print, select each one and delete it.

Share your Printer with Other Macs

Any printer can be set up to share, meaning any other computer in your office or home network can print to it without having to be directly plugged in to the printer. This is great because until Mac OS X came along, you had to buy a special networkable printer. Now you can have one little, inexpensive color Epson in your office and everyone can print to it.

If the printer you want to share is plugged directly into the router or switch for your network, anyone can print to it no matter which other computers are turned on. Typically, that means it's an Ethernet printer, probably a laser printer.

If the printer is plugged directly into a particular computer, that computer must be turned on for others to print to its connected printer.

To share a printer:

1   Turn on the printer that you want to share. The computer it's directly connected to must also be on, of course.

2   On the Mac that is directly connected to the printer, go to the Apple menu and choose "System Preferences…."

3   Click the "Sharing" icon.

4   In the pane on the left, check the box for "Printer Sharing." Then you should see the printer that is connected to your computer in the box on the right. Make sure there's a checkmark next to the printer you want to share.

—continued

5 At the bottom-right of the Sharing pane, click the button to "Open Print & Fax Preferences."

6 In the "Print & Fax" preferences, shown below, select the printer in the pane on the left, and then in the pane on the right you should see a checkmark next to "Share this printer." All is well.

Actually, you could skip Steps 3 and 4, and just go straight to the "Print & Fax" preferences to turn on Sharing. But I think it's important to know about the Sharing preferences.

To print to a shared printer:

1   The Mac that is directly connected to the shared printer must be turned on. That computer must have chosen to share the printer, as explained on the previous page. The printer must be turned on.

2   On your other Mac, open your document. Press Command P to get the Print dialog box.

3   In the "Printer" menu, the shared printer's name should appear and you can print to it. If the printer name is not in the menu list, see below.

If you don't see the printer in that list, click the "Add Printer…" option in the menu and add the shared printer just as you would add any other printer, as explained on pages 292–293.

If you don't have an "Add Printer…" option in the menu, go to the "Print & Fax" preferences as explained on the previous pages and add the shared printer. You might have to quit the application you're trying to print from and open it again to see the added printer.

Once you have added it, that printer will be in your Print dialog box whenever that printer and its connected Mac are turned on.

4   After you choose the shared printer, click the "Print" button.

Fax From and To your Mac

If your Mac has a modem built in or attached to it, you can fax from any application and you can receive faxes. But many Macs today do not have modems built in!

If you use a dial-up modem with a phone cable to connect to the Internet, then you are all ready to fax, as explained below.

But if you have a broadband connection to the Internet, you must first get a phone cable (a standard RJ11 phone cable like you use for your telephone). Plug it into the phone port on your Mac (if you have one!) and into a phone jack in the wall—you cannot fax over a broadband connection.

Send a fax from your Mac

1   Make sure you have a telephone cable connecting your Mac to a working phone outlet. (This assumes you have a modem built in to your Mac.)

2   Open the document you want to fax.

3   From the File menu, choose "Print...."

4   In the standard Apple dialog box, click the "PDF" button in the bottom-left corner and choose "Fax PDF...."

If you're using an application that has its own print dialog box, such as Adobe InDesign, you'll usually find a button at the bottom of the dialog box that says something like "Printer...." Click that button, and there you should find the "Fax PDF" button.

5 A dialog sheet appears (shown below) where you type in the fax number of the person you want to send the fax to.

If necessary, the "Dialing Prefix" is where you enter any number that gets you "out" of the office building. Typically it's 9. If you need to wait a couple of seconds after the 9 before the phone starts dialing, put one or two commas after the 9. Each comma makes the Mac wait two seconds.

6 If you want a cover page, check the box to "Use Cover Page," then enter the subject and message. The preview pane on the left displays what you're sending.

This button opens your Address Pane so you can automatically enter the fax number. See the steps on the following page.

7 Click "Fax" and off goes your page. You'll see the Fax icon in the Dock.

Enter fax numbers in your Address Book

You must **enter the fax number into your Address Book** properly before the Address Pane shown on the previous page can supply it for you.

To enter a fax number into your Address Book:

1 Open your Address Book.

2 Find the person whose fax number you want to enter.

3 Single-click the "Edit" button at the bottom of the pane, as shown below.

4 There are two fields at the top of the card, both pre-programmed for phone numbers. This is where you will enter the fax number.

5 Single-click on the tiny double arrows next to the field where you will enter (or have already entered) the fax number.

6 In the menu that pops up, choose "home fax" or "work fax."

7 Click the Edit button again to set your changes. Now when you click the little Address Pane icon when faxing, as shown on the previous page, this fax number will appear in the pane.

Receive a fax on your Mac

Set up your Mac to **receive faxes** using the "Print & Fax" pane in System Preferences, as shown below.

Check the box to "Receive faxes on this computer," then enter your fax information. Choose which actions your Mac should take when you receive a fax.

Remember, if you use a broadband connection to get to the Internet, you'll need to connect a phone line to your Mac (if it has a modem port) before you can send or receive a fax.

If you choose "Faxes" or "Shared Faxes," your Mac instantly makes that folder for you and puts it in your Home folder.

18

GOALS

Undersand why it's useful
to have multiple users
for one Mac

Learn to create new users

Know how to log out
and log in

Enable fast user switching

Allow other users to be
Administrators

Teach users to adjust some
of their own settings

Learn to share files with
other users on one Mac

Apply parental controls
from mild to serious

Share One Mac with Multiple Users

Mac OS X is specifically built for what's called a **multiple user environment;** that is, Apple *expects* that more than one person is probably using the same computer, whether it's in a school, office, or home. You can set up another user so no one else can access your personal letters, change your sound level, poke around in your financial files, put up a dorky picture as the Desktop background, or change any of your settings.

If you are the only user who ever has or ever will use this Mac, you can skip this lesson altogether. But are you really the only user? Perhaps your grandkids come over and want to use your computer. Or maybe your husband uses your machine from time to time. Or sometimes you have relatives staying for a week who just want to use your Mac to get their email. Or you're a teacher who wants a place on your computer safe from your students. If so, set up another user.

Overview of Multiple Users

First, let me explain the **concept and advantages of having multiple users** on your Mac so you can decide if you need or want to create other users.

You already have one user, **you,** which was automatically created when you first turned on your Mac and went through the setup process. You are the main user known as the **Administrator.** The password you set up when you first turned on your new Mac or installed Leopard is your **Admin password.**

You might not have noticed that you are a "user" because Apple sets a default so when you turn on your Mac, you are automatically "logged in" without having to type in a password. Once you have other users set up, you can change this default so everyone must log in with a password. If others use your Mac only occasionally, like your grandkids, you can leave it set to automatically let you in daily; then when the kids come over, you go to the Apple menu and **log out,** which means they must then **log in** with their own settings and yours will be protected.

One user, the first one (which was you, if it's your own Mac), is automatically created as the original, main **Administrator (Admin)** of the computer. If you are the *only* user, you are still the Administrator.

Limitations of other users

So you are the **Admin** and other people are either **standard users** or **managed users.** All other users are limited in certain ways:

- Applications can be made available to everyone, *or* limited to specific users. This means you could install a game in your child's Home folder and it won't clutter up your own Applications folder. If the game has to change the resolution of the monitor and the number of colors and your child cranks the volume way up, it won't affect what you see and hear when you log back in. You can install your financial program in your own Home folder so others cannot use it or access your files.

  You can create managed users for young kids and grandkids, where you can customize their Docks so they only have access to their own programs. You can seriously limit with whom they chat and email and to which web sites they can go.

- Even if an application is available to everyone who uses the machine, an individual user can set his own preferences because the preferences are stored in the user's personal Library folder.

■ Every user can customize the Mail program, and all of a user's email is privately stored in each user's personal Library folder.

■ Every user can set up her own screen effects. Fonts, window and Desktop backgrounds, Sidebar, Dock placement, Spaces, and preferences are individually customizable. Preferences are also individual for the keyboard, mouse, web browser bookmarks, international keyboard settings, applications that start up on login, and QuickTime.

■ The features that make the Mac easier to use for people with challenges can be customized by each user. This includes the Universal Access settings, full keyboard access, Speech preferences, VoiceOver (having your Mac talk you through doing things), etc.

■ Users who need international settings for such things as date, time, numbers, or for typing other languages, etc., can customize the Mac without bothering other users. If you have a laptop that you travel with, you can set up yourself as another user, such as "Carmen in Paris," and customize those settings for that country without affecting all your settings for home.

■ **Standard users cannot** change the date or time (except for the menu bar settings), nor can they change the preferences for energy saving, file sharing, networking, or the startup disk. They cannot add new users nor can they change certain parts of the login process.

■ **Managed users** have all of the above limitations, *plus* they have parental controls applied. You can severely limit a managed user, as explained on pages 324–329.

■ The **Guest account** is a special and very temporary account. Everything A Guest user does on the Mac while logged in completely disappears as soon as he logs out. This is great for someone who says, "Can I use your Mac to check my web mail?" He can log in as Guest, use Safari to check his mail, and leave no trace.

More than one Admin

As the Administrator, you can **assign Admin status to any other user** (see page 319). When that Admin user logs in, he can make system-wide changes that standard users cannot; he can create and delete other users, and do most of the things you can do. But your personal Home files are still protected from everyone else, including other Admins.

Guest Account Is Already Created

Apple has already created a special Guest account for you. This is a very temporary account! It's for those times when someone comes over to your house and wants to use your Mac to check their mail or write a quick TextEdit report. As soon as this person logs out, everything they did on the computer is completely erased.

There is no password for a Guest user. As soon as you **enable login** (shown below), anyone can log in as Guest, but has no access to any of your files.

To log in as Guest, from the Apple menu, log yourself out. The login window that appears has a "Guest Account" option. Just click once on it.

To log out as Guest user, go to the Apple menu and choose "Log Out Guest Account." There will be a warning that all files that have been created will be deleted.

1. Click the lock to allow you to enable login for the Guest Account. If you don't, a Guest can use the network to share public files, but cannot log in to your Mac.

2. Click the "Guest Account" on the left, above, to see this pane shown to the right. Put a check in "Allow Guests to log into this computer."

3. Click the lock again.

Create New Users

If you are the Admin (as explained on pages 308–309), you can create standard or managed users (also explained on the previous pages). You'll create the user in the "Accounts" pane in the System Preferences, plus you'll assign a password and a login picture. In the "Login Options" pane, you can make adjustments to the login window.

To create a new user:

1 Go to the Apple menu and choose "System Preferences…."

2 In the System Preferences pane, single-click on "Accounts." You'll get the dialog box shown below, except it probably has only two users listed, you and Guest Account. Your user account is also the **Admin.**

3 Click the lock icon in the bottom-left corner. In the dialog box that appears after you click the lock, enter the Admin password (the one you chose when you set up your Mac), then click OK. The lock in the bottom-left corner is now open, as shown below.

4 To add a new user, click the "plus" button. This makes a sheet drop down (as shown on the following page) where you will add new user information.

—continued

Type the full name (or any descriptive phrase) in the "Name" edit box. A short name is automatically created for you, but you can edit it. *You will never be able to change the short name after you leave this pane!* The only way to "change" it is to delete the entire user and make a new one.

The short name should be short, you can't use spaces, and you should avoid non-alphabet characters (like * ! ? or /).

Mac OS X can use either the short name or long name. But the short name is sometimes necessary if you use FTP, Telnet, or other applications that let you log in to your Mac from some other location.

For Group accounts, see page 316.

Click this to get secure password suggestions.

5 Enter a **password** for the user. **Write this down somewhere.** As you've probably seen before, you need to type in the password twice to make sure you've spelled it right, since you can't see it. If you like, click on that tiny key icon to get some suggestions for passwords that are very secure.

Passwords are "case sensitive." That means capital or lowercase letters change the password: "ChoCho" is not the same password as "chocho." So be darn sure when you write down your password somewhere that you make note of any capital letters.

It is possible to leave the password blank, but that makes the entire computer easier to get into. If privacy is an issue, be sure to assign a password.

You can, if you like, enter a **password hint.** On login, if a user enters the wrong password three times, a message appears with this hint (see the following pages to make sure the box is checked to make the hint appear).

6   If you know how to use **File Vault,** click that option. Don't click it if you don't know how it works! (See Lesson 24).

7   Click the "Create Account" button. You will be asked about Automatic Login, whch lets you turn on your computer and automatically logs you in without a password. If you have security issues with your Mac, turn off Automatic Login.

8   **To choose a login picture,** do one of the following:

   ▪ Single-click the existing picture you see in the window and choose another from the collection that appears.

   ▪ **Or** do the step above (click the picture), then choose "Edit Picture...." Then skip to "Edit the image," below.

   ▪ **Or** drag a photo or other image from a Finder window and drop it on top of the existing picture.

   ▪ **Edit the image:** Resize, reframe, take a new photo, or choose a different image. You can edit this at any time in the future as well.

If you have a camera attached, click this button to take your photo.

Press-and-drag on this image to position it within the frame.

To resize the image, drag the blue slider.

To choose another image from your Mac, click here.

When you're happy with the image, click "Set."

—continued

9 Enter the user's .Mac account name if she has one.

If you want to allow this user administration privileges so she can change preferences, install software, etc., check that box.

If you want to enable parental controls, check the box, then click the button to go to the Parental Controls preferences (see pages 324–329).

10 In the Accounts window, single-click **Login Options** to assign a user the ability to automatically log in, as explained below. This pane is available only to Administrators (that is, standard and managed users will not be able to change anything on this pane).

I just set up several new users, but my Mac will **automatically log in** to "Robin Williams," meaning I do not have to go through the login screen and enter a password whenever the Mac starts or restarts. This is good for me on my big tower Mac in my office because I work by myself; for my laptop that I travel with, I **disable** automatic login.

Because the Mac will automatically log me in on my tower, the only way the other users can get to their Home folders is if I go to the Apple menu and choose "Log Out…," *or* if I uncheck the automatic login on this pane. Which one you choose depends on how often the other user needs your machine; if it's infrequent, you can let yourself automatically log in daily, then log out when the other user arrives to log in.

Only one user can be assigned the automatic login. Any time you like, open this pane and choose another user from the menu shown above to give that person the automatic login privilege.

This is a login window.

If your password isn't working, check to make sure this Caps Lock symbol is not in the field! If Caps Lock is on, your password will be typed in all caps and might not work.

To take it off, press the Caps Lock key again.

If you checked the box to "Show password hints," this button will give you the clue you entered for your password.

Display login window as: The "List of users" displays a list of all accounts. The pictures that were chosen appear next to the names of the users. It's really cute. At login, click a picture, then type the password. (If you have a very young user who can't type and you feel your Mac is safe from strangers walking by, do not assign a password; she can just click her picture to log in.)

The "Name and password" option displays a small window with two edit boxes, one for the user name and one for the password. A user will have to type in both name and password. This makes it one step more secure.

Show the Restart, Sleep, and Shut Down buttons: This adds a wee bit more security to your Mac. You see, when you log out, your computer does not turn off. It sits there with a little window where you can log back in again, and there are buttons in the window to "Sleep," "Restart," or "Shut Down." If your Mac is set to automatically log you in on startup, then an unauthorized user can walk by after you have logged out, click the Restart button, and your Mac will restart and automatically log you in. Or someone could shut down your Mac, insert an OS X CD, boot up the Mac, and get access to your whole computer. By disabling these buttons, your Mac is one step closer to being protected.

—continued

However, there is nothing to prevent anyone from pushing the Restart button on the Mac, so if you really don't want people getting into your Mac, do not enable automatic log in, and do not leave your OS X CD laying around.

Show Input menu in login window: This gives you access to the language options that you may have set up in the International system preferences.

Use VoiceOver at login window: This turns on Apple's built-in spoken user interface so a visually impaired person can log in. It reads everything on the login screen out loud to you and tells you what is highlighted so you know where to type your name and password.

Show password hints: If a user enters the wrong password three times, the hint that was provided in the password pane when the user was created is displayed. Or you can click the button (shown on the previous page) to provide the hint immediately.

Enable fast user switching: This is so cool—see page 318 for details.

11 **To limit** what the new user can access, see pages 324–329.

To choose login items that automatically open, see page 321.

When done, close the Accounts preferences pane. You can always make changes at any time. To make changes to other users, they must be logged out.

Create a Group

You can create a Group account that consists of individual users. This makes it even easier to share files with a group of people who are all using the same network, such as students or co-workers.

Simply choose the "Group" option when making a new user (see pages 311–312). You will get a pane in which you can add other existing users to this Group.

To maximize the file sharing capabilities, use the Sharing preferences to turn on various sharing possibilities, then add this Group to the list of sharing users.

Log Out and Log In

Automatic login allows *one* selected user to use the Mac without having to enter a password. If automatic login is enabled (page 314), then you must make sure to **Log Out** (*not* restart or shut down) before another user can log in. This is because the computer will automatically log you in again when it starts up.

If automatic login is *not* enabled, then it doesn't matter how you turn off the Mac—it will always display a **Log In** screen where every user, even Admins, will have to enter a password.

When you log out, all of your documents will close and your applications will quit. If this is inconvenient, read about "fast user switching" on the next page.

To log out, go to the Apple menu and choose "Log Out *User*...." "*User*" is the name of the currently active user. All applications will quit, the current screen will disappear, and the login window will appear waiting for the next user to log in.

To log in, click your name and then type your password. If the password is incorrect, the login window shakes back and forth, as if it's saying "No! No! No!" After three wrong passwords, it will show you the hint you assigned (see pages 312–313). Or you can click the "Forgot Password" button and it will provide the clue immediately.

Switch Users with a Click

The Mac has a feature called **fast user switching** that allows multiple users to stay logged in at the same time without having to close files or quit applications. If you're working on a newsletter and your teenager needs to do her homework, she can switch to her personal user environment, do her work, then you'll switch the Mac back to your user space—with your newsletter sitting there waiting for you. The important thing is that you didn't have to close your documents and quit your applications to log out.

When fast user switching is turned on, all users are listed in the top-right corner of your screen, next to the menu clock. The currently active user's name appears in the menu bar.

To see other user names and to see which ones are logged in, single-click on the current user name in the menu; a menu drops down showing all users. Users in the list that have a checkmark next to them are already logged in. The currently active user is grayed-out.

To enable fast user switching, click the checkbox "Enable fast user switching" in the "Login Options" pane of the Accounts system preferences (see page 314).

To switch to another user, choose one from the user menu, as shown above. If you (the Admin) assigned a password to the chosen user, a login window opens so the user can type a password. Enter the correct password and the user's own personal Desktop environment opens.

If a password was not assigned to a user, that user's Desktop opens immediately, without a password-protected login window. Actually, it doesn't just open like some ordinary computer; the entire Desktop rotates like a cube to the new user space.

To open the main login window, choose "Login Window..." from the user's list in the menu bar, as shown on the previous page. This is a convenient way to leave the screen if you have multiple users. The next user that sits down at the Mac just clicks her name to log in and start work (or play).

Allow Other Users to be Admins

An Admin can select another user and give that user Administrator privileges. In the Accounts preferences, select the user in the left panel, then click the button to "Allow user to administer this computer."

A standard user can give himself Admin privileges if he knows the name and password of an Administrator. All he needs to do is click the lock icon and enter the correct information.

Adjust User Settings

You, as Admin, cannot make changes to another user if that user is already logged in. So if you try to make changes and it won't let you, log out that user.

TIP ——— If the rotating-cube effect isn't happening for you during fast user switching, the graphics card installed on your Mac might not be able to handle the intense processing that this effect requires. Fast user switching will still take place–it's just not quite as sexy.

Let Users Adjust their own Settings

Once a **standard user** is logged in, she can adjust some of the login settings, even if she's not the Administrator. She can change her password (she has to know the current password before she can assign a new one). She can change the login picture, apply parental controls to herself, and choose which applications open automatically when she logs in.

Below you see the applications that my mother likes to have open automatically when she comes to visit and uses my Mac. See the opposite page for details about Login Items.

Set Up Login Items

In the **Login Items,** any standard or Admin user (including yourself) can choose to have certain items automatically open during the login process. You can open your favorite applications, utilities, documents, even movies or music. If you choose to have a document open, the application it was created in will have to open as well, even if you don't have it in the list.

This pane applies only to the user who is currently logged in! No other user even has access to the Login Items pane for someone else.

To add items to the Login Items list, click the "plus" button circled below. A dialog box opens to let you choose any file or application to add to the Login Items. To add more items, click the "plus" button again.

The files will **open in the order in which they are listed.** Drag any file in the list up or down to change the order.

If you don't want to see a certain application right away every time you turn on your Mac, click in the checkbox to **hide** it. It will still open, but its windows won't be visible on the screen. The application icon in the Dock will have the blue bubble under it, though, so you know it's open and you can access it at any time.

The current user is always at the top of this list.

To delete items from the Login Items list, first select the item, then click the "minus" button.

Share Files with Other Users

Once users are set up, other users can only access each other's Public folders, the Drop Boxes inside the Public folders, and the Sites folders. But the Shared folder (which is in the Users folder, which is on your main hard disk) is available to everyone who uses the Mac. Here's how it works:

- Put files in your own **Public folder** that you want others to be able to read, copy, or print. They have to open your Public folder to do so.

- Other users can put files *for you* into your **Drop Box,** which is located inside of your Public folder. They cannot *open* your Drop Box, not even to see if their file successfully transferred.

- Put files in the **Shared folder** that you want everyone who uses the Mac to have access to. This is a good way to distribute something to everyone on the Mac without having to copy it to each individual's Drop Box.

- The **Sites folder** is where you can store a web site or files that you want people to access through the Internet.

You can also change the sharing "privileges" for any folder in your Home. That is, you can turn *off* the sharing privileges for the Public folder and the Drop Box so no one can access them, and you can also choose to share *any* or all of your other folders, with varying levels of access. Please see the following page for details.

All users can access items in the **Shared** folder.

Every user has a Drop Box located inside his Public folder.

Set Permissions for Shared Files

Every file on your Mac has "permission" settings. Some of these permissions you can change, if you like. For instance, you might want to send a memo to all users of this Mac, but you don't want them to be able to edit it. So select that document and give the others a permission of "Read only." Or perhaps you don't want anyone to access your Sites folder; give it a permission of "No Access." Maybe you want to share your Movies folder so another user can drop movie files into it; select the folder and change its permission to "Read & Write" or "Write only" (which means they can put files *into* your folder but can't take them out.)

To change permissions on a file or folder:

1   Single-click on a file or folder to select it.

2   Press Command I to display the Info window, as shown below.

3   Click the disclosure triangle next to "Sharing & Permissions."

4   Click the lock icon and enter your Admin password. Click OK.

5   Click the little menu next to user names or groups to change the permissions.

6   When you're finished, just close the Info window.

Documents and folders have different sorts of permissions available.

Add users or a Group to this list and assign permissions.

To revert changes or to apply the permissions to all items in a folder, use the Action menu.

Parental
Controls

Apply Parental Controls

There are several levels of limited user access you can create. Once you apply any of these parental controls, the user changes from a "Standard" user to a "Managed with Parental Controls" user. Choose the level of access you want to control. Each of these options is explained on the following pages. Only an Admin can apply or change parental controls. You can even manage these controls from another computer.

You can limit the applications a user has access to, the content of the Dictionary and web sites, whether or not a user can burn CDs or modify their Dock, and more. You can set time limits and check logs to see where a user has been.

The **Simple Finder** is the most serious limitation. This is appropriate for very young children who want to use their educational software and games on your Mac and really don't know how to surf or chat anyway. It makes the Mac very easy for them to use and they can't do any damage.

Set limitations on a user

1 Set up a new user, as explained on pages 311–316, if you haven't already.

2 Make sure that the user is not logged in. If he is, log him out.

3 Go to the Apple menu and choose "System Preferences...."
Single-click on the "Accounts" icon.

4 If the lock icon in the bottom-left corner is locked, single-click on it and enter the Admin name and password. Click OK.

5 Select the user in the left-hand pane.

6 Check the box to "Enable Parental Controls."

7 Click the button to "Open Parental Controls...."

8 You'll see the window at the top of the next page, asking you to choose the account to which you want to apply parental controls.

Choose an account and you immediately get the screen shown at the bottom of the opposite page.

9 The rest of the process is pretty self-explanatory. Go through the next few pages for some clarification. Essentially, you're going to choose what you want to limit. Don't choose the **Simple Finder** until you read page 328.

Use the back and forward buttons to go back and forth between panes.

Click these tabs to limit other features.

Choose which applications you will allow.

Don't neglect these options; uncheck any you do *not* want this user to access.

—continued

This is the "Mail & iChat" pane. You can add the individual accounts that you will allow, or click the disclosure button to access your Address Book and choose from there.

This is the "Content" pane where you can hide naughty words in the Dictionary and limit access to the web.

This is the "Logs" pane where you can keep track of every web page this user has visited, as well as with whom they've chatted and what applications they've used. Wow.

Be sure to check the "Time Limits" pane where you can limit the amount of time the user can use the computer, and turn it off at a certain bedtime.

—continued

Simple Finder

The Simple Finder is the most serious limitation. The illustration below shows what a user logged in using **Simple Finder** might see.

■ The Applications and Utilities are limited to what you allow.

■ The user has no access to a Desktop, hard disk, or other partitions.

■ The user cannot move files from one folder to another.

■ The user has three folders in her Dock: My Applications, Documents, and Shared. The Shared folder contains items placed in it by other users of the computer, as explained on page 322. Anything anyone puts into the Shared folder (shown in the Dock) will be available even to users running Simple Finder.

■ The Finder windows have no Sidebars or Toolbars.

My Applications folder.

Shared folder.

Documents folder; all saved documents will be in this folder.

In Simple Finder, click an icon just once to open it.

To set up a user with Simple Finder:

1   Follow the steps beginning on page 324 up through Step 9.

2   Click the button to "Use Simple Finder."

3   In the list of applications, uncheck the boxes to deselect applications.
Every checked item will be available to the user in Simple Finder.

> **To deselect some applications,** click the small disclosure triangle next to the different sorts of applications to see an itemized list of individual applications, each with its own checkbox. Uncheck a box to deselect an item.

Override the Simple Finder

While in the Simple Finder, an Admin user (or anyone with an Admin name and password) can go to the Finder menu and select "Run Full Finder." A dialog box opens that requires the Admin name and password, and then the current user has access to a complete menu bar, hard disks, and Finder windows with Sidebars and Toolbars.

Delete a User

Any Admin can delete a user. You have three choices about what to do with all the files that belong to a user when you delete her account:

Save the home folder in a disk image. The contents of the user's Home folder will be compressed as a disk image format (.dmg) and saved into a "Deleted Users" folder located in the Users folder. This is a nice safety net in case you need to access that user's files later—just double-click the .dmg file, it opens to a hard disk icon (as shown on the opposite page), and all the files are restored in that hard disk icon.

Do not change the home folder. This stores the entire Home folder and all its contents in a folder called "*username* (Deleted)." All of the folders except Public and Sites are locked, however. You, as Admin, can open a folder's Info window and change the permissions to give you access to it, as shown on page 323.

Delete the home folder. Choose this if you're certain you don't need anything the deleted user may have in her Home folder. The user account and all files in the user's Home folder will immediately disappear.

To delete a user:

1   From the Apple menu, choose "System Preferences...," then click the "Accounts" icon.

2   If the lock icon in the bottom-left corner is locked, single-click on it and enter the Admin name and password. Click OK.

3   Click once on the name of the user you want to delete. If the user name is gray and you can't select it, that means that user is logged in. She must log out before you can delete the account.

4   After you select the user, click the "minus" button at the bottom of the list of users pane.

5   A sheet drops down, shown at the top of the next page, asking what you want to do with the files belonging to this user. Make your choice based on the information above.

If you choose to *not* save the Home folder, this is the deleted user; the files are all in this folder, but they are all locked. Use the Info pane, as described on page 323, to unlock the folders.

To access the saved user files later, double-click the .dmg file. It will open to a hard disk icon. Open the hard disk icon and you'll find all the files.

19

GOALS

Find What You Want, Fast—with Spotlight

Spotlight is not just a search feature, it's a way of working with your Mac. Once you get accustomed to its speed, versatility, and usefulness, you'll find yourself using Spotlight regularly instead of opening and closing folders and windows.

If you find you perform a certain search often, save it as a Smart Folder. Files that match the search criteria are automatically listed in the Smart Folder and the folder updates itself every time a matching file is created or changed.

The Many Faces of Spotlight

Spotlight really has **five** different ways of working. You'll find yourself using them in different ways at different times. Experiment with each one so you'll know which is the most appropriate for what you need to do. Details for each option are on the following pages.

1. Spotlight menu

Click the Spotlight icon in the upper-right of the menu bar,
or use the keyboard shortcut, Command Spacebar.

Type your query into the field that appears and Spotlight instantly starts presenting results. As you type more letters, the search narrows and updates.

Access to the Spotlight menu is available no matter which application you're using—you don't have to go to the Finder to run a search. See pages 342–343 for all the details.

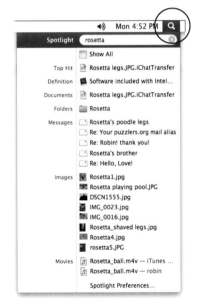

2. Spotlight window

To get the Spotlight window below that displays more information:

> **Either** click the option to "Show All" at the top of the Spotlight menu after you've made a search, as shown on the previous page.
>
> **Or** use a keyboard shortcut:
>
> > If you're in the Finder, press Command F.
> >
> > If you're in an application, press Command Option Spacebar.
>
> See pages 345–346 for details.

3. Spotlight-powered search in the Finder

When you type into the Search field in a Finder window, Spotlight instantly kicks in and shows you simple results directly in that window. It automatically looks in the last "location" that was chosen ("This Mac" in the example below). See page 344 for details.

4. Quick "Search For"

There is a section in the Finder window sidebar called "Search For." Apple has created several pre-defined searches for you. If you're looking, for instance, for a file you used yesterday but you can't remember what you called it, check the "Yesterday" search and see if it jumps out at you.

You can't change these search parameters, but you can get take them out of your sidebar if you're not using them. Just drag them off to the side and let go—they'll go up in a puff of smoke. If you want them back, use the Finder preferences (go to the Finder menu, choose "Preferences…," and click the "Sidebar" tab).

5. Spotlight-powered search in many applications

You can find Spotlight-enabled searches in many other applications. Some applications also let you create other forms of Smart Folders.

Mail and Smart Mailboxes, pages 88–91.

Address Book and Smart Groups, pages 116–117.

Spotlight on text, page 350.

System Preferences, page 279.

Open and Save As dialog boxes, page 351.

Safari, page 350.

But Before You Begin

There are several things you might want to know before you start using Spotlight. In the Spotlight preferences, you can choose which **categories** of items you want Spotlight to search through. You can also choose certain disks and folders that you (or anyone using your machine) *cannot* search through, giving you some extra **privacy.**

And on the following pages are some tips for searching.

Choose the categories for searching

1   From the Apple menu, choose "System Preferences...."

2   Single-click on the "Spotlight" icon.

3   Click the "Search Results" tab if it isn't already highlighted.

4   *Uncheck* boxes for categories you *don't want* Spotlight to search.

5   Click the Back button (the triangle in the upper-left) or "Show All" to go back to the main preferences pane.

Create some privacy

1   If you haven't already, open the Spotlight preferences, as explained on the previous page.

2   Click the "Privacy" tab.

You can change these keyboard shortcuts if you find they interfere with your favorite applications.

3   Click the **+** sign to open a dialog box where you can choose any folder or disk on your Mac that you don't want Spotlight to search.

Or drag any folder or disk icon from the Finder and drop it into this pane.

Note: This isn't a very *safe* privacy feature because anyone using your computer can just open the preferences and remove these items.

Keyboard shortcuts to open Spotlight

Notice in the illustration above that these preferences also include options for you to change the existing keyboard shortcuts or to turn them off altogether (uncheck the boxes). Some applications might use those same shortcuts; Spotlight will override the applications' shortcuts, so if it creates a problem for you, go to the preferences above and change them.

Don't search just file names

Spotlight doesn't just search file names. It searches the contents of email messages, it knows who sent you email, it can look through the contact information in your Address Book, images and graphics, calendars and events and to-do lists, System Preferences, PDF text, the contents of TextEdit pages (but not text clippings), even iChat logs (if you previously chose to log them).

Expand your repertoire of searchable items

You're not limited to searching just for *words* that might be found in a file. In the Finder Spotlight search, you can use the existing parameters to find particular categories of files. For instance, you can look for "music" to find all your music files, or "images today" to find all the images you have opened today.

Leave the search field empty when you use these parameters if you want to find all files of a particular type.

Expand the search with metadata

Spotlight also looks in the **metadata** that every file contains. Metadata includes information about who created the file, when it was created and modified, the copyright date, the file type, the color space for a photo or image, even what kind of camera a particular photo was taken with. Different kinds of files have different kinds of metadata associated with them.

To make a metadata attribute appear in the parameter menu, check the box in the column labeled "In Menu."

Click a plus sign to add another parameter; click a minus sign to delete that one.

In the Find window, single-click any of these parameter menus in the left-hand column and choose "Other..." to get a list of metadata options to search for.

Add keywords to files

There are some files that, even with all the options in Spotlight, still won't be found because there is nothing associated with them that Spotlight can decipher. For these files, you can add your own **keywords.** For instance, the example below is a music file of an Elizabethan song written in the 16th century. I can search for "music," "Hecate," and other data, but if I search for "elizabethan," this piece of music won't be found. So I added a number of keywords that I might use in a search to the Get Info window for this file and for all the other Elizabethan music I have on my Mac. Now Spotlight can find them.

To add a keyword to a file:

1   Single-click on a file to select it.

2   Then press Command I to get the Get Info window.

3   Type your keywords into the "Spotlight Comments" area.

If you have more than one file to which you want to add keywords, select one file, then press Command *Option* I. Now as you select other files, this Get Info window automatically displays the information for the currently selected file.

Spotlight Menu

The Spotlight menu is available no matter which application you are using at the moment (although this is *not* the tool to use to search within your application, such as searching the text on a visible web page or in your word processor).

To open the Spotlight menu:

1   Simply click on the Spotlight icon in the upper-right of the menu bar, **or** press Command Spacebar to open it.

2   A small field appears. Start typing in it.

Results appear instantly in the Spotlight menu, as shown below. The more letters you type, the narrower the search becomes.

To use the Spotlight menu:

Below are callouts of the various parts of the Spotlight menu. Use the Spotlight menu for a quick search for something you think can be easily found.

Single-click the **X** to delete everything in the search field.

Single-click "Show All" to display the Spotlight window, as shown on the following page.

Single-click any item to open it.

These are the categories that Spotlight is searching. See page 337 for a list of the categories possible.

This opens the same preferences you see on pages 337–338.

343

Spotlight in the Finder

There are two ways to use Spotlight in the Finder, both of which use your Finder window. You can do a **quick search** by simply typing in the search field that appears in the upper-right corner of every Finder window, as described below. *Or* press Command F to go straight to a more **specific search** window with options to narrow your search, as described on the following pages.

Quick search in a Finder window

Below are the **results** of a quick search for "death." As soon as you start typing in the search field, results appear. Also, a bar appears that tells you where Spotlight looked (in the example below, it searched the *contents* of "This Mac").

In this window, you can easily choose another location for Spotlight to search— just single-click one of the locations in the bar, shown below. If you select a folder before you begin the search, it will limit the search to that folder.

You can also click the **+** button that now appears (circled, below) to add more parameters for narrowing your search, as shown on the opposite page.

To see where a file is located, single-click any result; the path to that file (the folders within folders) appears at the bottom of the list.

To open the folder that holds the selected file, press Command R (or Control-click, right-click, or use the Action menu to choose, "Open Enclosing Folder").

To open that file, double-click it.

To quickly view the file, click the Quick Look button (the eyeball in the toolbar).

Specific search in a Finder window

On the Desktop, press Command F and the active window will switch to what you see below. If no window is open or active, a new one will open automatically. This window includes the search field, and the location bar is already visible.

The only difference between this window and the one on the opposite page is that this Find window automatically provides parameters for you to work with.

To add more parameters to narrow your search, click the plus sign; to delete one, click its minus sign.

To change the parameters, single-click on a parameter menu to choose a different option. Start with the menu on the left, as shown below, which will change the specifics in the next menu to the right, which might then create a new field for you to enter a new parameter, also shown below.

As in the example on the opposite page, you can choose to search the "Contents" or just the "File Name."

Choose a location to search and whether to search the contents or the file name.

You can narrow your search even further with Boolean operators, which are not as scary as they sound. See the next page.

Use a Boolean search

A Boolean search simply means that you limit the search by using the words AND, OR, and NOT. As you can see below, a search for "mabel" showed me three files. But a search for "mabel AND love" found exactly the one I was looking for, and only that one.

The Boolean operator (the AND, OR, or NOT word) *must* be typed in all caps or it won't work.

You can also use quotation marks, just as you probably do when searching the web. For instance, if you search for *knitting yarn* without quotes, you'll get every document that has the word knitting in it and every document that has the word yarn in it. But if you search for *"knitting yarn"* in quotes, you will only find pages with that exact phrase.

Smart Folders

Once you do a great search in the Finder via Spotlight, you might like to create a **Smart Folder** that automatically keeps track of every file that fits that search. This folder doesn't store the original files—the originals stay in their original folders, and the Smart Folder just keeps a list of everything so it's easily accessible to you.

For instance, you might want a Smart Folder that contains all the various presentations you've made so you don't have to go looking through numerous folders to find a particular one. If so, make a Smart Folder that just stores presentation files.

Or you might have used the Labels feature on your Mac (see page 264) to color-code all the files that belong to a certain project. For instance, your newsletter might include a **document** in the application Pages, **images** from the last event, **word processing files** your authors have sent you, and a **spreadsheet chart** from the Apple spreadsheet software called Numbers. And you used the Labels to give them all a label color of orange. Your Smart Folder can keep track of all the orange-labeled files in one place for you, even though the files themselves are organized into their own particular folders. The Smart Folder updates automatically as new files are labeled or old files are trashed.

To create a Smart Folder:

1   At the Finder, press Command F to open Spotlight in a Finder window.

2   Define your parameters. Below is a simple search of all files in my Home folder that are presentations. Notice there is *nothing* typed into the search field at the top of the window because I want to find *all* presentations regardless of their names.

—continued

3 Click the "Save" button, which is just below the search field. You will be asked to **name** this Smart Folder and **where** to save it. In the example below, I saved this into my Documents folder.

If you want this folder to be visible in your Sidebar, check the box to "Add To Sidebar." Click "Save."

I saved this Smart Folder into my Documents folder.

4 Now that the Smart Folder is saved, all you need to do is double-click on it and your Mac will display all the files that match the criteria you originally set. (If the Smart Folder is in the Sidebar, just single-click on it.)

To edit this Smart Folder search at any time, double-click on its folder and set new parameters. Files will automatically update.

System Preferences

As explained in Lesson 15, Spotlight also works in System Preferences. This is great when you know you need a System Preference to do something in particular, but you're not sure *which* one you need.

To search in System Preferences, simply type into the search field. As you type, Spotlight highlights all the possible preferences that might help you.

When you click on one of the options in the menu that appears, Spotlight highlights the best preference for that option in a bright white spotlight, as shown below, then opens it for you automatically.

This preference is where you can monitor Internet activity, as selected in the menu above.

Spotlight in Text

In some applications on your Mac, you can select a word or phrase and let Spotlight find other occurrences of that word or phrase on your Mac. This might be useful when you're browsing the web and find the name of someone in the news and it makes you say, "Hmm, didn't she send me an email last month?" Or if you're in your word processor and you're writing an essay and you want to find the article you saved earlier on a topic that's mentioned.

For instance, try this in Safari or TextEdit:

1 On a web page, press-and-drag to select a word or phrase.

2 Control-click (or right-click) on that selected word or phrase.

3 From the contextual menu that appears, choose "Search in Spotlight." Remember, Spotlight searches your Mac, not the Internet!

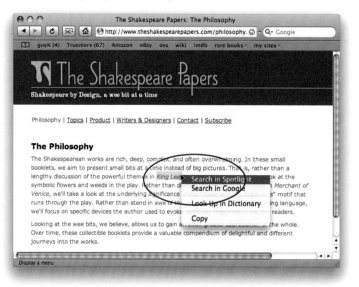

Open Dialog Box

In any Open dialog box, as shown below, you can search for a **file name.** Spotlight will locate all files that your open application thinks it can open and display, plus all folders with that search phrase in the name (it does *not* search contents or to-do list items, etc., in this dialog). Any Smart Folders you have placed in the Sidebar will also appear here.

After you start typing a search entry, this bar appears.

Narrow or expand your search by clicking on one of these locations.

Save As Dialog Box

You can do a search in the Save As dialog box and Spotlight will find **folders** for you to save into. Any Smart Folders in the Sidebar will also appear here.

Click the X to delete the entire search string.

20

GOALS

Learn about Time
Machine

Create a backup of your
entire hard disk

Find and restore files

Search and switch
to Time Machine

Time Machine Backup

We know we should back up important files every day, but really, "It's just too much trouble." Surely everything will be okay for a couple of days until we have time to make backups. Months later we finally have some extra time and the files are nowhere to be found. Or the original version has been overwritten by a newer version with unwanted changes in it. Oh, if only we had a time machine that could go back in time and grab earlier versions of files. And wouldn't it be nice if the time machine did this without us doing anything—except maybe turning it on?

Wait . . . there *is* such a thing! And, amazingly, it's called . . . Time Machine!

About Time Machine

After you set up Time Machine, it backs up your computer regularly. For the initial backup, Time Machine backs up everything, including system files, applications, etc. After that, only files that have changed are backed up. Hourly backups are stored for twenty-four hours, daily backups are stored for a month, then weekly backups are stored until the backup disk is full. Because backups are stored by date, you can restore files or folders (or your entire system) exactly as they were at certain points in the past.

When the backup disk fills up, Time Machine deletes the oldest backups to make room for new ones. It could take a long time to reach this point, but be prepared to either replace the Time Machine disk with another one, or to let Time Machine delete older files when necessary.

While Time Machine is a good solution for temporary storage of backups and a great way to restore files that have been thrown away, lost, or changed, it isn't a final solution for creating permanent archives of your files. If you plan to keep using the same backup disk and let Time Machine delete the oldest files to make room for new backups, be sure to use other backup methods to create permanent backups of important files and folders (burn files to CDs or DVDs, copy items to your .Mac iDisk, or copy items to other external drives). Remember, it's safest to create *multiple* backups of items that you absolutely cannot afford to lose, and be sure to store those multiple copies in several different place—if your office burns down or floods, it won't matter if you had sixteen backups in that office, they're all gone.

What kind of disk to use as backup

You must use a disk for Time Machine that is separate from the hard disk you work on. An extra internal hard disk is great, and peripheral hard disks work fine too. The disk needs to be big enough to backup the drive it's assigned to. For best results, use a disk dedicated only to Time Machine backups. If you use this backup drive to store other files, you lose that storage space for Time Machine.

Both FireWire and USB disks work with Time Machine, including most disks that might be available on your local network. Disks used for Time Machine backups must be formatted as Mac OS Extended (journaled), and have Access Control Lists (ACLs) enabled. Time Machine will erase and reformat the disk if necessary.

Create a Time Machine Backup

It's very easy to start the process. Make sure you have an appropriate disk installed.

To set up Time Machine backups:

1   Once you have an extra **internal** hard disk installed *or* you've connected an empty **external** hard disk, open the Time Machine system preferences: Either click its icon in the Dock, then click the button to "Open Time Machine Prefs," *or* go to the Apple menu, choose "Preferences...," and click on "Time Machine."

2   Click the "Choose Backup Disk..." button. You'll get a list of possible drives that can be used; choose one and click "Use for Backup."

   If you're using an external disk, Time Machine will probably automatically ask if you want to use that disk for backup.

3   Once a backup disk has been assigned, Time Machine automatically switches itself ON and displays information about that disk, including when the first backup will start.

4   Click the Options button to display a sheet (shown on the next page) in which you can designate items you want to *exclude* from Time Machine backups.

See the next page.

—continued

5 To add items to the "Do not back up" list, click the plus (**+**) button, circled below.

Another sheet slides down from the title bar, covering up the one shown below. Select the items (drives, volumes, files, or folders) that you do NOT want Time Machine to back up. Click the "Exclude" button. This returns you to the first sheet, shown below.

To remove items from this list so that Time Machine WILL back them up, select them and click the minus (**−**) button from the sheet shown below.

Choose to receive a warning when Time Machine needs to start deleting the oldest backups.

6 Click "Done."

Time Machine makes an initial backup that includes everything on your computer (below). This backup can be time consuming, depending on how many folders, files, and applications are on your Mac. Subsequent backups are faster since only changed files are backed up.

To stop a backup, click the gray **X.** *Or* slide the ON button to OFF.

Backup failed?

If a Time Machine message tells you the latest backup failed (see below), click that red info button (*i*) for an explanation. The disk may be too small or perhaps you're out of room on the chosen disk.

To switch to another disk, click the "Change Disk..." button, then select another connected disk.

If Time Machine alerts you that the new disk must be erased (far below), click "Erase." This will of course destroy everything that's already on that disk! If you don't want to lose information on that particular disk, connect another hard disk and click "Choose Another Disk."

How to Use Time Machine

Once you've got Time Machine all set up, as explained on the previous pages, there are several different ways to use it to find earlier versions of files that have changed or to find missing files.

To find and restore a file:

1   On your Desktop, single-click a file or folder in a Finder window to select it.

2   Click the Time Machine icon in the Dock. The Time Machine universe is revealed in the background. It shows the current Finder window in the foreground, with earlier versions of that same window receding into the recent (or distant) past. The selected file is prominently displayed in Cover View and is also shown highlighted in the List View in the bottom section.

Notice that the bar at the bottom of the star field universe is labeled "Today (Now)." In other words, any files shown or accessed through this particular window are the most current versions.

3   To go back in time and find *previous* versions of the selected file, click the back-in-time arrow (called out, below). The star field zooms back in time through the floating windows until it reaches a window where an earlier version of the selected file exists.

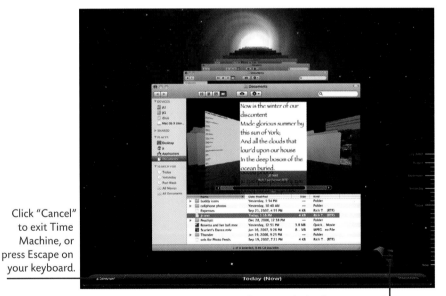

Click "Cancel" to exit Time Machine, or press Escape on your keyboard.

These are the back-in-time and forward-in-time arrows.

The file is selected and displayed, as shown below. Notice that the bar at the bottom of the window now says "Today at 8:50 AM," which is about twelve hours earlier than my current time. And you can see that the file had different formatting in this earlier version.

If this isn't the version of the file you're looking for, click the back-in-time arrow again to find earlier versions. *Or* drag your pointer over the timeline on the right edge of the screen and select a backup time or date.

4   **To restore the version of the file** you want, first make sure it's selected. Then click the "Restore" button on the right side of the bar at the bottom.

To go directly to a specific backup date or time, click in this timeline.

5   A message asks if you want to keep the original version of the file (instead of the backup), keep both files, *or* replace the original with the backup version.

If you choose "Keep Both," a restored copy of the backed-up file is made and put in its original location on your computer. The word "original" is added to the original file's name (right).

Do a Spotlight Search in Time Machine

When you use Spotlight to search for items on your computer, the search naturally takes place in the "Now" time frame; in other words, it finds files in their current versions. But if you've lost or deleted files, Time Machine can zoom into the past and find the files in the various states in which they were saved.

Search, then switch to Time Machine:

1   Start a Spotlight search in the Finder (see Lesson 19). If Spotlight doesn't find the item you're looking for, click the Time Machine icon in the Dock.

    The Time Machine universe appears, with Finder windows receding into the past. The window in the foreground is labeled "Today (Now)." Your search term is in the Spotlight search field, circled below.

2   Click the back-in-time arrow. Time Machine zooms back in time until it finds the item. To look for an even earlier version of the item, click the back-in-time arrow again, *or* click in the timeline along the right edge of the screen. Notice that the time label in the bar at the bottom of the screen shows when the *selected* item was backed up.

3   When you find the item you want, click "Restore" on the right side of the bar at the bottom of the Time Machine screen.

You can also go straight to Time Machine (click Time Machine in the Dock) and initiate a Spotlight search—enter a search term in the foreground search field.

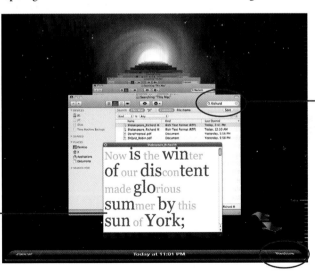

To show a Quick Look of the item, make sure the item is highlighted, then tap the Spacebar.

To close the Quick Look preview, tap the Spacebar again, or click the Close button in the top-left corner of the Quick Look window.

Enter a search term here in this Finder window search field.

Tech Stuff

21

GOALS

Troubleshoot your
network settings

Create a new connection

Use the Network
Diagnostics tool

Connect two or
more Macs

Share files on a network

Send files to anyone
through Bonjour or iChat

Share the screen of
another computer on the
network or in the world

Get Connected and Share Files

On a Mac, you have various ways to connect to the Internet. You might have a dial-up account that goes through your phone line, a cable modem, a DSL modem, a wireless connection, an Ethernet office connection that plugs into a broadband setup, or some other arrangement.

And you have various ways to connect your Macs together in a home or office. Once your computers are on a local network, you can transfer files between them and even access your own Mac from another computer.

The feature that most amazes me is screen sharing, where you can connect to someone else's computer and actually see her screen and use her computer!

How your Mac Connects to the Internet

When you first turned on your Mac and walked through the setup process, you probably filled in the information for your Internet connection. The Network preferences is where your Mac stored that information and where you can change it, adjust it, or troubleshoot it.

The Network preferences lists all of the ways that your Mac might be connected and displays the current status of each option. You can configure all interfaces for all your possible connections from this one window.

Network

To open the Network preferences, go to the Apple menu and choose "System Preferences...." Single-click the "Network" icon.

When you first open the window, it probably looks something like the one below, showing you the status of any possible connections your Mac might have access to.

These are the available "network port configurations" on your Mac.

This pane instantly shows you how you are connected to the Internet and to the other computers in your office.

Change the order in which your Mac looks for an open connection; see the next page.

Check the port configurations

You might have several options for connecting. For instance, your Mac recognizes a modem port, if you have one (whether or not you use it), and it might find a wireless card and an Ethernet port. Every possibility it finds is listed in the Network preferences, in that pane on the left side.

As you see on the opposite page, you can click the Activity button (shown circled) and choose to "Set Service Order...." This is the first place I go if there is a connection problem because the Mac goes down this list in order and chooses the first interface that works. **If you're having problems making a connection,** make sure your *preferred* connection is at the top of the list—just drag it to the top. Click OK, then click the "Apply" button to force the change.

Choose the order in which you want your Mac to try to connect. Drag these services into your preferred order.

Establish a new connection

If you didn't set up your Internet connection when you first installed Leopard or turned on your brand-new Mac, you can always do it in this Network preferences pane. Just click the button (circled above), "Assist me...." A sheet drops down from the title bar (as shown on page 367). In that sheet, click the button labeled "Assistant...." It will walk you through the process.

Troubleshoot your Internet Connection

If your connection doesn't work when you first turn on your Mac, perhaps the information you entered in the setup process wasn't correct. Or if you changed Internet Service Providers or changed your connection process, you might need to change the information. Now, most of the information is supplied automatically, but if your provider says you need to change a setting, this is where you'll do it. There is also a little trick you can do here that sometimes kicks things into gear.

Network

1   From the Apple menu, choose "System Preferences…," then click the "Network" icon.

2   In the left-hand pane, you can instantly tell whether or not your Mac thinks your connection is working. (Sometimes the Mac swears it's working, but it isn't and you know it.) Choose the connection that you need to fix or change.

You can always click the Revert button, which will restore the settings to how they were before you started messing around.

3   First, use the technique on the previous two pages to make sure the connection you want to choose is the first one in the list. Click "Apply." Wait a minute or two and see if your browser will connect to the Internet. If not . . .

4   This trick often works if all the settings are correct and there's no major problem with your modem box or router (if you have one): Change any setting; for instance, if you see "Using DHCP," change it to "Manually." Then immediately switch it back. This makes the "Apply" button available. Click the Apply button. Sometimes all it needs is a kick in the pants to make it take effect.

5 If you think the settings need to change, do so here; you need to click the "Advanced..." button to get to the rest of the settings. If you're not sure what the appropriate settings are, you have two choices:

a Call your **ISP** (Internet Service Provider) and ask them what to enter in which panes. Your ISP is the company to whom you pay the monthly fee for your connection to the Internet. Although these windows look scary, there are only two or three settings you need. If you use cable or DSL with "DHCP," it probably sets it up for you automatically. Click "Apply."

To check, open Safari and see if it goes to a web page. If it does, you're done.

b Use the **Network Diagnostics tool,** as described in the following steps. This tool automatically appears when your connection goes down, but you can also call on it here whenever you need it.

6 Click the "Assist me..." button at the bottom of the Network pane. This drops down a sheet from the title bar, as shown below. For troubleshooting help, click the "Diagnostics..." button.

Click the "Assistant..." button if you want to create a **new** connection.

7 The diagnostics tool will check all the relevant settings on your Mac and ask you simple questions. If it can't fix the problem, it will at least pinpoint it so you can call your ISP with the specific issue.

Use the AirPort Admin Utility

If your connection is through an AirPort wireless setup, use the AirPort Setup Assistant and the AirPort Admin Utility to see if you can figure out what's wrong. You'll find those tools in the Utilities folder, which is inside the Applications folder. Use the same trick as on the previous page—make a change that you don't need, immediately switch back to the one you know is correct, then click the "Apply" button.

Unplug everything and reboot

Your modem box, whether it's a dial-up, cable, or DSL, usually has a tiny **reset button.** It's so tiny you need to poke it with a pin. That can sometimes get things going again.

If not, do the unplug routine (I have to assume you're got all the wires in the right places). If you have a number of devices in your system, such as a switch, a router, and a modem box, unplug the items starting with the smallest one, the dumbest one. That would be the switch, if you have one. Next the router (which might be your AirPort). Last unplug the modem itself. Let everything sit for at least a minute or two. It's not a bad idea to shut down your Mac as well.

Then plug everything back in again in the opposite order—start with the most important item first, the modem box. Let it get going and make sure all the lights are green. If the problem is in your modem box, call your provider.

Then plug in the router, if you're using one, and let it get going. Then the switch. Let everything get running, then turn your Mac back on. And pray.

Sometimes we go through all this and give up. Shortly thereafter it starts working again. Sheesh.

Talk to your ISP; check your cables

If everything seems okay on your end and you still can't get connected to the Internet, call a friend who uses the same ISP and see if she is connected (actually, we do this first). If her connection is down as well, then just let go and wait until they fix it. But if her connection is working, call the ISP. They can check your modem from their office and help pinpoint the cause. Also check your cables—they might have wiggled loose or one might have gone bad. They do that sometimes. If you're setting it up for the first time and using Ethernet cables, make sure they're the right kind; see page 372.

Troubleshoot your Mail Account

If you have problems getting your email, there are several things you can do. Make sure your Internet connection is working, of course (check by making sure your browser can get to the Internet.) Then check your account information in Mail (go to the Mail menu, choose "Preferences," and click the "Accounts" tab):

The **Description** is anything that will tell you which account this is.

The **Email Address** and **Full Name** describe your mail to those you send it to so they know who it's coming from.

- The **Incoming Mail Server** is information that you have to get from whoever hosts that particular email account. I have more than a dozen email accounts, not one of which is with my ISP. So I need to get the Incoming Mail Server of each of the hosts where I have the email *coming from.* Typically it's *mail. domain.com* or *pop.domain.com.* And as I mentioned in the Mail lesson, some providers don't allow you to get your email through a mail application like this; see page 75.

- Keep in mind that some ISPs have a different **User Name** and **Password** *for your account with them* than the user name and password to get your email. This is especially true if you've had the account for a long time. If your email account is not with your ISP, then of course the account information in your Mail window is definitely not the same as for your ISP. You might have to check their web site or call your email host and ask what to enter here.

—continued

- The **Outgoing Mail Server (SMTP)** is always from your ISP, no matter where your email account is located. Well, there are exceptions, like you *can* use a mac.com SMTP, but in general, you are always assured of being able to *send mail out* if you use your ISP's SMTP. If you don't know what the SMTP is, call and ask them or check their web site—it should be listed. For all fifteen of my email accounts from a variety of servers, I use the same Comcast SMTP because that's who connects me to the Internet.

  To change your SMTP setting, click on the SMTP menu and choose "Edit Server List...." Click the **+** button to add a server. Double-click the blue bar to add the SMTP name. Make sure that is the selected server, then click OK.

  Some cheesy companies will not give you an SMTP address. For instance, if you get a Qwest broadband account here in New Mexico, you'll discover they are in cahoots with Microsoft and provide no SMTP unless you pay an extra fee. You cannot use the Mail application—you are forced to go to the MSN web site and do all mail online (where Microsoft can keep track of you). Change providers.

Reminder: where to get the information

Your email provider's web site should include the information for the *incoming* mail server, user name, and password. Your ISP's web site should provide the SMTP (*outgoing* mail server) information.

If you have a **free webmail account** like Yahoo or Hotmail (which is Microsoft), you might not be able to set up Mail to check your mail. However, the free services often have a paid option as well, and with the paid service you can usually get the specs to set up your account in the Mail program. (But if you have to pay for it, why not get a .Mac account?) Check this wonderful web site for details on how to set up most webmail accounts to appear in Mail: www.EmailAddressManager.com.

Use the Mail Connection Doctor

If your account information is correct but email still isn't working, check this utility: In Mail, go to the Window menu and choose "Connection Doctor." You'll get the window shown below; it will automatically check your accounts. If it finds a problem, the dot is red; depending on the problem, you may be able to click the "Assist me..." button to help pinpoint the issue further.

In this case, I had the wrong information in the Accounts pane.

Share Files on a Local Network

File sharing on a local network is so great—as Apple says, your Mac just "discovers" other Macs. But it can't discover them unless the computers are connected in some way. So first, a wee bit about networking.

Simple networking

The Macs you want to share files between must be **networked** together—you must have some sort of cable connecting them to each other or both to the same printer, or AirPort cards installed so they can connect to each other wirelessly.

Networking can get very complex and specialized! I am only going to explain the simplest method to get a couple of Macs talking to each other.

Ethernet cables

You might have to buy Ethernet cables.

- If the cables are going from the computer into a hub, router, or switcher, or into a cable or DSL modem, you need **straight-through cables**—not crossover. Straight-through cables are the most common.
- If the cables go directly from computer to computer (or any two Ethernet devices, like a Mac to a printer), you need **crossover cables** (see below).

To tell if an Ethernet cable is crossover or not, hold both ends up, facing the same direction, with the locking clips facing up. Look at the colored wires coming through the end.

- A straight-through cable has the colored wires in **exactly the same order.**
- A crossover cable does **not** have the colored wires in the same order.

Just two computers?

Two computers can be connected with one crossover Ethernet cable **or** a FireWire cable for easy and instant file sharing on two working Macs.

If you have one Mac that is having trouble and you want to grab files off of it onto a working machine, use a FireWire cable and Target Disk Mode, as explained on page 412. Target Disk Mode uses the target computer as a hard disk, without having to get its operating system working.

What else you need

If you have a number of machines in your office, you will need something called a **switch** or **Ethernet hub** that can connect all of your machines, including your modem. The switch/hub will have a number of Ethernet ports; you connect each Mac *to that box* with straight (not crossover) Ethernet cables. (If you want to share printers, see pages 299–301; it's easy once you have your network working.)

If you have several computers in your office, a broadband connection, and all your Macs get on the Internet at the same time, you're probably using a **router**—you're already set up for networking. An AirPort base station can function as a router.

If the router doesn't have enough ports for the items in your office, buy the small **hub** or **switch** mentioned above and connect the router to it with an Ethernet cable.

Peer-to-peer network

This simple network in a small office is called a **peer-to-peer network,** where every computer is considered a "server," which is a computer that can "serve" files to others. This is different from a client-server network in a large corporation, where lots of computers connect to one huge, main server and everyone gets files from that main server, rather than from each other's computers.

Turn on Personal File Sharing

Now that your computers are connected, you need to tell them it's okay to share files. On each Mac, go to the Apple menu and choose "System Preferences...." Click the "Sharing" icon. Put a checkmark in "File Sharing."

Give each Mac a name that clearly identifies it.

This is the name that other computers will see when networking.

Connect to Another Mac

Once the Macs are connected in some way and you've turned on File Sharing in the Sharing preferences (as explained on the previous pages), you're ready to connect.

Make sure you are in the Finder (single-click on any blank space on the Desktop). Then follow *either* Process **A** or **B**.

Process A, directly through the Finder window:

1   Open any Finder window. Click the Column View icon (circled below).

2   In the Sidebar, if your "SHARED" group is not visible, click its triangle to display the other computers on the network.

3   Single-click the name of the computer you want to connect to.

You are automatically connected as a Guest. What you see in the window above is the Home folder of another computer, and that's actually his Public folder in the second column. As a Guest, that's all you have access to. You can take copies of any folder in the Public folder, and you can put files into his Drop Box.

4   To access the rest of this other computer, you need to know its name and password (the same name and password that the Admin uses to log in with). If you have them, click the "Connect As…" button and log in.

If there is more than one volume on that other computer, you can Command-click on any of them that you want access to.

Now the tricky thing is to keep straight which machine you're working on or which machine you are viewing in a window! It's a good idea to stay in Column View so you can always see where a folder originates.

Process B, through the Go menu:

1 From the Go menu, choose "Connect to Server...." The little window shown below appears.

If you know the name of the Mac you want to connect to (as shown in the Sharing pane of the *other* Mac; see page 373), type it in the "Server Address" field, with ".local" after its name.

Or, what usually works more consistently, enter the afp:// number that you see circled on page 373.

2 Click the "Connect" button. You'll see this window:

To connect as a **Guest,** you don't need a name and password; see page 377.

To connect as a **Registered User** so you will have access to the whole computer, you need to enter a name and password. **Important!** Even though this window shows up with *your* name in the field, it doesn't want *your* name and password! It's asking for the name (long or short) and password *of the computer you're trying to connect to!* Guess how long it took me to figure *that* out.

3 Enter the name and password of the other computer, then click "Connect."

—continued

4 The next window that appears lists the hard disk, the Home folder, and any partitions or other hard disks attached to the other Mac. Double-click the name of the one you want to connect to.

To have access to more than one of the partitions, hold down the Command key and click on as many as you want to connect to, then let go of the Command key and click OK. You can also repeat this entire process if you decide later you need to connect to another volume.

5 On the Desktop of the computer you're working on, you'll see a network icon for each volume you're connected to, shown below-left. Double-click that icon to open a window to that drive, shown below-right.

It's not an easy task to keep track of which windows are on which machine since they all have the same names! Don't *open* any applications or documents from the window of the other Mac because you will actually be working on the other machine at that point, which might affect the person using it. It's best to drag the necessary documents to your own computer before you open them.

Connect as a Guest

Follow Step 1 on page 375. When you get to that window shown in Step 2, click the "Guest" button. Then click "Connect."

The Mac opens the **Public folder** of the computer you are connecting to, shown below. The only things you will have access to on the other computer are the files that user has put in her Public folder for you. The only place you can move documents *to* on the connected Mac is the Drop Box, shown below.

Create Favorite servers

In the "Connect to Server" window (choose it from the Go menu at the Finder), type the name you want to connect to. Click the **+** button to add that server to your favorites in the list below. Now you can just double-click on a server name to connect to it.

Bonjour–Share Files Locally

Once your Mac is on a network of computers running OS X, version 10.2 or later, you can send files back and forth to everyone through Bonjour, which is part of iChat (in OS X versions earlier than Tiger 10.4, it's called Rendezvous, not Bonjour). The iChat icon should be in your Dock; if not, it's in your Applications folder. See Lesson 9 for details about iChat and Bonjour.

If you didn't **turn on Bonjour** the first time you opened iChat, you can do it in the iChat preferences, in the Accounts pane:

But you can also turn it on with this shortcut:

1   Open iChat.

2   From the Window menu, choose "Bonjour List" (or press Command 2).
    If you're not already logged in, it will ask if you want to start it up.

3   Click "Login."

And now the Bonjour List window is open as well, as shown on the next page.

Send a file to someone on the network

This is so easy it will boggle your mind.

1   First open the Bonjour window, if it isn't already: Open iChat, then press Command 2 (or from the Window menu, choose "Bonjour List").

2   Now drag a file and drop it on someone's name in that list. That person will get a message that she has an incoming file.

3   She clicks once on that message, then she has a choice to "Decline," in which case the message will disappear, or "Save File," which downloads the file to the Downloads folder.

Here's another way to send a file (this also works in iChat). Just open a chat with someone in either Bonjour or your Buddy List (double-click a *name*, not a phone or camera icon, to open a text chat). Drop a file in the text field and hit Return.

What's even more amazing is the screen sharing feature through iChat and Bonjour, as explained on the following pages.

> **TIP** —— If you need to share files on a local network regularly, you can drag a folder from another computer and put it on your computer and even in your Sidebar. Then you can move and save files directly into that folder on the other computer. You don't even have to go through the connection process—as soon as you put something in that folder, it acts as an alias and makes the connection.

Screen Sharing

Screen Sharing enables you to share not only your screen but your entire computer either through your Finder on the local network, or through iChat with a buddy anywhere in the world. Through iChat, you can choose to either share your own screen (and computer) or share the buddy's screen (and computer).

This is great for anyone who has experienced the frustration of trying to give Mac support and instruction over the phone or through email. Now you can just activate Screen Sharing and watch as you give instructions. Or control the buddy's computer while she watches and listens. When Screen Sharing is activated through iChat, it automatically starts an audio chat so you can discuss whatever matter is at hand.

> You can screen share over a *local* network using Bonjour or the Go menu; if the other user is running 10.4 Tiger, tell him to go to his Sharing preferences and turn on "Apple Remote Desktop."

> You can use Screen Sharing over the *Internet* through iChat; both computers need to be running Mac OS 10.5 Leopard.

Set up screen sharing

Before you start Screen Sharing, make sure both computers have "Screen Sharing" selected in the Sharing pane of System Preferences:

1   From the Apple menu, choose "Preferences…." Click the "Sharing" icon.

2   Put a checkmark in the option called "Screen Sharing"; see the callout on the opposite page.

3   If you have other users on the network, you can choose to allow only certain ones: Check the button, "Only these users," then click the **+** button to add the ones you want.

4   Close the preferences and carry on.

Check the network for local screen sharing options

Below is the simplest and fastest way to connect to another monitor in your home/office to screen share and access the computer.

1 In your Sharing group, select another computer running Leopard on the network.

2 You will probably see a "Share Screen…" button, as shown here. Click it, and a window immediately opens displaying the other computer. Amazing.

3 To stop screen sharing, close the window that the other computer is in.

Now, if you don't see the "Screen Sharing…" button, as shown above, don't despair. The process on the following page works very well.

Screen Share locally through the Go menu

This method is a quick and easy way to get to another user's screen who is on the same network. You can also use Bonjour, which looks a little different, as explained on the following pages. Using Bonjour, you'll be able to talk to each other as well.

1 First make sure you get the vnc address from the computer you want to connect to. This address appears in the Sharing preferences pane when you turn on Screen Sharing—you can see it circled on the previous page.

2 At the Finder, go to the Go menu and choose "Connect to Server...." You'll get the window shown below.

3 Type in the vnc address as shown below. Hit the "Connect" button.

4 A window will appear on your Mac and inside that window is the other person's entire computer! You can open his iTunes and play a song for him, or open Sticky notes and leave a message. It's freaky.

5 **To turn off screen sharing,** close the window of the other computer.

If you need to go to this computer often, click the **+** button to make the address a favorite. It will appear in this pane under "Favorite Servers" whenever you open this window.

Screen Share globally through Bonjour and iChat

Of course, the buddy whose screen you want to share must have first turned on Screen Sharing, as explained on the previous pages.

1 **To screen share through iChat,** open either your Buddy List to screen share with someone over the Internet, or open your Bonjour List to screen share with someone on your local network.

2 You can tell which buddies have turned on Screen Sharing: When you click a name in the list, the Screen Sharing button at the bottom of the Buddy List or Bonjour List is black (instead of gray) for those who have turned it on.

  This is the Screen Sharing button.

3 Click a buddy's name. Click that Screen Sharing button and choose "Share My Screen…" or "Share (Buddy Name's) Screen…."

In this example, the user chooses to share his own screen with his buddy instead of sharing his buddy's screen.

4 When you receive and accept the invitation to share someone's screen, the other (remote) screen (the flower Desktop in the example) appears full-size on your screen, while your own Desktop appears as a miniature. When you mouse over the miniature screen, a "Switch to My Computer" message pops up.

To enlarge your own Desktop to full-size and miniaturize the remote screen, click anywhere on the miniature screen. Meanwhile, the buddy who initiated Screen Sharing doesn't see any change on his own screen, even though you can now control his computer, grab files, open applications, or do anything he can do.

To copy files between computers: Simply drag a file from one screen to the other. If the file you want is on the miniature screen, just click on the miniature screen and it will become large enough to find the file you need. Drag it to the [now] miniature other screen; as you drag, hover over the miniature screen for a few seconds until it enlarges to full-size, then drop the file wherever you want to place it.

To end a Screen Sharing session: Click the circle-**x** in the top-left corner of the miniaturized screen. **Or** go to the iChat icon in the menu bar and choose "End Screen Sharing."

Disconnect

Disconnect from any connected servers in the same way you disconnect from any other hard disk.

- Click the Eject symbol next to the server name in the Sidebar.

- **Or** if the server is visible on the Desktop, drag its icon to the Trash.

- **Or** select the server icon. Go to the File menu and choose "Eject."

- **Or** select the server icon and press Command E for Eject.

- **Or** Control-click on a server icon to get the contextual menu; choose "Eject *'disk'*."

```
         Open
rob      Eject "robin"

         Get Info
         Duplicate
         Make Alias

         Copy "robin"

         Clean Up Selection

         Label:
         ×  ▪ ▪ ▫ ▫ ▫ ▪ ▪

         More                    ▶
```

To hide or show the servers on the Desktop:

1 At the Finder, go to the Finder menu and choose "Preferences...."

2 Click the "General" tab, if it isn't already selected.

3 Check or uncheck the box to show "Connected servers." When it's unchecked, you won't see the server icons on the Desktop, but they will all be accessible in the Sidebar.

4 However, you can go to the Sidebar pane in those same preferences, (click the "Sidebar" icon in the toolbar) and choose to take server icons out the Sidebar and leave them on the Desktop.

22

GOALS

Know what to do and
what information to have
on hand before you install

Understand whether
to upgrade, archive,
or clean install

Customize the installation

Go through the
setup process

Become familiar with the
utilities available from
the startup disk

Upgrade your Mac and Migrate your Files

You may have just gotten a brand-new Mac with Leopard already installed, in which case you can skip this chapter altogether, unless you need to learn about transferring your files from an old machine to your new one.

If you just got a new DVD with the Leopard installation, Mac OS X version 10.5, then you have a few choices to make before you upgrade. This chapter explains the choices you will need to make along the way and walks you through the process.

Remember, before you do anything serious like upgrade your operating system, first back up your important files. The easiest thing to do is drag your entire hard disk onto a FireWire hard disk. Always create at least two backups and store them in a different places—it won't do any good if all your important backups are in the same office that gets burglarized or flooded!

The Installation Process

Of course you need the DVD installation disk from Apple to start the process. Put the DVD in. This is what you'll see:

I strongly suggest you read the file called "Welcome to Leopard." And the file called "Read Before You Install" has up-to-date technical details that I haven't been able to include here. For instance, it might be good to know that you can't upgrade from Mac OS X 10.2.8 or earlier (you can replace, but not upgrade).

It's always a good idea to read the "Read Me" files before you do something like install a brand-new operating system that can potentially destroy everything on your Mac. So I suggest you read all those files. In fact, I suggest you **print them** before you start to install so you can have them to refer to.

Write down the specifications for your Internet connections and email accounts. Better yet, make a screen shot of the dialog boxes with their info so you can recreate it. To make a screen shot of the entire screen (with your specifications displayed), press Command Shift 3. Save those files (named Picture1.png, Picture2.png, etc.) onto another disk. If you have a .Mac account, sync everything to the .Mac server.

If you think your machine is capable and ready **to start the installation process,** double-click the file "Install Mac OS X." This will restart your Mac and make it boot up with the install disc. If you are upgrading a Mac running some version of OS X, you will be asked for the Administrator name and password.

Or you could do this: Insert the DVD into your Mac. Then **restart and hold down the C key,** which will force the Mac to boot from the DVD.

Welcome to the Installer

The first thing you will be asked to do is choose the language in which you want to see all the menus and dialog boxes. Choose it and then click the button to continue.

Become familiar with this first Installer screen because you may need to come back here again someday. Check out the Utilities menu and all the options available there. This is a wonderfully useful troubleshooting stop—when things go really wrong with your Mac, restart from the Installer DVD and use one of these utilities. They are described in a little more detail on pages 396–397.

If you need to quit

If you decide you need to quit the installation process at this point—*after* you restart with the disc but *before* you actually click the "Install" button—you can do so (do not quit once you start the installation process!):

> From the Installer menu next to the Apple icon in the menu bar, choose "Quit Installer." A dialog box appears with buttons labeled "Restart," "Startup Disk," and "Cancel." Read the following before you make your choice.

Once you quit, your Mac will restart with the install disc again because it always looks first in a disc drive to see if it can find an operating system. So you need to force the DVD to restart from the internal hard disk on your Mac. You can do either of the following:

- Choose "Restart." As soon as you hear the bong, hold the mouse button down *and keep it down.* (On a laptop, hold down the bar beneath the track pad.) This forces a CD or DVD to pop out, at which point you can let go of the mouse button. Without the disc, your Mac will start as usual.
- **Or** choose "Startup Disk" before you restart. You will see at least two options to choose from—the internal hard disk that you've been using, or the DVD that is currently in the drive. Choose your hard disk and click "Restart."

If you absolutely *must* quit the installer while it's running, understand that all the files on your hard disk will have already been destroyed.

Choose an installation option

When you click the "Continue" button in the Installer screen, you will be asked (as usual) to agree to the software license agreement. If you don't, you can't install the operating system.

Once you agree, you see a screen where you can choose the hard disk on which to install Leopard. If you have more than one choice, your Mac will usually choose the best one, but make sure it's the one you want. It must be an internal hard disk.

This screen has a **very important button!** Click the **Options...** button! You have several options for the installation process.

1   Upgrade Mac OS X *or* Install OS X for the first time

If your Mac is running an earlier version of OS X, you can choose to **upgrade;** the installer will **replace** your earlier version with this new one, Leopard. Your files, applications, preferences, and everything else will not be touched. Essentially, the next time you start your Mac it will look just the same, but will be running the new system with the added features.

If you've never installed any version of OS X before, the option you have is to install it for the first time. If your hard disk is currently running Mac OS 9, that operating system will be left intact—you'll now have both.

2a   Archive and Install

If you choose this option, the Installer will save your existing operating system and its related files into a folder called "Previous System Folder." Then it will proceed to install a brand new operating system, but all of your own documents and applications and files will be left intact in case you need to copy them over later. You will not be able to start up your Mac from the "Previous System Folder."

This is a good choice if you're not sure about replacing your previous operating system. For instance, maybe you're not sure if you have copies of all the fonts in the various font folders or preferences that you need for different applications. By leaving the "Previous System Folder" on your Desktop, you can work in the new system for a while until you're sure you haven't forgotten anything important. Eventually, delete the "Previous System Folder" because it takes up a heck of a lot of room on your hard disk.

2b Preserve Users and Network Settings

Once you choose to "Archive and Install," another option is available *if your previous operating system was OS X:* **Preserve Users and Network Settings.** If you created multiple users on your Mac, this option will save them so everyone's Home folders and preferences will be intact.

Even if you have no extra users on your Mac, this option is still handy because you won't have to go through the Setup Assistant during the installation process—the Mac will pick up your Internet settings and automatically apply them. By the time you see your new screen, you will be connected to the Internet as usual.

3a Erase and Install

If you have backups of all your important files and applications, you can choose *to completely erase your hard disk* and install a brand-new version of the operating system instead of updating the old one. This is called a "clean install." This is particularly great, as I mentioned, if your Mac is starting to act a little peculiar and you'd like to just start over, fresh and clean.

Of course, if you do a clean install, **you will destroy every single thing on your entire hard disk!** So make sure you have backups of anything you want to keep. My favorite method these days for temporary backups is a little FireWire drive. I have one right now from SmartDisk.com, a little FireLite that fits in a shirt pocket, plugs into the FireWire port on the back of my flat-screen monitor, and holds 40 gigabytes. I love it.

3b Format disk as

Once you choose to "Erase and Install," your Mac asks how you want to format (reformat, actually) the hard disk. Your two options are "Mac OS Extended (Journaled)," which is most likely what you want, or "UNIX File System." If you want the UNIX File System, I highly doubt that you are reading this book. Trust your Mac that it is correct in already choosing Mac OS Extended for you.

Make your choice of installation option, and then click the OK button. The "Destination" screen confirms the option you just made, so click the "Continue" button.

Customize your installation

The next screen you see is the "Easy Install." But you *can* customize your installation, which lets you delete unnecessary printer driver files and language files. This can be useful if you don't have a lot of room on your hard disk (which is unlikely). If you need *lots* more room, this won't help, but if you're worried about space, try it.

Now, you can only customize this **if you did not choose to upgrade!** That is, you can only customize the installation if you previously choose to "Archive and Install" or "Erase and Install."

If you chose one of those options, or if the Installer tells you there is not enough room on your hard disk to install, click the button to "Customize."

- In the list that appears, check the "Languages" checkbox. This displays all the foreign languages your Mac is going to install in case you ever want them. If you feel pretty confident you're not going to be needing a number of those languages in the near future, uncheck their boxes.

- Then check the "Printer Drivers" box. You can safely uncheck the drivers for printers you've never heard of. If you ever need a driver for a printer you've unchecked, you can always find it on that vendor's web site.

Install!

Now you're ready to actually start installing. Click the "Install" button to continue. Actually, this button will say "Upgrade" if you chose to upgrade the previous system.

Customize the Setup Assistant

After your Mac installs the operating system, but before it takes you to your Desktop, you will go through the Setup Assistant. Well, as I mentioned on page 391, you will *skip* the Setup Assistant if you chose the options to "Archive and Install" and then "Preserve Users and Network Settings."

The Setup Assistant asks for information that will get you connected to the Internet and make sure the email program, Mail, can get your email for you.

VoiceOver option

During the Setup Assistant, one of the options you'll see is **VoiceOver.** This is part of the enhanced Universal Access capabilities of Mac OS X. VoiceOver provides a spoken user interface (English only), which means the *computer* speaks to the *user* and describes what is going on. People with visual impairments can access just about everything on the Mac using the keyboard instead of the mouse. It's quite amazing.

In this introductory process, VoiceOver walks a user through keyboard practice, moving around the screen using the keyboard, typing in text fields, as well as selecting items in pop-up menus, scrolling lists, and control panes.

If you choose not to practice VoiceOver at this point, you can always do it later at your leisure. See the VoiceOver preferences.

The welcome screen

Most of the next few screens are self-explanatory—choose your language, the time zone, etc.

Migration Assistant

You will be asked if you want to **transfer your files** from another, separate Mac or from a separate partition on the same Mac. This feature, called **migrating,** transfers over most of the files from your old machine to your new one. You can either follow the simple, on-screen directions and migrate your files right now. **Or** you can skip to page 397 and read about migrating before you do it. **Or** you can skip the entire process right now and do it later at your leisure, using the Migration Assistant (it's in the Utilities folder, which is in the Applications folder.

The network setup

You will be asked how you connect to the Internet. If you know how you connect and you know all the pertinent data that needs to be entered (it's not much), follow the on-screen directions. If you run across information you don't know, call your Internet Service Provider (the one you pay your monthly connection fee to) and ask them what to enter.

If you have a .Mac account, all you need to enter is your email address and password and the Mac sets up everything for you instantly.

If you don't know the information at the moment, **you can skip this part** of the process altogether. You can always set your connection up later; it only takes a few minutes. If you want to do it later, check the button, "My computer does not connect to the Internet."

If you want to set it up now, select your connection method and then follow the directions. If you run across places where you need to enter information and you don't know the information, call your ISP or click "Continue." Either it will work without that particular information, or you can fill it in later (see Lesson 21 for details on filling it in later).

Your Apple ID

You will be asked to enter your Apple ID. If you have a .Mac account, your email address and password is considered your Apple ID. Use your entire .Mac email address, including your member name, the @ symbol, and "mac.com."

If you've ever bought songs on iTunes or photos from iPhoto, you have an Apple ID.

If you do not have a .Mac account or any other Apple ID that you know of, leave the fields blank and click the "Continue" button.

Other details

There are a few more screens asking for information from you, like personal details and where you will use this computer. It's easy.

Create your account

This is **very important!** What you are creating here is your **Administrator account** as the primary user, as well as your **Administrator password.** Write down this password because your Mac will not let you install new software or upgrades or make specific system changes unless you can provide this password. The hint you provide is important, also—if you forget your password and enter the wrong one three times, this hint will appear on the screen.

You can leave the password field blank if you have no worries about anyone ever using or stealing your Mac. But I suggest you write down that you left it blank; it is just as easy to forget that you did *not* enter a password as it is to forget which one you used. You might spend hours trying all kinds of different passwords only to finally realize you didn't give it one and all you needed to do was hit the Return key. Guess how I know this.

Make sure the **short name** is something you want to keep because you will never be able to change it. When asked for your Administrator name, you can usually use either the long name or this short name.

Done!

It takes just another minute or two to finish it up. Apple will try your modem connection and register you instantly. (If it can't register because your connection is not set up yet, it will save the information and do it the first time you connect.) Continue on and you will see your new Desktop!

Take Advantage of the Utilities in the Installer

When you run the Installer and get to the first screen, you'll see a menu item called "Utilities." This menu gives you access to a number of troubleshooting features on your Mac. If you like, you can stop here before installing Leopard and use the Disk Utility to partition your Mac.

All of the utilities mentioned below, except "Reset Password," are in your Utilities folder, which is in your Applications folder. You don't need to use the Install disk to access them. **But if your Mac has totally crashed** and you can't get anywhere at all, insert the original Leopard install DVD, then restart your Mac. Immediately hold down the C key to make sure it boots from the DVD. Do not click any of the installation buttons, but use the tools that are available here.

From the Utilities menu, choose the appropriate tool:

- **Startup Disk:** Choose which disk you want your Mac to check first when starting up. Only disks that contain operating systems can be used as startup disks.

- **Reset Password:** Here you can reset not only the Administrator password, but the passwords for every user on the Mac. You do not need to know the original passwords to set new ones.

- **Firmware Password Utility:** This option prevents others from starting your computer with a different disk. If someone stole your laptop, this won't get it back for you, but it does make it much more difficult for anyone to log in and get your data.

- **Disk Utility:** Select your hard disk and use the "First Aid" pane to see if anything's wrong with the hard disk. The "Repair Disk Permissions" feature has solved some odd problems for my Macs. This is where you can partition the hard disk before you install.

- **Terminal:** The Terminal lets you use UNIX commands to do all sorts of things. If you don't know anything about UNIX or how to use the Terminal, skip this altogether.

- **System Profiler:** The System Profiler tells you all the gory details about your Mac, the CPU type, the audio, what kinds of devices are attached to your Mac, the speed of everything you can think of, and oh so much more. It will even tell you the serial number of the computer. This is also available at your

Desktop: Go to the Apple menu, choose "About This Mac," and click the button labeled "More Info...."

■ **Network Utility:** This utility has a number of great tools. If you know what it means to finger someone, ping your modem, run a lookup or a port scan, or when to use whois, then you'll have fun with this utility. It's also in your Utilities folder (which is in the Applications folder) in case you need it.

■ **Restore System From Backup...** uses Time Machine, which is a big clue that it can't restore the system from a backup until you've first put it all on Time Machine (see Lesson 20). But once you've done that, you can use this option.

Do you Now Own Two Macs? Migrate!

If you have important information on another Mac (a completely different machine from the one you are installing Leopard onto) or a partition or volume on the new Mac, you can transfer the information from the older machine, partition, or volume to this new Mac. You'll use a feature called **migrating** and the **Target Disk Mode.**

You can either use the Setup Assistant during the Leopard installation, or at any time in the future—open the **Migration Assistant** and do it; the instructions on screen are easy to follow. You can choose to migrate the files from the Administrator (main user), from any individual user, or from both. The information on the old Mac or partition is not affected at all.

Migration Assistant

The migration process can automatically transfer:

■ Network and computer settings.

■ User accounts, preferences, and email.

■ Documents and other files.

■ Applications.

Some applications, however, will need to be reinstalled from their original disks because they install necessary files in different system folders. All you can do is transfer them, then open them and see if they work. The more expensive and complex an application, the less likely it will transfer perfectly.

—continued

Requirements for the Migration Assistant

The old Mac must:

- Be running Mac OS X version 10.1 or above.

- Have a built-in FireWire port.

- Support "Target Disk Mode." Apple says that "most do."

You'll also need:

- A standard FireWire cable long enough to reach between the two computers. Or move the computers so they can connect via the cable.

- An Administrator name and password (unless you're doing this during the Leopard installation).

Be aware that:

- This process will tie up both your Macs for hours!

- This process will *not* automatically migrate songs that you bought from the **iTunes Music Store.** If you want to migrate *all* of your songs, including those you bought at the Music Store, first deauthorize the old Mac before you migrate files:

  1   Open iTunes.

  2   From the Store menu, choose "Deauthorize Computer...."

  3   Enter your account and password. Click the button to "Deauthorize," then click OK.

  4   To deauthorize any Audible content (books) to migrate over to the new machine, go to the "Advanced" menu and choose "Deauthorize Audible Account...." You'll need your Audible.com name and password.

      Be careful with your **iPod**—if iTunes on your new Mac has no music in it when you plug in your iPod, everything on your iPod will probably be erased to match your empty iTunes!

Migrate additional users

At any time you can migrate additional users and their files from other computers. Just follow the directions on the previous pages.

You can also use this **FireWire Target Disk Mode** at any time to transfer files from one Mac to another; see page 412. This technique is especially useful if one Mac is dying, because in Target Disk Mode, the target computer does not use its operating system—it acts like a plain ol' hard disk.

What to do after migrating

It's a good idea to do a quick check of the files on your new Mac after migrating. Open every application to make sure it works okay—make a quick file and try to save it. If an application doesn't work, you will just have to reinstall it from the original disks.

Open sample files by double-clicking on them to make sure they can open in the correct application and that their fonts appear correctly.

Connect to the Internet, check your mail, and take a peek at your System Preferences to make sure things are really how you like them.

TIP —— Do not unplug the FireWire cable before you unmount the icon of your old Mac from your new Mac running Leopard! Even though it's "hot swappable," which means you don't have to shut down, it's still possible to lose data if you unplug it while the icon is still visible on the screen.

Find the hard disk icon of your old Mac on the Desktop of the Leopard computer. Drag it to the Trash before you unplug the FireWire cable.

Other Ways to Transfer Files from Mac to Mac

The migration process can take quite a long time because it gathers up thousands of files. If you want to transfer just selected files, you might want to consider these other options. Some you can do before you install Leopard; others are new techniques that can only be accomplished in Leopard.

Use an external disk

Use a portable hard disk with a USB or FireWire connection. It's worth it to buy one just for this process. Copy the files onto the disks as you usually would from your old machine (drag them from the hard disk of your old Mac onto the disk icon). Then connect the drive to the new machine and copy them onto your hard disk. If you have a *very* old Mac, the trouble, of course, is finding drives that work on both an old Mac and the new one (or finding software on that old Mac that will run on the new one). The actual disks should work on both Macs, even if the drives you use are different.

Burn a CD

If your old machine can burn a CD (or a DVD) you can transfer quite a few files by burning disks and moving them to the new machine. Plus you'll have ready-made backups (always the smart thing to do).

Send attachments in email

If you don't have huge files, send them as attachments through email. It's kind of funny to send your files around the world to get to the machine sitting two feet away.

Use your .Mac account

If you have a .Mac account, put the files from your old Mac onto your iDisk (see www.Apple.com/dotmac). On your new Mac, download them from your iDisk. Also take advantage of syncing your Macs through .Mac—a terrific option.

Send files through the network

If both machines are on the same network, connect the two computers and copy files directly from one to the other. See Lesson 21 for all the details. It's really easy and you'll love knowing how to do it.

Use a FireWire cable

Connect a FireWire cable between two Macs. The other Mac will appear in the "Shared" group in the sidebar of a Finder window. You will probably be able to screen share (see pages 380–385). Or at least you can connect to each other and easily move files back and forth (see Lesson 21). Also look at the FireWire Target Disk Mode option; see page 412.

23

GOALS

Basic Troubleshooting

When things go wrong, here are a few simple troubleshooting techniques you can try.

Force Quit an Application

Sometimes just one application has trouble and you need to force it to quit. There are two ways to **force quit** any application. This doesn't affect any other application or the system. If an application isn't responding to anything you ask it to do, if it's hung up and the wheel keeps spinning, or it won't let you quit, then force quit the app. After you've force quit an application, try restarting it. It should be fine.

■ Hold down the Option key and **press** *(don't click)* on the application's icon in the Dock. A menu pops up with a choice to "Force Quit." Choose it.

■ **Or** press Command Option Esc. The window called "Force Quit Application" appears. From this window, select the application you want to force quit (if it isn't already selected), then click the "Force Quit" button.

Relaunch the Finder

You can't force quit the Finder, but you can **relaunch** it, which only takes a minute. If things are acting a little squirrely, try this. It doesn't hurt anything.

- Hold down the Option key and **press** *(don't click)* on the Finder icon in the Dock. A menu pops up with a choice to "Relaunch."

- **Or** press Command Option Escape, as explained on the opposite page, to open the "Force Quit Applications" window. Select the Finder in the list, and the button changes to "Relaunch." Choose it.

Restart

It's amazing what a simple **restart** will fix. Especially if you rarely turn off your Mac (like me), sometimes little things may start acting a bit quirky. Perhaps your Mac can't find the printer you've been using for months, or icons for new files don't appear. For little unexplainable things, restart.

- **To Restart,** go to the Apple menu and choose "Restart...."

- On most laptops, **press the Power button for one second** and you'll get a little message with a button to restart.

If you **can't restart,** then Shut Down; see below.

Shut Down

Sometimes shutting down fixes small problems that a restart doesn't fix. This is especially useful when you're having connection problems.

- **To Shut Down,** go to the Apple menu and choose "Shut Down...."

- Sometimes things are so bad you can't even get to the Apple menu. In that case, **hold down the Power button** (the one you push to turn on your Mac) for at least five seconds. This forces it to shut down.

Delete the Application Preference File

Another tip to troubleshoot an application that isn't acting right is to delete that application's **preference file.** This is perfectly safe—when the application opens up again, it will recreate a new preference file from scratch. You will lose any preferences you had personally changed in the application, but it can be worth it because this works pretty well to solve inexplicable annoyances in applications.

1 Quit the application.

2 Open a Finder window and view it by columns, as shown below.

3 Single-click your Home icon in the Sidebar.

4 In the column that appears to the right, single-click the "Library" folder.

5 In the next column to the right, single-click the "Preferences" folder.

6 In the next column to the right, find the ".plist" file for an application that's giving you trouble. That is the preferences file. Some vendors include their own preference files as well that might be named something else, as shown below.

7 Drag the application's preference file to the Trash. Empty the Trash.

8 Restart the application and hope it works better.

The preferences for Apple applications have an extension of .plist.

The preferences for non-Apple applications may also have their own names for their preferences. These are the prefs for the Mariner Write word processor.

Safe Boot

This is one of my favorite troubleshooting techniques. During a safe boot the Mac actually goes in and fixes little things. If you've ever used the terminal commands to do the fsck technique, you'll be pleased to know the safe boot does the same thing. This is safe and easy and comfortable and fixes lots of mysterious problems.

1   Go to the Apple menu and choose to "Restart...." If you're having such problems that you can't even get to the Apple menu, hold down the Power key for five seconds to shut down the machine. Then restart.

2   Immediately upon hearing the startup bong, hold down the Shift key and keep it held down. This might take a while, like five minutes or even more. Be patient. Keep that Shift key down. You'll probably come to a log in screen that says, in red, "Safe Boot." If not, no worries; go to the next step.

3   When you get to the Desktop or to the log in screen, restart immediately (either click the restart button if you see one, or go to the Apple menu and "Restart"). The Mac needs to restart to put everything back and turn everything on. See if things work a little better now.

Repair Permissions

For some reason (unbeknownst to me), something called "permissions" can go bad and cause trouble. Repairing the permissions solves many mysterious things.

Disk Utility.app

1   Open Disk Utility: Go to the Applications menu and open the Utilities folder. In the Utilities folder, find the Disk Utility and open it. You'll see this:

2   Select the hard disk in the left pane. Make sure the "First Aid" tab is selected.

3   Click the button to "Repair Disk Permissions."

Depending on how much stuff you have on your hard disk, this can take up to twenty minutes or so. If the Mac finds any permissions that need to be repaired, it will repair them.

If it finds things it can't repair, as you see above, then you need to go to the next step and verify and repair the disk. See the following page.

Verify and Repair Disk

First, go through the steps on the previous page to repair permissions, just to clear any little things up. Don't quit the Disk Utility yet.

If you think the disk might need to be repaired, or if you just want to check to see if the disk has a problem, click the button in Disk Utility (shown on the previous page) to "Verify Disk." This will make sure that the disk really does have a problem that it might be able to repair.

If the disk needs to be repaired, you can't do it with this Disk Utility. You need the original OS X install disk because *Disk Utility can't repair the disk it's stored on.*

So get the original install disk that came with your Mac. It's a CD or DVD. Then:

1   Insert the original install disk. Double-click the "Install" icon as if you were going to install the system again.

2   At the Welcome window, DO NOT INSTALL! Go to the Utilities menu at the top of the screen. Choose "Disk Utility...."

3   You get the window shown on the previous page. *Now* you can click the button to "Repair Disk." Let it run through its process. It might take up to a half hour or more. Be patient.

4   When it's done, it will probably tell you it has repaired the disk. If it can't, it must be a serious problem and you need to take it to a repair shop.

5   Quit Disk Utility and quit the installer.

6   It might ask you to choose a startup disk because if you don't, when you restart your Mac it will boot up from the CD again. If it asks, you will see the disk options; single-click on your hard disk, then click the "Restart..." button.

   Or restart without choosing a disk and hold the mouse button down until it has restarted. Holding the mouse button down forces the CD to eject so it can't be used to boot the machine. (If you're on a laptop, hold down the bar under the trackpad.)

Check for Software Updates

Make sure you are using the latest versions of all your software. For your Mac OS software, use the Software Update preferences to see if everything is up to date (open it in the System Preferences, as described on the previous pages). It's especially important to check for updated application software when you update your operating system, like when moving from any other OS to Leopard.

TIP —— If your connection to the Internet is a dial-up through a telephone modem, do *not* check the box to "Download important updates automatically" because it will tie up your phone line for hours. Check for updates manually (click "Check Now").

Create Another User and Test

If you install new software and it just won't work right, or perhaps it won't even open, one good troubleshooting technique is to create another user (see Lesson 18) and install the software in that user's Home. See if it works. If it *doesn't* work for the new user, the software itself has a problem—check the package it came in or with the vendor you bought it from to make sure it is the correct version for your operating system.

If the software does work for the other user, that indicates there is something in your system that is conflicting. Try throwing away the preferences, as explained on page 406. If it still doesn't work, you may need to contact the vendor to find out what sorts of cache files or other files may be conflicting with that particular software.

If you Forgot your Password

If you forgot the password you entered when you first set up your new Mac or installed your new system (called the Admin password), you'll have to use the original install CD to fix the problem. (I think someone told you that you should have written down your password.) If you have created more than one user for your Mac, you can use these steps to change the password of any user.

1   Get the original CD. Put it in and double-click the "Install" button. Follow the directions to restart. No, you are not really going to re-install the entire system.

2   All you need to do is wait until the Welcome screen appears. Then go to the Utilities menu at the top of the screen and choose "Reset Password...."

3   Enter your new password—twice. And add a hint. And write that password down where you can find it again. Click OK.

4   Quit the installer from the Installer menu. Your Mac will restart (it might ask you to choose a startup disk—choose your hard disk).

If you did not enter a password when you first set up your Mac, then you can leave the password field empty and just hit the blue "OK" or "Continue" button and it will work just fine (although it's not secure at all).

Report Crashes

Often when an application crashes, an alert box appears and asks if you want to send a report to Apple. Now, Apple is not going to write you back—this is just an anonymous report you send in so Apple can figure out if there are common issues among many users, enough to warrant looking into. It's good to go ahead and send in the report.

Use Target Disk Mode

It's not unusual to need to move lots of files from one computer to another. If both computers are working fine and you just need to share files, there are lots of ways to do it. Please see Lesson 21, and check the index for "sharing files."

But sometimes one computer is just about defunct or maybe won't wake from sleep and you've got to get the files off quick. Use **FireWire Target Disk Mode.** You'll need a FireWire cable that can connect to both Macs. A FireWire cable with 6-pin on both ends will probably fit both computers, but check your ports before you buy.

This is the FireWire symbol.

- Unplug all FireWire devices from both computers that you are going to connect to each other.

- If FileVault is enabled on the computer you want to take files from, turn it off (if you can).

- If either machine is a laptop, it's best to plug in its power source.

- The machine you are going to transfer files **to** is the **host** computer. The machine you are going to take files **from** is the **target** computer.

In this process, the *target* computer will appear as a hard disk on the *host* computer and you can move files to and from it.

1 Turn off the *target* computer (the one that's probably going bad). The *host* computer can stay turned on.

2 Connect the two computers with the FireWire cable.

3 Turn on the *target* computer and immediately hold down the T key and keep it down. Keep it held down until you see a FireWire symbol (shown above) moving about its screen.

4 On the *host* computer, you will see a hard disk icon representing the *target* computer. You can copy files from the *target* computer and put files onto it.

    If you don't see the *target* computer's hard disk on the host screen, make sure all the cables are securely attached and reboot the *host* computer.

5 When you're finished copying files, eject the *target* hard disk icon from the *host* computer—drag it to the Trash, or select it and choose "Eject" from the File menu.

6 Press and hold the *target* computer's power button until it turns itself off.

7 Unplug the FireWire cable.

Force a CD or DVD to Eject

If a CD or DVD is stuck in the drive and won't come out, this trick almost always works:

1   First make sure you've unmounted the disc: Click the eject icon on the screen, or drag the CD icon to the trash, or Control-click on the CD icon and choose "Eject disc."

But you're probably reading this page because you already did that and there is no icon on the screen but it won't come out. So . . .

2   Restart your Mac. As soon as you hear the restart tone, hold the mouse button down. Hold it down until the disc pops out.

On a laptop, press the bar beneath the trackpad instead of the mouse (unless you have a mouse attached to your laptop).

If that doesn't work, see if there is a tiny hole next to the CD drive slot. Not all Macs have a tiny hole here. But if you see one, that hole is specially made for a paper clip (not the kind with the plastic coating). Unfold a metal paper clip and gently but firmly press it into the hole to snap open the mechanism.

One thing that can cause a huge problem in a CD/DVD player is a disc with a paper label glued to the top. If the tiniest little edge peels up, it can get stuck in the drive and ruin not only the disc but the drive itself. So don't be buying those CD labels that you can print yourself, and don't put any disc with a paper label into your Mac!

24

GOALS

Secure your Mac and its Files

In these days of identity theft and with so much of our personal and financial data being stored on our computers, it's important to take some precautions to make it more difficult for unauthorized creeps to gain access to our Macs.

Know your Security Options

There are a number of **security features** on your Mac. Apple has installed lots of security stuff like Kerberos, Secure Shell, Wired Equivalent Privacy data encryption, Virtual Private Network, firewalls, and other features. It doesn't matter to most of us what those are—they work behind the scenes. Your Software Update (one of the System Preferences) will automatically update security features as Apple releases them.

The above features work without you having to do anything. The features that require your participation are explained on the following pages:

- There are a number of **password**-protect options on your Mac that make it difficult to gain casual access.

- You might need security from humans who walk past your desk when you're not there. Your Mac has a number of **low-level security features** to protect your information from the curious. These are good for laptops as well.

- **Keychain Access** stores many of your passwords in locked "keychains." This includes passwords to your .Mac account, servers, eBay account, PayPal, and more. Keychain Access also lets you store passwords and codes for other things, such as credit card numbers you might like to use while shopping online. Keychain Access does double-duty—it makes things easier for you and harder for thieves. Please see pages 424–425 for details.

- If you have highly personal or valuable stuff on your Mac, you can use **FileVault** for maximum security. If you have a laptop, this is especially important to prevent thieves from accessing your data.

- And don't forget about the feature to **Secure Empty Trash.** This deletes files from your Trash in such a way that no one can retrieve them again. See page 423.

Passwords on your Mac

You have several different passwords on your Macintosh.

- **Administrator password:** When you first turn on your Mac, you are asked to create a password. Write this down in a safe place! You will need this password whenever you install new software or when you make certain system-wide changes.

You can choose *not* to have a password. Your Mac will still *ask* you to enter a password, however—if you never entered one, just leave the password field blank, and click the OK or "Continue" button. But keep in mind that it's not very safe to neglect this password.

If you forget your Admin password, you will need to reset it:

1   Insert the original Mac OS X installer CD.

2   Double-click the "Installer" icon to start the process of reinstalling. You are not really going to reinstall!

3   When you get to the Install screen, go to the Utilities menu. Choose "Reset Password...."

4   Enter your new password. Write it down in a safe place!

5   Quit the Installer from the Installer menu.

- **Login password:** If you have set up multiple users on one Mac, each user has her own password to log in. *An Admin password is also the login password for that Admin user.* By default, your Mac is set to auto-login the Admin so you don't need your password at startup, but you can turn this off to make the computer less accessible (see Lesson 18 for details about multiple users and log in).

—continued

If a standard user forgets his password, the Administrator (or anyone who knows the Admin password) can reset the user password in the Accounts preferences.

- **Keychain Access password:** This is the same as the login password, whether you are a standard user or the Admin (you can change it to create a special keychain password). Keychain Access is the application on your Mac that keeps track of a variety of passwords for you. If you can remember your login password, then Keychain Access can show you the rest of your passwords. See pages 424–425.

- **Master password:** An Administrator can set up a computer-wide password in case he forgets the login password. Master passwords are usually used in conjunction with FileVault; see pages 426–427. The Admin's Master password can override a standard user's FileVault password.

What to do if you forget the Master password? Well, you can scream. It won't help, but you can scream.

Password tips

- A password should be difficult for others to guess, but easy for you to remember.

- Don't use a word that can be found in a dictionary. Some hackers use software that tries every word in the dictionary in a matter of minutes.

- Combine caps and lowercase and numbers.

- Most passwords are case-specific, meaning a lowercase "r" is completely different from an uppercase "R." Take advantage of this and put capital letters where someone wouldn't expect them.

Security System Preferences

Apple makes it easy for you to turn on a number of the low-level security features in one place, the Security system preferences.

Go to the Apple menu and choose "System Preferences…."

Click on the Security icon.

Click the "General" tab, as shown below.

For details on how to create multiple users, see Lesson 18. Even if you are the only user, you have what the Mac considers to be an "account."

Require password to wake computer: See page 422.

Disable automatic login: See page 421.

Require password to unlock every System Preference: This would prevent any user from changing any of the preferences without a password.

Log out automatically after a certain period of time: This does just what it says. Combine this with "Disable automatic login," so when the Mac logs you out after this amount of time, no one can get back in without a password.

Secure virtual memory: In the Mac's process of swapping data between RAM (random access memory) and virtual memory, it's possible that sensitive information that you assumed was deleted from RAM was actually written to the hard disk through virtual memory. Using secure virtual memory ensures that the sections of the hard disk that were used in the memory-swap process get overwritten, thus protecting your privacy. This is turned on by default.

The **Firewall** pane of the Security preferences is not something you will mess with very often, if at all. The most important thing to understand is that as you use Sharing features (turned on and off in the Sharing preferences), the Mac lets down the firewall (a protective barrier) for the features you have turned on so others can access your machine to share. This means you are at a little more risk than if that feature was not turned on. So if you're not using a feature, turn it off so the firewall goes back up.

You can't turn any of these features off in this pane—go to the Sharing preferences pane and uncheck them. When you do that, they automatically disappear from here.

Low-Level Security Features

Here are some simple and quick features to take advantage of if you have any worry at all about casual access to your computer.

Auto login

■ **Turn off auto-login:** Auto-login lets your Mac start up without a password —it automatically logs in the person who has "auto-login" turned on in the Accounts preferences "Login Options."

So turn off auto-login and then be sure to **log out** before you leave your computer for a while. This ensures that people walking by will need a password to log in to your account, even if they restart your Mac. Laptops should always require a login password.

You can also disable automatic login for all users in the Security preferences pane, as shown on the previous page.

■ **If you don't want to turn off auto-login,** you might want to at least take the extra step to uncheck the box to "Show the Restart, Sleep, and Shut Down buttons." Because if auto-login is on and you log out and leave your Mac, the login screen appears and you think you're safe. But someone can just click the Restart or Shut Down button and the computer starts back up again and auto-matically logs in to your account. By unchecking this box, no one can restart your computer so easily.

This precaution isn't going to help much if your laptop is stolen because someone can just reboot the computer. Nor will it help if the Restart button is accessible on your desktop machine!

—continued

■ Mac OS X lets you have multiple users on one computer, and each user has a separate, private Home area (see Lesson 18 for details). Even if you are the only one using this Mac, you can **create another user,** a standard user who has no administrative privileges, and regularly log in as the standard user. This is a simple step that just makes it one level more difficult for someone to get into your main account and make system-wide changes. It won't protect any data that you create as that user, but it will make it more difficult to get into your Mac as the Administrator with privileges.

Require a password to wake your Mac

To prevent access to anyone walking by your computer, you can use these simple yet effective features. Open the System Preferences from the Apple menu, and then:

1 Use the "Security" preferences to **require a password to wake up the Mac** from sleep or from the screen saver.

2 Then go to the "Desktop & Screen Saver" preferences to choose a screen saver and tell it when to start.

3 Then go to the "Energy Saver" preferences to tell your Mac to put either the computer and/or the display (the screen) to sleep after a certain amount of time. Now when the screen saver comes on or your Mac goes to sleep, you'll have to enter your password to get back to it.

An alternative to the above technique is to set up your Mac so you can **lock it with a mouse click** whenever you choose, not just when the screen saver comes on or when it goes to sleep.

1 Open Keychain Access (first open the Applications folder, then open the Utilities folder; Keychain Access is in the Utilities folder).

2 From the Keychain Access menu across the top of the screen, choose "Preferences...."

3 Check the box to "Show Status in Menu Bar." A padlock icon appears on the right side of your menu bar, as shown on the next page.

4 Quit Keychain Access.

•

5 Click the padlock icon that now appears in your menu bar to get the menu shown below.

6 Choose "Lock Screen." The screen saver will start and no one can access your Mac unless they know your login password.

Higher-Level Security Features

■ **Secure Empty Trash:** You might think that after you empty the Trash, it's gone. But it's possible to recover many deleted files using special data-recovery software. If you are selling or giving away your Mac, you might want to make sure no one can recover your old, trashed files. To completely overwrite files so no one can ever get to them, go to the Finder menu and choose **Secure Empty Trash.** This might take several minutes, depending on how much stuff you've thrown away since you got the computer!

■ **Encrypt a disk image:** Using the Disk Utility (found in the Utilities folder, which is in the Applications folder), you can protect all or part of your hard disk by making a selected portion of it into a password-protected "disk image," which looks like a hard disk icon. It has its own password; if your Keychain is locked (see the following pages), this image is really safe from prying eyes and fingers because someone would need both passwords to access the disk. When unlocked, this disk image acts just like any other hard disk and you can move files in it, copy files to it, and delete files from it. I recommend you read all about this feature in the Disk Utility Help files before you start using it.

Use Keychain Access for Protection

Keychain Access provides a secure place to store information that can only be accessed with a user name and password. Keychain automatically and safely stores the passwords you create on your Mac, like those for web sites you go to, servers you connect to, email accounts, etc. Every time you see one of those messages that asks if you want your Mac to remember this password in your keychain, it gets stored here in Keychain Access.

You can also add your own secure collections of Keychains to store your credit card numbers, PINs, bank card information, private notes or messages, and other things that you want easy access to, but you want them to be secure. They won't be entered automatically anywhere—it's just a safer place to store them than on a sticky note.

Keychain Access sets up your initial Keychain file, the one based on your user name and password, as the default Keychain. This default Keychain automatically opens when you log in. To make other Keychains more secure, such as your list of credit card numbers or banking passwords, be sure to make *new* Keychain files for them instead of *adding* them to your default file.

To open Keychain Access, first open your Applications window. Inside you'll find the Utilities folder. Keychain Access is inside the Utilities folder.

Click this button to show the list of Keychains, now showing at the top of the sidebar. Any new keychain you create will appear in that area.

To access any password Keychain has been storing for you:

1   Find the item in the list of "Passwords," as shown on the opposite page.

2   Double-click that item. You will be asked for your Keychain password, which is the same as your login password. If you are the only user of the Mac, it's the password you assigned yourself when you first set up your Mac, the Admin password. A window like the one below appears.

3   Click in the box to "Show password." Your password appears!

You can create a new Keychain: Go to the File menu and choose "New Keychain…." Give it a descriptive name *and a password you will remember.* This Keychain will appear in the top portion of the sidebar, as shown on the opposite page. You will need to know that Keychain's password if you want to access things in it!

With that Keychain selected, go back to the File menu and choose to create a new password item or a new secure note to store in it.

Oh, Keychain is a very powerful and fairly complex application! To use it wisely and well, please study the Keychain Help files.

Consider FileVault for Heavy-Duty Protection

FileVault encrypts, or scrambles, the data in your Home folder so unauthorized people or software cannot get to it. While you are working on your Mac with FileVault turned on, you won't notice anything. But everything in your Home folder will be safely protected from prying eyes, both in your office and from remote connections. **Don't ever forget the Master password,** though, or you will never again see anything in your Home folder!

To turn on FileVault:

1   Before you begin, make sure you have the Admin name and password, as well as the password for this user (if it's separate from the Admin user).

2   Also before you begin, make sure all other users are logged out.

3   Check to make sure you have enough hard disk space available for the process—you'll need as much free hard disk space as there is data in your Home folder.

> To check the file size of your Home folder, single-click the Home icon in the Sidebar of any Finder window.
>
> Press Command Option I to display the Info window.
>
> Check the "Size" of the Home folder.
>
> Now check to see how much free hard disk space you have: Single-click the hard disk icon in the Sidebar. In the Info window (which has now switched to show you the info for the hard disk), find the amount "Available." About 1024 megabytes fit into one gigabyte, so unless you've been making movies on your Mac, you probably have plenty of space.

4   You must first set a Master password. Keep in mind that once you set a Master password, you can never get rid of it. *If you forget your login password and you also forget the Master password, everything in your Home folder is lost forever.*

> **To set a Master password:**
>
> **a.** From the Apple menu, choose "System Preferences...."
>
> **b.** Single-click the "Security" icon to get the Security pane shown on the opposite page. Click the "FileVault" tab.
>
> **c.** Read the warning! Then click "Set Master Password...," enter your password and hint, and click OK.

5 Now click the button "Turn On FileVault...."

6 Read the warning! If this is what you really want, click the OK button.
   It may take a few minutes. Your Mac will log itself back into this account
   and FileVault will be on.

7 Close the Security preferences window.

Laptop Precautions

One out of ten laptops in this country gets stolen, which means about 600,000 a year. They get stolen not only for the hardware, but more and more often for the valuable data that is stored on them. So it's particularly imperative that if your laptop does happen to get stolen or lost, that the data inside of it is as safe as possible. Here are a few features I discussed in this lesson that you should make sure you take advantage of.

- Use a password to log in. Do not set auto-login for your laptop.

- Set a firmware password; see page 396. It prevents someone from booting your computer with another disk.

- Password-protect the screen saver and sleep so if the screen saver turns on or the Mac goes to sleep, you need a password to get back in.

- Turn on FileVault (but never forget its password!). When your machine is off or sleeping, all of your data in the Home folder is encrypted until you enter the password to start working again. This is the strongest protection you can have for the data itself on your laptop.

- There are devices you can buy that can alert you to when your Mac is moving away from you. And services you can subscribe to that can track the stolen computer as soon as a person logs on to the Internet with it. Search the web for laptop security devices and services.

Mini-Glossary ❧ *Most words are defined as I use them. Please see the index!*

active window

The *active window* is the one that is in front of everything else and is selected. You can tell if a window is active because the three little buttons in the top-left corner are in color, and the title bar icon is not shaded. It's important to become aware at all times of which window is active because that is the window that will accept any command. For instance, if you press Command Shift N to create a new folder, that new folder will appear in the active Finder window (or on the Desktop, if the Desktop is active). If you press Command W in just about any application or in the Finder, it will close the active window. **To make any window active** (or the Desktop), single-click on it.

alias

An *alias* is a "go-fer"—it goes for things and gets them for you. It's nothing all by itself; it's merely a representative icon (only 2ᴋ or 3ᴋ in file size) that is *linked* to the original. You double-click the alias and it goes and gets the real thing and opens the real thing for you. The advantage of this is that you can put aliases in multiple places for easy access; in fact, you can have as many aliases of an item as you

Methinks I scent the morning air

want. Some applications cannot open properly if you move them out of their folders, but if you make an alias of that application, you can put it anywhere.

An alias icon has a visual clue, a tiny arrow in the bottom-left corner of the icon (shown below) so you know it's a go-fer.

You can throw away an alias and it does not affect the original at all. You can move an original or rename the original or the alias and everything still works fine.

To make an alias, select a file; press Command L. *Or* hold down the Command and Options keys and drag the file into another folder or onto the Desktop. As you drag, you'll see the tiny alias arrow that tells you that you are indeed dragging to create an alias.

colored labels

To *color-code* a file, Control-click on it and choose a "Color Label" from the menu that pops up. Once a file is color-coded, you can search for it by its label, organize your files, etc.

To change the names of the labels, use the Finder preferences: Go to the Finder menu and choose "Preferences…." Click the "Labels" menu and change the names. For more details, please see page 264, and check the index for "color labels." This is a great organizational tool.

default

A default is something the Mac has chosen for you, until you make your own choice. For instance, TextEdit it must have a font chosen to type in, so your Mac chooses one for you. A default window view is chosen for you. But you can at any time change just about anything to something of your own choice.

extension

A *file extension* refers to the short code at the end of a file name. It might be from two to six letters. This extension tells the Mac what to do with that file.

ApplePro Tip of
the Week.webloc

The extension, .webloc, tells the Mac this is a web page location.

You might not see the extensions. If you like to have them visible all the time, go to the Finder preferences (from the Finder menu, choose "Preferences"). Click on the "Advanced" tab. Put a check in the box to "Show all file extensions."

To show the extensions temporarily or to check to see what the extension is for a particular file, use the Info window (explained in this mini-glossary). You'll see an option for "Name & Extension" that will tell you what it is and let you hide or show it for that selected file.

Do not add or change the extensions yourself! The Mac has become very fussy about these extensions and you run the risk that the file will not open if you change its extension without knowing what you are doing.

Info window

The *Info window,* as shown on pages 323 and 341, has a secret **Inspector** mode: If you select a file and press Command I, the Info window appears *for that one particular file.*

But if you select a file and press Command Option I, you get the *Inspector* window, which looks exactly like the Info window *except* the Inspector window changes depending on what you click. That is, if you display the info for one file, then select another file (single-click on another file), the content of the Inspector changes to display the next file. Try it.

You can also open the Inspector with a contextual menu: Control-click on a file, then hold the Option key down and you'll see "Get Info" change to "Show Inspector."

screenshots

To make *screenshots* (pictures of the screen), use these shortcuts:

Full screen: Command Shift 3

Selection: Command Shift 4, then let go. Use the target cursor that appears to select the area you want to capture as an image: just press in one spot and drag to another spot, catching the image inside of this invisible box.

Window: Command Shift 4, then let go. Tap the Spacebar and a camera icon appears. As you move the camera icon over different windows, even those that are hidden, you'll see that window highlight. Click on the one you want an image of.

> *The above screenshots land on your Desktop labeled "Picture 1," "Picture 2," etc. They are in the PNG file format.*

Selection you can paste: Press Command Shift 4 and the target cursor appears. Hold down the Control key and drag to select the area, which *copies* that screenshot image. Now you can paste the screenshot somewhere else.

string

A *string* is simply a line of characters that you type. If someone tells you to "enter a search string," all it means is to enter the words you want to search for.

Symbols

Each key has a **symbol** by which it is known. These are the keyboard symbols you will see in menus and charts:

⇧	**Shift**	↺		**Escape (esc)**
⌘	**Command**	⬍ ⬍		**Page Up or Page Down**
⌥	**Option**	⌫		**Delete**
^	**Control**	↑↓←→		**Arrow keys**
↵	**Return**	⌤		**Enter**
▲	**Eject**			

O

online forms, fill in automatically, 128

Open dialog boxes
search for files within, 351
Spotlight search in, 351

Option key
symbol for, 24, 433
use in copying documents, 253
use in copying one column of text in Preview, 204
use in copying text, 249
use in Dock menus, 404
use in resizing columns in Column View, 16

orange arrows in Safari fields, 129

Outgoing Mail Server,

ownership and permissions, 323

P

padlock icon in menu bar, 423

page proxy, tiny icon in title bar, 253–254

Page Up and **Page Down keys**
symbols for, 24, 433

parental controls
overview of and where to set, 324–329
in Safari, 137

partition your hard disk with Disk Utility, 396

passwords
Administrator password, 417
forgot your Admin password? 396, 411, 417
no password assigned, 395, 417
set it up on installation, 395–396
where it came from, 308
blank passwords can be used, 312, 395
case-specific, case-sensitive, 312, 418
forgot your user password? 396, 411
help for good passwords, 312
hints for user passwords
add one, 312, 395
when they appear, 316
lock your Mac, require a password to unlock, 422
login password, 418
login password doesn't work, 315

Master password, 426–427
no password assigned, 395, 411
online, fill in passwords automatically, 128
on your Mac
Administrator password, 395, 417
Keychain Access password, 425
login password, 426
login passwords for users, 312
Master password, 426–427
PDFs, password-protect them, 217
require a password to wake your Mac from sleep
or a screen saver, 422
reset your password, 396, 411
user passwords
Admin password is user password, 395, 418
if you forget yours, 396, 411, 418

Paste and Match Style, 61, 249

PDFs
what are they? 217
create a PDF, 217–218
annotate a PDF, 200–201
bookmark multi-page documents, 199
copy text from a PDF page
to paste in another document as editable, 204
to paste in as a graphic, 204
crop PDFs in Preview (non-destructive), 196–197
fax a PDF
from your Mac, 302–305
straight from the document, 218
forms, fill in PDF forms, 206
iPhoto, save a PDF to, 218
links, create them in TextEdit, 68
open a PDF in Safari, 132, 254
password-protect a PDF, 217
PDF-X, save as, 218
save PDF to Web Receipts folder, 219
search a PDF, 198
view PDFs in Preview, 194

peer-to-peer network, 373

permission settings in Info window, 323

Personal File Sharing, turn it on, 373

phone cable to fax from your Mac, 302

Colophon!

I wrote and indexed this book directly in Adobe InDesign on an Intel Mac Pro. The fonts used are Warnock Pro for body copy (9.5/14) and Today for the heads, subheads, and captions. I wish I could have been allowed to use something really sassy here and there. Some fun face from MyFonts.com, like Flyswim, above, or Cocktail Shaker from Veer.com, which is what you're reading now.

Although the indexing feature in InDesign is fabulous, this new version of CS3 broke the index. I am deeply indebted to **Ole Kvern** for writing me a script that did magical mystical things and let me get this book to press on time. Bless your heart, Ole—I adore you. I hope you enjoy the Calvados. :-)